A CHARMED LIFE

NEVER TAKE NO
FOR AN ANSWER!

EVELYN PREBENSEN HARRISON

Available on Amazon.com or by contacting
evelynharrisonpb@gmail.com

Print ISBN: 978-1-09832-970-9

Printed in the United States of America on SFI Certified paper.

First Edition

ENDORSEMENTS

Evelyn Harrison has written an elegant account of her life in diplomacy, living across cultures and coming to terms with contemporary America. From her days as hostess for her father, The Norwegian Ambassador and Dean of the Diplomatic Corps in postwar London, to navigating today's high society at age 89 in Palm Beach. This is a riveting read.

Richard L. Jackson, writer
Retired U.S. Diplomat
President of Athens College,
Greece

I am very pleased to have been asked to write this note for Evelyn Prebensen Harrison, a true, dear friend who has had her share of ups and downs! She has never complained, and has now put her "Charmed Life" on paper for all of us to enjoy and admire!

Louise Hitchcock Stephaich
Proud Benefactor
Hospital Albert Schweitzer,
Haiti

TABLE OF CONTENTS

INTRODUCTION

This book is a reflection of what I consider to have been a charmed life, in spite of innumerable uphill battles. My father, who meant more to me than I can possibly describe, impacted my life enormously. I was especially proud of him when, in 1945, I watched him come out in public with the armband of the Civilian Leaders of the Resistance. That was when he gave me his gold Naval Academy bracelet.

On this gold chain are many charms which have been given to me over the years. Each one represents a chapter in my life. Each chapter tells a story of incredibly supportive friends from all over the world. These stories are written to inspire the reader to never give up, regardless of their challenges, and also to remind them that every day of this incredibly beautiful journey is brimming with the prospect of joy and adventure.

My adventures began in Moscow, Russia, where I was born the daughter of a Norwegian diplomat in the British Embassy. We returned to Norway when I was three. There I enjoyed a rich childhood with family and friends. When I was ten, WWII broke out. Five dreadful years of German occupation left me with a serious—and at times life-threatening—circulatory illness. Having survived the war, I decided to face these medical difficulties head on and seize every hope of a cure to regain my health. Throughout Europe and later the United States, I sought out medical professionals who were willing to experiment outside of the box, like Professor Enocksson in Sweden and Dr. Frias Fereira in Portugal. My worldwide quest for healing led me to experience many marvelous moments with outstanding friends.

I have also been fortunate to have pursued numerous artistic endeavors, including painting, gardening, fashion design and travel writing. Without the inspiration of art and music, as well as a deep childlike faith, I don't think I would have survived. Throughout my years, I volunteered in education and a variety of charities, which has also been a source of pride and strength.

My parents and maternal grandfather, as well as my two brothers, taught me many life lessons, including the importance of a sense of humor as well as a sense of duty. It was essential to draw upon all available resources and possess a stubborn will in order to survive. Even more importantly, they taught me the priceless gift of friendship and to welcome friends of any age or country. Wisdom of our elders should be cherished and the twinkle of youth never lost.

After all, I have always said that charm has no age!

FOREWORD

I have had the pleasure of knowing the author for more than 80 years, with some clear memories for the last 77. I was a disappointment to my eight-year-old sister that I was not the little sister she had wished for. She already had a brother five years her junior, so she decided to turn me into a long-haired sibling, which involved endless hours of hair dressing. At a certain point I did get up and walk away to join my brother in boys' games, but a very firm bonding had taken place and lasts to this day.

Evelyn was leader from an early age and gave herself the Russian name, Evy Sama, which means "Evelyn, do it herself". To this was added, when she got back to Norway at the age of three, Kruttone—that is to say "Powder Keg Prebensen". Evelyn was born in Moscow in 1929 to a Norwegian Foreign Service couple who later served for many years as Norwegian Ambassador in London and Rome. In our youth, our family survived five years of German occupation in Norway during World War II. At that time, Evelyn contracted a serious blood circulation illness, which turned into her life's challenge for survival.

She became a citizen of Europe and a global traveler in her search for a cure. In the process she has become an author and artist. She became familiar with the country houses, old palaces and embassies around Europe which birthed many a story to pass on. It was European history in the making. It was meeting many of the day's actors, from royalties to the politicalleaders such as Winston Churchill and Ernest Bevin. During her search she was helped on her way by special people from all walks of life. Several gave her lucky charms which formed a bracelet and a story of a life well-fought and a good example for us who follow in her wake.

With a lot of love and admiration from a little brother who is also in the process of growing up.

Christopher Fougner Prebensen- Career Diplomat
Executive Secretary
North Atlantic Council (1988-1993)
Secretary General
Norwegian Atlantic Committee (1997-2010)

ACKNOWLEDGEMENTS

There are so many people to thank for this full life I have lived, without which there never would have been a story to write. I am profoundly grateful to my parents, Per and Ragnhild Prebensen. The two set the foundation for my character and drew the blueprint of determination, loyalty and a sense of humor—traits necessary to sustain one through life's ups and downs. My grandfather, Christopher Fougner, also influenced my path by introducing me to horses, books, and drawing—all of which became life-long passions.

My architect husband, Billy, was my partner for over twenty years in the building of dreams and several houses. Our two daughters, Alexandra and Elizabeth brought us tremendous joy.

The many friends I've met around the world were the décor and beauty of my cosmopolitan, political and social life—without whom this story would be rendered monochromatic and ordinary.

I am deeply indebted to my two brothers, Peter Nicolai and Christopher Prebensen. As my best friends, they always believed in me, and have kept in contact with me wherever our lives took us. Chris is there to this very day, and his encouragement has helped see this book through.

Many thanks to Natalie and Russell Walden who provided the creative environment of their Santa Fe home where I worked on my book for several months.

My grateful thanks go to Joan van der Griff, for her suggestion to build this life story around each charm on my bracelet.

Thanks to Michael Martin who helped bring my cover concept and images to life with his expert photo and computer skills.

A huge 'thank you' is extended to my special friend, Louise Hitchcock Stephaich, for her priceless friendship and support for over three decades.

Special thanks goes to my daughter, Alexandra, who has walked with me through thick and thin and helped me continue my artistic endeavors.

Angela Shaw is most appreciated for her editorial work and warm interest in this project. Her technical support was of great help in getting this book published.

I appreciate and love you all!

Russia – Caviar in the Morning

GOLD 1769 RUBLE

I first saw the light of day on August 24, 1929 in Moscow, Russia at the British Embassy with the help of a French-speaking Russian doctor and a German-speaking Lithuanian nurse. It made my life quite cosmopolitan from the very beginning. As a daughter of a Norwegian diplomat, my life was certain to continue its international path.

My father, Ambassador Per Preben Prebensen, was not the first in our family to be appointed as a diplomat to Russia. He was inspired by his uncle, Nicolai Christian Grove Prebensen who had led a distinguished career as a civil servant. Uncle Nicolai held office as County Governor of Finmark (an area located in the High North near Russia), a member of Parliament and as the Chairman of the 1905 Independence Committee. He was largely responsible for the special Pomor commerce trade between Bodø in Norway and Murmansk, Russia. After Norway's 1905 independence, Uncle Nicolai also helped build the new diplomatic service, and was later appointed as Minister to St. Petersburg where he remained until the 1917 Russian Revolution. With this kind of influence, it's understandable why my father—on finishing his duty as a naval officer in WWI—wanted to join the diplomatic service. After hearing so much about the Russian post in Moscow, he made a formal application. When my father started his post eleven years after the 1917 revolution, he found a very different Russia than his uncle had known. By this time, both my parents spoke Russian, and the ensuing four years proved to be very interesting.

I, Evy *Sama* ("Evy do it myself" as they called me because I was a very willful little lady) grew up on British soil in Russia. My mother recorded how I stood up in a pram at eight months old and took baby steps before my first birthday. Once, on a walk with my father to the Minsk Train Station, I insisted on wearing raffia slippers instead of regular shoes! I blew kisses, curtseyed and took tea in fine teacups before age two. While such willfulness exhibited itself as both delightful and difficult, I'm convinced my innate determination is precisely what has brought me to over nine decades with body and soul intact.

At the end of the 1920s, the British broke off diplomatic relationships with the Soviet Union due to the so-called Zinoviev Letter. The Norwegian Legation was asked to be in charge of British affairs. Hence, I was born in the British Embassy. Minister Urbye, the Norwegian Envoy, gave my father the official responsibility. Concurrently, Urbye engaged the Captain Vidkun Quisling as an extra secretary. Quisling knew the Russian language and was an expert on Russian conditions. He had been a young assistant to the Norwegian arctic explorer, Fridtjof Nansen. In 1919, after WWI and the Russian Revolution, Nansen became head of the Humanitarian Aid Delegation during the terrible famine in Ukraine. Apart from being a well-known explorer and the Norwegian Envoy to Great Britain, Fridtjof Nansen was famed for procuring passports for political refugees after WWI. Following his time with Nansen in the Ukraine, Quisling traveled to Moscow, married a lovely Russian lady named Maria, and the two remained in Moscow for a few years. There had not been a British ambassador residing in the Russian capital since the Revolution. The British Mission, however, had left a very distinguished house to the disposal of the Norwegian government.

When we lived at the British residence located at 46 Ulitza Voroskovo, we shared the house with the Quislings. Each family ran separate households, but ate in the same dining room with each couple at opposite ends of the long table. Although he was an introvert and a man of few words, Quisling was fond of children and often smiled at them. On the august occasion of my christening, he bestowed a bouquet of flowers in a handsome sterling goblet. I own the goblet to this day and feel it is part of history. As is the silver terrine in which I was baptized!

Because of his experiences in Russia, Quisling became an anti-Bolshevik par excellence. He tried to mount a front against the Soviets, but to no avail. Only Adolph Hitler paid attention, and in 1933, Quisling set up his own Nazi Party. There is no doubt that he was an ardent anglophile at the time. However, he became a notorious WWII traitor when the Germans invaded Norway in April 1940.

At the close of 1929, the British resumed diplomatic relations with the Soviets. My parents rented half of one of the last privately owned houses in Moscow. It was a single story, stucco, brown frame house. I still remember its lovely pear tree and lantern on the corner! The other half of the house was occupied by the Russian landlord, "a former human being"—as we referred to him. The landlord and his family were charming, and we all became good friends. There was a hidden door between the two kitchens. Every time the secret police made one of their surprise razzias (or raids), the landlord would shove the family's valuables through the secret door until danger had passed.

Their great dog, an Alsatian, was my best friend and guardian. During the extremely cold winters, snow filled the walled garden where we played. I was given my first pair of skis when I was eighteen months old so as not to be engulfed by the deep drifts. Once, I braved the elements at minus 22 Celsius by putting goose fat on my cheeks. This was probably where my severe allergy to the cold began.

I remember the first time I visited my godfather, Uncle Nicolai, outside Arendal in southern Norway. He was such a charming old gentleman, and we got along like a house on fire. He showed me a curious small bridge that crossed the ditch on the roadside between the gate and his house. When I asked him where the bridge went, he answered, "My dear, that is my bridge from nowhere to nowhere!" I adored the Chippendale bridge so much that

I copied it years later at *Shenandoah,* my beloved Tuscan villa and favorite home.

When I later left Russia, my parents gave me an Empress Caterina gold coin dated 1769. It has stayed with me all my life, and I wear it daily for good luck. The coin was too large for my charm bracelet, so I attached it to a necklace. This lovely Santa Caterina gold coin ignited my fascination of Catherine the Great.

During twelfth-century Moscow, a frontier outpost fell to the rule of local princes under the Mongols. By the sixteenth century, Ivan the Great had made Moscow the capital of a growing Russia. Tsar Peter the Great, however, wanted to live by the sea. So, after his victory over Sweden, he built a new capital on the Baltic. It provided him with a seaport and a window to the "west." He named it St. Petersburg.

In 1744, the 14-year-old Catherine traveled from Germany to Russia to marry Peter's grandson, the future Tsar Peter III. It was no secret at the time, however, that Peter III had intended to make his current mistress the empress. Catherine quickly arranged a military coup, and had her cruel and mentally subnormal husband assassinated after an unhappy 16 years of marriage. Catherine, on the other hand, idolized Peter the Great and lived her life on and off at the beautiful *Peterhof.* Situated 20 miles outside of St. Petersburg, the palace had been Peter's favorite. Catherine the Great was a powerful personality who ruled for 34 years from 1761 until her death at age 67. During her reign, she dismembered Poland, and through wars with the Turks, helped Russia obtain Crimea, as well as an access to the Black Sea. She was an avid patron of the arts and amassed a great art collection.

Catherine hated Moscow; it was too chaotic, too barbaric and too Asiatic for her. So it was from the cold grandeur of the *Winter Palace* in St. Petersburg that the Empress Catherine oversaw the expansion of her empire. Across the river Neva, the old white stock exchange gleamed in its neo-classic splendor. To the right jutted the gilded spire of the Peter and Paul Cathedral. On the island sat the Peter and Paul Fortress. Waterways linked over 100 islands known as the Venice of the North. Catherine's idealistic reign was tempered with her deep sense of responsibility—a trait highly valued by the Russians. History, however, is somewhat mixed in its appreciation. Only after the Russian Revolution did Moscow again become the capital of all of Russia.

Although I was only three years old when we left Moscow, I have vivid memories of that time. The great cupolas of St Basil's Basilica on Red Square made a huge impression on me. I viewed the Russians as a people with big hearts and a deep adoration for their native music and literature. I have never forgotten the beloved family who owned the house we rented. Their wonderful dog instilled a love for large endearing canines! Those early life impressions have followed me throughout my rather international life. I'm reminded of them every time I wear my beautiful 1769 Caterina gold coin.

Our family saw a good amount of White Russians when we later lived in Oslo and London. These were people who had been forced to leave during the Revolution. One of the White Russians in London was Prince George Galitzine who died in March of 1992. Prince George had opened Russia's cultural doors to the west. Both his wife and daughter, Katya—whom I subsequently knew when they visited Palm Beach—were determined to perpetuate Prince George's great achievement. The women wanted to honor the Prince's memory by providing sustaining help to the people of St. Petersburg during their difficult transition. They created the Galitzine-St. Petersburg Trust to provide grants for the arts and crafts. After 75 years of communism, the city was hungry for modern knowledge. The women established the Prince George Galitzine Memorial Library in the lovely Niva riverfront home of Prince Galitzine's mother. George Galitzine's maternal grandfather, Grand Duke George of Mecklenburg Strelitz, sold the Michael Palace in 1895 to the Tsar who used it as a storehouse for Russian art. In its stead, the Grand Duke bought 46 Fontanka. One hundred years later, this beautiful palace houses the Galitzine library and the British Consulate.

After my parents returned from a six-week assignment in Tehran, they took me to Oslo to visit my grandparents. I was one year old. To prepare for the great occasion, my grandmother, very much an imposing lady, wrote to ask Mother, "What does the child eat?" Mother named all sorts of delicacies, and added with tongue in cheek, "And then, of course, every morning she has a large soup spoonful of the very best caviar. So much better for you than cod liver oil!"

At our final departure from Moscow, we went by train to Helsinki where the tracks changed from the Russian wide gage to the European narrower gage on the Finnish-Russian border. From Helsinki we crossed by ship to Stockholm. A Swedish dance band played on board. I had tried to talk to the musicians, but they responded coldly. Even at that young age I was taken aback by the difference between my warm Russian friends (whom I called uncles) and these strange, impersonal Swedes. Apparently I returned very disappointed to my parents' table and complained, "These are not my uncles!"

Norway – Childhood and World War II
THE GOLDEN STIRRUP

When my parents' work in Moscow came to an end, the family moved back to Oslo where my parents started their life together. I was only three years old, but remember it all so well. We continued to speak Russian in the home. But from the day I arrived, I spoke only Norwegian because I wanted to fit in with the other children—with the sole exception of calling my father *Puschka*.

Our first Norwegian home was a white frame house with a large garden at Slemdal, in the hills just above Oslo. The landlady, Mrs. Nandrup, was a fierce old battle-ax. I used to hide from her at the bottom of the garden. As Beatrice Lilly—the famous English singer and actress—declared it, "There are fairies at the bottom of my garden!" From there I would be lifted over the fence to play with the neighbor's daughter. Her name was Signe, and all the neighborhood children gravitated towards her enchanting playhouse. Our house was not far from the Slemdal tram station. Every afternoon my father would come home from the office on the tram, 15 minutes from downtown.

When I was five years old, one day my mother let me walk to the station alone to meet Father. I was waiting on the platform when a tall man in a dark suit approached me. He politely said that my father was going to be late and that he was supposed to take me home. I followed him, but this man did nothing of the sort and tricked me instead. As soon as we turned a corner away from the station where someone might recognize me, he put his hand over my mouth to muffle my cries for help. He forced me to go into a wooded area and started to fondle me and expose himself. I remember fighting him with all my might, kicking and trying to bite his hands. He was a disgusting man. After what seemed like forever, he finally stopped. He snarled that he was tired of fighting such an unwilling and unruly child. On our way back toward the residential area, we met my mother and the police who were already out looking for me. The man was obviously caught, but never prosecuted. In those days, even though the police believed me, unless there was complete penetration, a "sexual maniac" could not be charged. A pedophile could be arrested, but was then quickly released back into the community. Nobody knew the suspect, and in those days my story was not made public. A month later, a little girl named Mary Hansen was found in a sack at the bottom of a pond after she had been raped. She, too, was barely five years old. The police identified the suspect as the same man who had accosted me! My parents read about it in the papers, and we later discussed it. The ordeal made a deep impression on me and I have never forgotten the girl's name. I realized how lucky I had been. As a result, I took other roads and climbed over fences to reach my playmates. When I started elementary school at age five, I walked with my friend, Grethe. That assault has haunted me ever since and colored many of my life-decisions—especially with male relationships. It also helped me appreciate good friendships. I certainly have counted my glass half full, rather than half empty. Hence, in first grade I met a wonderful group of girls and am still in touch with several of them—even though I've lived most of my life far from Norway.

Soon after the attempted kidnapping, we moved to a brown, two-story frame house with a large garden and an orchard full of apple trees, cherry trees and even pear trees. The landlord gave me a couple of my own apple trees, which made me very proud. I used to sit on a high branch of a tall cherry tree and indulge my love for reading undisturbed by the invading world. Two brothers were born in that brown frame house. The boys and their friends could be annoying, so I adored my hiding place. However pesky my brothers were as children, throughout my adult life, they've become my very best friends and supporters.

The plan was to stay at Slemdal for just a few years because Father expected to be sent to Brazil in 1939. Instead, we ended up living there for over ten years due to World War II. Our landlord joined the Norwegian Nazi party, which made it dangerous for us as children because Norwegians did not usually associate with Nazis. In fact, I was nearly arrested at the age of twelve. I had told my younger brothers not to play with the neighbor boys' electric train because they were members of the Norwegian Nazi Party. They wore Nazi uniforms and great big Nazi party buttons on their lapels. When my politically dissident behavior got to certain officials, they took action. I still have the letter written to my father from a higher-ranking Nazi. The official's threat stated that if didn't stop terrorizing the children on the street, they would send me elsewhere for a *different* kind of education! While I avoided arrest, my grandfather became a prisoner of war at Grini in 1940. His stint was short and he was released early. His son, my uncle, however, was later sent to Germany as a POW for the duration of the war.

When WWII first broke out in 1939, Norway had hoped to stay neutral, just as they had in WWI. But on April 9, 1940—after a British ship was hidden in the nonaligned waters of Joessingfjord on the south coast of Norway—the Germans launched a surprise attack. They simultaneously bombed Oslo, Bergen, Trondheim and Narvik. That morning as we slept in our beds at Slemdal just outside Oslo, we hadn't heard the first air raid sirens. At 4 a.m., however, Mother woke Father and asked him if he had heard planes overhead. A moment later, the telephone rang informing us that the Germans were on a mission to occupy Norway. Father learned that our King Haakon and the government officials were leaving town. Unlike the others, Father was given orders to remain in Oslo and to continue as head of the Forsynings Departementet (the Supply Department). I shall never forget when the news of the raids came over the radio. My parents decided we should evacuate. Mother summoned a driver who lived upstairs. Within no time the car was packed, and we were driving north toward my uncle's farm called *Staur*.

The expansive farm bordered Norway's largest lake, Mjoesa. Lillehammer, a town known for hosting the Olympics, sat at the northern end of the lake. That momentous morning, everyone was gripped with sheer terror. The Germans were employing a deliberate panic tactic which they had used in Poland and Spain, and later perfected when they invaded Holland, Belgium and France. It was April, and a steady stream of cars moved northward over slush-covered roads. From time to time officials stopped us. I can still picture women emerging from their cars dressed only in nightgowns and boots with fur coats thrown over. Fear and alarm overwhelmed us. But when we finally crossed the bridge at Minnesund at the south end of the Lake Mjosa, a sense of relief and good fortune ensued. We felt even luckier when we arrived at the family property and approached the drive between the two white gatehouses. From there it was only another kilometer through the fields. The birch trees along the driveway greeted us, dressed in their white and black gear. We entered the courtyard and drove up to the heavy wooden front door. When it opened, warmth and security enveloped us. Mother left us in the care of my aunt and uncle, then immediately returned to Father in Oslo. Fortunately, she and the driver got back across the Minnesund Bridge before it was blown up.

The main building at *Staur* was a large, beautiful three-story, white frame house with a sloping black slate roof. Dormer windows peeped out like square eyes from the top floor. They seemed to smile to us in the gray spring light of that April day. A large fire in the main hall was a comforting sight, as was my aunt's smile. She was dressed in a tailored, pastel-colored skirt, a silk blouse and matching cardigan. We felt safe in these familiar surroundings. My uncle was my father's oldest brother and my godfather. He always seemed like our grandfather, as Father's own dad had died in 1911. I was ten years old and my brothers were not quite five and three. Our nanny was totally hysterical, because she had to leave her twin sister with my father in Oslo. The boys became partly my responsibility in the days to come. One entered this lovely house through an outer hall where furs, coats and boots were shed. A big central stair hall invited guests with its big fireplace. To the left, one passed through the library to the ballroom, which occupied that whole end of the wonderful house. Straight ahead of the hall, the drawing room led to the dining room. To the right of the hall there was a huge pantry and an enormous, but cozy kitchen where Big Anna reigned as queen. Beyond the kitchen lay the servants' hall and the refrigeration room. Outside, one of the farm buildings served as the larder, or *stabbur* in Norwegian. This structure was raised on huge stones to defend against rodents and other pests. The bedrooms had the Austrian white-tiled, floor-to-ceiling corner stoves, which would be lit early morning. The brass doors at the bottom were left open. I used to watch the flames play shadows on the ceiling. The top floor had more bedrooms, one of which was used to store apples. Each fall, apples were piled high as they were harvested. By Christmastime, the aroma was heavenly.

Along the entire length of the garden façade of the house, Aunt Margit planted rectangular beds of multi-colored snapdragons. Other planters were on a lower level. Oline, the gardener, was in charge for as long as I can remember, and continued to be after I left the country. Across the glassy water of the Mjoesa, on the island of Helgoen I could see Aunt Sisken and Uncle Jacob Hoel's white manor house. Their lovely estate was called *Hovinsholm*.

The front door to the main house at *Staur* faced the handsome courtyard which was flanked on one side by a large red barn with its two bridges to the hayloft. One of the many Christmas Eve traditions was to leave rice pudding on the bridge for the Nissen, the gnome. About 25 to 30 horses occupied half of the barn, and 100 head of cattle lived in the other half. All the horses, cows and calves had names.

Throughout my childhood, horses were among my best friends, and riding my favorite pastime. That is why the gift of the gold stirrup charm on my bracelet has given me lifelong inspiration. This charm reminds me of my grandfather who was one of my dearest friends in my youth. He headed up our cavalry, which led to our mutual love of horses. Since the age of five, Grandfather would take me to horse shows and to riding school. I remember how he would come home from the office on horseback in the 1930s. His aide-de-camp would then return the horse to the stables while bringing Grandfather's document case. During difficult moments in my childhood, I would confide with Grandfather, the old Colonel—the *Oberst*. When I was

21, he permitted me to dine and dance with my friends in the evenings. But lunch was his! He would treat me like a girlfriend and bring flowers, perfume and wine with which to skaal, or toast. Sadly, he died unexpectedly at the embassy in London later that year. I shall never forget this remarkable friend.

At *Staur* there was another barn-red building on the north side of the courtyard where the manager and grooms lived. To the south was a tall stone wall, and beyond it was the spacious chicken coop. During the war, my brothers helped Aunt Margit feed the chickens. One day, the chickens discovered some fermented rhubarb wine. They got totally drunk, which made the funniest sight as they weaved about with their heads dangling. A little way off was the old racing-horse stable that had been converted into a "pig palace."

One of our horses named Apollo hated three things: locomotives, baby-prams and pigs! This presented a slight problem when I was sent to fetch the mail at our local railway station. It was eleven kilometers from our property.

Throughout the endless months of evacuation, these experiences and environments nurtured my love for rural living and helped relieve homesickness for Mother and Father.

While in the country, there was no communication from Oslo for three weeks. Rumors ran rampant. On one hand, in the country, we were told the capital was in ruins. On the other hand, the people in Oslo were told that the Germans had bombed the entire countryside. The enemy had followed the path of the king's flight to the north. One rumor declared that a German military bus was coming across the ice-covered lake. All the men on the farm brought out their guns and lay in wait along the shore to protect their property and families. Someone had to bring the men food, but their wives did not dare, for fear of being raped by the Germans. In those days, it was commonly thought that children were immune from attack. Plus, I wasn't afraid to go down through the horse pastures. So, another girl (who also had evacuated from Oslo), and I got the meal delivery job. Together, we faced the dusk together, braved those cold April evenings, and felt extremely important bringing food baskets to the men on the beaches.

My cousin—my uncle and aunt's only son—was an officer in the cavalry assigned to fight the German tanks. My beloved grandfather also rode in the cavalry. He was captured by the invading Germans and sent to a prison camp. It was soon obvious how inadequate our weapons were against the Germans. My cousin was sent home to *Staur* along with his horse, Erma. After a few weeks, the Germans, in badly fitting green uniforms, came to pick up Erma. She belonged to the cavalry, ergo state property. But the Germans did not just take one horse; they took several including my favorite beautiful three year-old purebred called Floridor. We had been friends since the day he was born. He was a leader, and with my help often guided the other horses to change pastures. It had always made me feel extremely grown up and proud. I will never forget that horrible day when the Germans stood in front of the red barn dressed in their hideous green uniforms. As they started to seize the horses, Floridor looked at me as if to say, "Are you really going to let these awful people take me away?" The pleading look in his eye has stayed with me forever. At only ten years old, I cried my eyes out, and from then on, began to hate the Germans. I will always remember my friend, Floridor. Decades later I recognized the same look in the eye of the horse in the film, *War Horse*. That movie brought back all the pain of losing Floridor.

When the Germans first attacked Norway, the king, the crown prince, the government, as well as several foreign ambassadors fled northward. On my first night in the country, I recall when the Finnish ambassador stopped by *Staur* at two o'clock in the morning. I watched and listened from behind the upper staircase railing. Aunt Margit gave the guests something to eat and drink before they continued on their way to rejoin the king. The royal party was routinely bombarded wherever they stopped for the night. For some unknown reason, we were spared. Weeks later, when the king and the crown prince finally reached Tromsoe in the north, it was decided that they would continue their fight for Norway from London. Together with the government, they were picked up by a British destroyer and brought to England. In the meantime, the crown princess and her three children fled to the United States via Petsamo, Finland. They spent the rest of the war in America under the special protection of President Franklin Delano Roosevelt. There was no doubt that the Germans had prepared this attack well in advance. In fact, a large ship carrying a German occupation government was already en route prepared to rule Norway the morning of the first surprise bombing. Their ship, the *Blucher*, had steamed up towards Oslo. Halfway up the Oslo fjord, however, it met trouble and sank with "man and mouse." I heard that a soldier stationed at Oscarsborg Fort, where the Oslo fjord is at its narrowest, grew so angry that he fired old cannon balls from an even older cannon. The fact is the *Blucher* was hit mid-ships and sank immediately with every man onboard. The war joke that summer was that some small fish with green bones had eaten not only the Germans, but their green uniforms as well!

Around this time, the infamous Vidkun Quisling took over as minister president with his Nazi cronies. Thank Heavens! Quisling never contacted us again. Only once did my father's name come up. It happened one day when the Germans tried to intimidate Father by telling him that he was an Anglophile because he had the CBE, Commander of the British Empire. My father immediately responded that he received his the same day as Quisling for their work for the British in Moscow at the end of the 20s. The question never came up again.

Since the evacuation period lasted several months, I was sent to the local country school along with the other children on the farm. We caught a ride on top of the 50-liter milk containers on the early morning horse-drawn milk run. There were no cars in the country, so we reverted to horse and buggy for transportation. Mail was also fetched on horseback. I loved to ride the eleven kilometers to the nearest railway station at Ottestad. If there was anything heavy, I was given a horse and buggy. Apollo, the tall three-quarter bred, was good both to ride and pull a carriage. As mentioned, Apollo was afraid of locomotives, which once almost caused a serious accident. We were stopped at a railroad crossing when a speeding locomotive steamed by. Apollo went insane and reared up on his hind legs, buggy and all. If it had not been for some very handsome boys—from the nearby Grimerud Boys' Boarding school—who intervened and grabbed Apollo, I don't know how it would have ended. I immediately fell in love with the four of them, of course. And they all turned up as fellow students at my high school later that year!

Two years into the war, my parents and I were granted special permission to go up to the country to celebrate cousin Iacob's wedding and later, Aunt Margit and Uncle Iacob's silver wedding anniversary. They still had food in the country, even up to Christmas of 1941, when a large part of our family gathered to celebrate the holidays at *Staur*. It was the last time that we were all together until after the war. Some of the cousins and friends fled either to England or Sweden because the resistance work became increasingly dangerous. But in December 1941, Anna, our wonderful cook, was still very busy in the kitchen with most of her traditional cooking. At the silver wedding anniversary, she served roast beef one night and legs of veal the next. I remember Father having nightmares because of the rich food which we no longer were used to living in town. Anna was making the most heavenly veal meatballs, cooking hams and traditional pork products. She also baked a large quantity of Christmas cookies. The memories of those feasts sustained us through the later lean war years. Yes, I shall remember that Christmas till the end of my days. We all journeyed together from Oslo on a dark afternoon. The train puffed its way north through a snowy white landscape. After a few hours we arrived at Ottestad, our small country station. Horses and sleds filled with bearskins and other furs were waiting to take us to *Staur*. I loved the sound of the horse hooves as they trotted on the snow covered road. The happy music of jingle bells rang out in the clear night air. We made our way by the light of flickering torches. The snow banks piled high on the banks of the road, and the shadows from the torches threw strange silhouettes. Once in a while, a faint light from a distant farm appeared. Even the countryside in Norway was under a blackout. After about ten kilometers we reached the white gatehouses. The doors were flung open and old and young streamed out to greet us. Olaf, the groom and his large wife, Anna lived on one side with their young son. The farmhand, Ole, his wife and six children lived on the other side. From the gatehouses we continued through the familiar majestic group of tall, white and black birch trees. A translucent veil of snow still covered the branches. The high stone courtyard wall was also blanketed in snow. Looming up in the dusk was the long red barn.

We entered the heavy front doors to the hall and shed our furs. A huge fire blazed in the main hall's fireplace, exuding a warm welcome. Anna reigned in the enormous kitchen. In keeping with Norwegian tradition, she had baked for weeks. Before the war began, people baked at least a dozen different varieties and shapes of Christmas cookies and biscuits. I loved the sweet aroma that permeated the house. After a tall evergreen was brought in from the woods, the ballroom was off limits for the children until Christmas Eve. Every grownup decorated the ceiling-high tree. December 24th was always full of happy duties. Aunt Margit took us by horse and sled to bring gifts to the farm workers' families. It was wonderful to help Santa Claus and wish everyone a Merry Christmas. I was as excited as they were. I can still hear the jolly jingle bells filling the air above the silent, snow-clad landscape of the cold Nordic winter. In the afternoon we brought a big bowl of rice pudding to the Nissen, the gnome-like little man of fairytales who lived above the stables. We left the bowl on the middle bridge of the huge red barn. By morning, the rice pudding was always gone, the bowl licked clean. I never saw the Nissen, but sensed he was watching. Then we made a special visit to the horses. Each of my 25 four-legged friends was given goodies, like apples, carrots, and an extra handful of oats. At afternoon tea, the family, house guests, farm manager and workers congregated in the dining room to taste all the wonderful cookies and exchange presents for a Merry Christmas.

Later, the family met in the drawing room. Father would read us the Christmas story while candles were lit on the tree in the festive ballroom. Carols filled the room as young and old walked around the tree. More presents were opened and then, in procession, we entered the marvelously decorated dining room, also lit by live candles. Outside, even the birds had a Christmas dinner of big bunches of grain tied to the trees and pillars. A wonderful sense of peace and goodwill reigned that night. Since every bedroom was occupied, I was given the privilege to sleep in the fragrant Apple Room—another happy memory of that holiday. On Christmas Day, everyone attended the little white church in the valley. People gathered from all the nearby farms. It was almost unreal in its beauty. We were very snug in our sleighs, covered in furs, as jingle bells sounded gaily from every corner. This is the picture I have carried with me ever since. My "White Christmases" are treasured heart-felt memories.

Although we had ample food in the country, in the towns there was severe rationing. Once or twice a year, food parcels arrived from our family in Denmark, which helped a lot. But generally speaking, recipes had to be very imaginative, to say the least. Sometimes our dinner consisted of oatmeal made with water without sugar or discarded old salted herrings fried in cod liver oil. Those were the evenings I was allowed to take a walk during the meal. I was unable to get it down. Sometimes we ate rutabaga. Mother varied the way she served it. When she fried them in cod liver oil, again, I was out the door. Other times she took a cheese cutter and tried to make pretty rosettes. Even though we had potatoes in the cellar all winter, we had to fight some rather big rats in order to fetch them. On occasion, toward the end of the war, Father managed to get packages of frozen cod. In addition, because both mother and I developed ulcers, we were awarded small rations of white flour. Organized food distribution began October 1, 1939. A supply department was created consisting of four different directorates: one for rationing and supply for the population, one for industry, one for import/export to foreign countries and yet another one for shipping. Prime Minister Nygaardsvoll asked Father to take over the import/export department—a very demanding job.

I remember a few days after the outbreak of WWII, both Britain and Germany sought to establish treaties. Puschka went to London with a delegation in December, 1939. The deliberations dragged out so that they had to spend Christmas and New Year's Day there. The Germans had planted magnetic mines in the North Sea, so the usual route to Great Britain was not an option. Puschka was against flying in those days and, as members of a neutral country, the delegation could still travel over land, via Berlin, Brussels and Calais. In London, the delegation lived quite comfortably at the Savoy, where they also held their meetings. London, of course, was under blackout.

Other than that, Britain acted like there was no war. 1939 New Years Eve at the Savoy, I was told, was as gay and festive as ever. The treaty with Germany was signed February 23, 1940 and the treaty with Great Britain the 11th of March, both in Oslo. The latter was signed by Lord Glenconner. I remember being allowed to serve the *hors d'oevres* at the dinner held in his honor. His lordship had long hair hanging down over his collar. I was fascinated. Times had certainly changed!

Less than a month later on April 9, 1940, the Germans invaded Norway. All treaties were void. Father's nomination as Director of the Supply Department meant that we could not buy anything on the black market. Puschka's connection with the underground leaders, however, was established through his good friend, Gunnar Jahn. He was one of the heads of the organization of underground leaders. When Gunnar Jahn, Nicolai Schei and Gunnar Schjelderup were arrested in the fall of 1944, Puschka was advised to go underground for a few days till the coast was clear. Every morning he would call us to find out if anyone had asked for him during the night. The Germans usually arrested people at 4:00 in the morning. After three or four days he was told to go back to the office because his absence might cause suspicion. He still slept away from home. It was rather strange to meet him on the tram in the mornings and appear as if I'd just seen him recently.

I'm not certain when Father was appointed as one of a Council of Eight— or the Raadmen—who would handle the post-war period in Norway, but it must have been near the end of 1944. It was Dr. Philos. H.O. Christophersen who contacted him. The eight men would govern the country from the day the peace treaty was signed till the government returned from their London exile. A certain Miss Storm passed on secret messages. After the war was over, we found that her real name was Stromme. She married Dr. Christophersen in 1947. We met the couple later when Father, as ambassador, received them at the London Embassy. I remember hearing them reminisce.

That last winter of the war brought especially frightening days. I recall our family discussing what to do in case of trouble. The plan was that my two small brothers would be driven up to *Staur*. Mother and I stowed our packed suitcases under our beds. We would be taken via an escape route to Sweden. Because of his illness contracted after a fall while in Moscow, Father could not have survived a concentration camp. In case of danger, there were Resistance people ready to spirit him away in an instant. What remains in my mind forever from those days was that the entire country opposed the German and Norwegian Nazis. Thank God, there were very few of the latter. The rest of us were called the "Joessings" because of the 1940 incident when the British ship attempted to hide in the *Joessingfjord.*

It is not for me to write about the actual occupation. Enough books have covered that subject. But I will mention one of many incidents that occurred when I was only twelve years old. I had been home with the flu and went out skiing to get some fresh air. As I glided down a ski trail through the woods, I suddenly saw a German officer and his girlfriend. The girl was in the typical "grey goose" uniform. The two appeared suddenly on foot in front of me on the narrow trail with two big dogs. It all flashed in front of my eyes, but it was impossible to stop skiing, so I shouted, "Ahoy!" No one was supposed to be on the trails without skis, but the couple did not budge until I was practically on top of them. The big officer swung around and gave me an uppercut. Falling backwards in the snow, I was more scared than hurt. I scrambled up to quickly ski away. The officer shouted something in German. I quietly answered, "I don't understand German." "All Norwegians pretend they don't understand," he said furiously. Then he unleashed the dogs after me. Their teeth clenched my arms as I struggled to free myself. Finally, his girlfriend spoke up in my defense and said, "Let her go! She is only a child!" Only then did the officer call off the dogs. I dragged myself to the tram terminal and there people tended to my arms, which were bleeding through the ski clothes. I still bear the scars of that terrifying incident. That was the last time I was allowed to ski alone!

One by one, our schools had been requisitioned and used as barracks by the Germans. We skied or bicycled long distances—sometimes in the dark of winter evenings—for a few hours of school. During the occupation, the Germans eventually arrested many teachers and university professors, as well as our clergy and doctors. They were taken as political prisoners and sent to concentration camps simply because of their profession! Every day, people quietly disappeared. We always hoped some would escape, but never knew for certain if they did.

In the middle of all this, possibly due to stress and lack of food, I developed a variety of health problems. I got water on my knees for no apparent reason and felt the cold more acutely. I could no longer ski or play tennis. My parents took me to see my father's cousin, who was a doctor. To avoid being arrested, many physicians went into hiding with the Underground Movement. Uncle Arne Klem was still free and examined me thoroughly. I will never forget his face as he took my parents aside and said, "This is very serious, and I don't know what we can do for her. She may not survive. However, do try a neurologist, or even a brain surgeon. She will probably lose her extremities because she has some unknown illness related to blood circulation, or the lack of such." There was a struggle on all fronts. I was in a lot of pain. The doctors were actually so pessimistic about my prognosis that the Underground Movement was asked to procure some pain medicine for me in Sweden. It came into Norway through special channels. When Halvard Lange, who became Foreign Secretary, came back from a concentration camp after the war with the same symptoms, I was referred to a famous neurosurgeon. He tried every new medicine in the book on me. One of his experiments involved a medication containing nitro-glycerin. When he applied it to my knees, it made me so depressed that I begged my family to sit on me to keep me from jumping out the window. I even spent a few weeks in the Swedish Red Cross Hospital. There I was introduced to morphine for the first time to relieve the pain. It felt so yummy. After ten days, I refused it for fear of addiction.

During the German occupation, no one over twelve was allowed to travel far from home. Sometimes I would take the train alone to *Staur*, like the time the Germans forced the schoolchildren into potato picking. The country women were so adept at their work, and because I was younger,

I lagged way behind. Fortunately, a good friend of mine, who was working on the farm that year, would go back over the field with me during the rest periods.

Father and I spent a few summers steaming down the south coast to his family town of Risoer. He occasionally received special permission to travel to his hometown, but mother was never allowed to go. Risoer was named "The White Pearl of the South Coast," because the little town on the Skagerak consisted of mostly white frame houses, which speckled a natural port. The market square lay on the inner harbor, with the *Konditori*—or Eeg's Tea House—on the banks. Our old family home was built on the market square up against the rocky mountain. My favorite yellow cherry tree stood on one of the upper terraces behind the house. Since I was the youngest of the cousins, Aunt Ellen always let me go up through the old attic and pick yellow cherries to my heart's content. It was in Risoer that I learned to swim before I was five so I could go sailing with the big boys. At times I would sail in a small dinghy in the wee hours just to meet the shrimp boats coming in with their harvest. They would throw me a bag of newly cooked shrimp.

Risoer is one of the oldest towns on the coast. During the 15th and 16th centuries, it boasted a flourishing timber trade with the Dutch. Of even greater importance was the income received from taxes in the 1700s. Risoer became a city in 1723 and boasted one of the largest fleets of sailing ships in the country. Many of them belonged to my grandfather and great grandfather. The ships sailed every ocean of the world. Unfortunately, with the introduction of steam—of which my grandfather did not approve—the fleet dwindled. My grandfather died in 1911 when my father was only 15. Father was the youngest of five sons. He was, therefore, designated for the navy or the diplomatic service. He happened to be one of two Norwegians who were both. Before father entered the Naval Academy, he was required to have about 365 days under sail. Once in Adelaide, Australia, he missed the connecting ship to meet one of the family ships, and had to take a train to Sydney. It was difficult because his English was poor then, and the distances were long. But he caught another ship on its way to Chile to pick up a cargo of saltpeter. In 1914, while they were in Chile, World War I broke out. His ship sailed back to Europe round the Cape Horn. Off the Falklands, a British Man of War hailed them asking the Norwegians whether they knew how things were going with the war. No radio communications existed in those days, of course. For five months, father's sailing ship had no other contact with land. As they came nearer Europe, having no idea whether they were on the side of the English or the Germans, they feared encountering either side. Finally reaching their home port, they found to their relief that Norway was neutral.

One summer during WWII, I traveled back from Risoer to Oslo on the coastal steamer by myself. It took 24 hours because we could not proceed at night. I had no cabin, but spent the night outside on a deck chair. My only food for the whole trip was a head of cabbage and a pound of blueberries, which I shared with a friend. The Germans were afraid someone might escape across the North Sea to England! In fact, the *Galtesund*, one of the coastal steamers had done just that. Most of my cousins either escaped to England, or joined the local resistance movements. Some escaped across the border to Sweden where they lived as refugees until the war's end. Others went to England or Canada. As a result of the emigration, *Little Norway*—a school for pilots—was established near Toronto, Canada.

As I mentioned previously, my wonderful grandfather had been released early on as a prisoner of war. I spent a lot of time with him and our horses in town where food was scarce, for as long as we could feed them. I cried when we finally had to say goodbye to the last one at the riding school.

The next five years passed painfully slow. My diary during the last days reads:

April 28, 1945: Himmler has sent a request for capitulation to the Allied Forces who have returned it saying it has to be sent to the Russians at the same time! Does this mean peace? Dear God, help all the people who suffer and make men act humane and end this horrific war as soon as physically possible.

April 29, 1945: In church they told wrong news from the pulpit. Rumors are flying about everywhere! Imagine if, at last, peace rumors would come true!

April 30, 1945: All rumors of peace are off!

May 1: No daily things matter, rumors continuing.

May 3: Only rain!

May 4: Once more, masses of rumors.

May 6: Fantastic news: The Germans capitulate in Denmark, Holland and Germany! But what will happen to us? Norway was not included in that treaty. We were told we have almost 400,000 armed Germans in Norway at this time. They might have been ordered to fight to the bitter end!

May 7: Gone to school early, it is all very exciting. We are having a party at home in the evening. Fortunately Nanny Jenny will be there. Puschka was very nervous as he knew all the secret facts. He went to listen to a secret radio under a Turkish rug in the chicken coop of our neighbor! We cried and laughed off and on. Then at five the telephone rang. Alf Roed said the news of peace had been on British radio! "Are you sure?" We still could not believe it. The telephone rang again. It was the Swedish Consul General Westring who told us it had been on both German and Oslo radios. We had no radio as the Germans had confiscated all private radios in 1941 or '42. It was six o'clock and the telephone rang again. I picked it up. "This is Dr. Christophersen." He had a message to Puschka from the leaders of the Resistance. The peace was for real, at last! Our joy was immeasurable. The guests arrived; the Skeis, the Joachim Ihlens and others. Embraces were exchanged in an atmosphere that was electric! FREEDOM!!!

The following morning, wearing a red Monty cap that had been smuggled in from Sweden, I went to town to celebrate. There were thousands of freed Norwegians, as well as young men who had been covertly waging a guerilla war in the woods. Still, the fully-armed Germans walked the streets and the Norwegian Nazis stood as sharpshooters on the rooftops. But it did not dampen the spirit of the people. Some German officers even appeared irritated over the open joy of the Norwegians. It was as if the Germans were thinking, "How rude, while we are still here!" The Germans had enlisted men—most of whom were extremely young—who could not wait to return home. They shouted to us from the school windows they'd previously taken over, "Der krieg ist fertig, der krieg ist fertig," or "The war is finished!" I saw trucks carrying prisoners from *Grini,* our concentration camp just outside Oslo. Norwegian flags fluttered from every flagpole and draped from every window. People sang the national anthem, *Ja vi elsker dette landet,* and there was a 17th-of-May (our National Day) atmosphere all over town. The boys of the Resistance, in their sports clothes, had taken over the watch at the royal palace. The Norwegian police were back in their national uniforms.

Six days later, Crown Prince Olav flew in from London and exhibited great courage to his people by riding in an open car through town. The jubilation was high. My father, along with the eight Raadmen, came forward to fulfill their important mission of running the country until the government returned from England. Three weeks after the signing of the peace treaty in Europe, the Norwegian government rolled down the gangway of the British ship, the *Andes.* Eight extremely thin men were among the welcoming committee. Another very lean man, H.M. King Haakon, received a real hero's welcome. I've always considered him my hero. Then the crown princess and her children returned from the States. Slowly, prisoners came home from their corner of the world, each carrying a unique story.

One homecoming in particular sticks out in my mind. A friend and his father, who was a doctor, had been sent to the Dachau concentration camp. Toward the end of the war, father and son were separated. The Americans liberated one half of Dachau concentration camp and the Russians liberated the other half. I don't remember the details of how my friend made his way through Russia and ended up in Murmansk in the very north. One day, however, he stood with several other people on the pier in Murmansk, when he discovered a Norwegian ship in the harbor. Nobody was allowed near it. Eventually, he spied his own brother on the bridge. Miraculously, his brother recognized him in spite of his being incredibly thin. The brothers joyfully united onboard and arrived home to Oslo soon after. Although, I barely recognized my friend, I was extremely happy, at long last, to see him again.

Throughout those five interminable years, grandfather was always there for me. He inspired me to keep reading by offering books from his vast library. Some I have to this day!

After the Liberation, my father became Permanent Secretary of Foreign Affairs. Trygve Lie was the Foreign Minister. Later, Lie became the first head of the United Nations. Trygve Lie often came to London in the 1950s, and we became good friends. We would dine out with Notti Bohn, one of father's good friends. I remember Father being horrified the first time he realized that I was on first name basis with Trygve, an older statesman. How times have changed!

In 1946, father was appointed ambassador to the Court of Saint James in London. We celebrated our last Norwegian Christmas in our Thomas Heftyesgate home, where we'd moved when father became head of the Foreign Office. Although we only lived there about a year and a half, I dearly loved that house. The two living rooms had paneled walls; one of polished walnut another of light birch. The attic was designed like a ship's corridor with doors labeled "Captain," "First Mate," etc., and the roof looked like a ship's bridge, complete with lifebelts, steering wheel and compass. I spent a great deal of time on the bridge, reading and enjoying the view of the Oslo fjord. Delightful parties were hosted on that rooftop, as well as on the ground floor. For several months, the ground floor was occupied by charming American Air Force officers. One officer named Mike helped me prepare for my final high school math exams. From that moment on I loved America!

What does Norway mean to me? It is the beautiful country of my ancestors. It is a rocky coastline with myriads of islands and jutting fjords surrounded by a powerful ocean. It is a land of people with a love that binds them through both prosperous and troubled times. Norway's people possess a passion for sport and life in the free outdoors, both on land and sea.

I returned several times to my dear homeland and savored the beautiful people and scenery from time to time while in London. Whenever we flew up the Oslo fjord and caught the first glimpse of white sails and my childhood city at the end of the fjord, I always got a fluttering feeling deep inside. One year the town was beautifully repainted and restored in honor of the 1,000 year anniversary of the city. Flowers abounded everywhere. It was also the 700th anniversary of the Akershus fortress, as well as the centenary of the National Theater.

One of Norway's famous actors who often played at the National Theatre was Per Aabel. He happened to be a neighbor and good friend. At age five, while we lived in the brown frame house with the orchard, I used to crawl under our fence to Per's parents' house. Per played the piano beautifully. I would sit and listen under his window for hours. He lived past the ripe old age of 90. Just before his last performance, I was privileged to talk with him. He said, "Do you think it would be all right if I could keep the book from which I am to recite on my lap when I am on stage, just for any eventuality?" He died two months later having led a rich and eventful life. He gave so much, and not just from the stage.

Finally, one of my dearest friends was my grandfather who was one of my dearest friends in my youth. He headed up our cavalry, which led to our mutual love of horses. Since I was five, Grandfather would take me to horse shows and to riding school. I remember how he would come home from the office on horseback in the 1930s. His aide-de-camp would then return the horse to the stables while bringing Grandfather's document case. During difficult periods in my childhood, I would confide with Grandfather, the old Colonel—the *Oberst*. When I was 21, he permitted me to dine and dance with my friends in the evenings. But lunch was his! He would treat me like a girlfriend and bring flowers, perfume and wine with which to skaal, or toast. Sadly, he died unexpectedly at the embassy in London later that year. My golden stirrup charm shall forever remind me of this remarkable friend.

Evy and Father, Moscow, 1932

Nicken, Evy and Chris, Norway, 1939

King Haakon VII, my beloved king, 1947   My grandfather, Colonel Christopher
                                            Fougner, 1957

A "Lenare" study of Madame Ragnhild Prebensen,
wife of H.E. the Norwegian Ambassador, Doyen of
the Diplomatic Corps. Her Excellency speaks many
languages, including Russian. The Prebensens have
one daughter, Evelyn (28) and two sons.

My mother in The Diplomatist   My parents, the Norwegian Ambassador
Magazine, London 1957   to the Court of St. James (1946-1958)
                                      and Madame Prebensen, 1957

Our 1957 Christmas card from Queen Elizabeth, the Duke of Edinburgh, Prince Charles and Princess Anne

Her Royal Highness The Princess of Berar, London 1937

Her Royal Highness Princess Fatima Zohra of Morocco, 1958

H.E. MONS. PER PREBEN PREBENSEN, G.C.V.O., C.B.E., has been Norwegian Ambassador in London since 1946, and on the departure, now impending, of H.E. Mons. Massigli, will become Doyen of the Diplomatic Corps here. During their years in this country M. Prebensen and his wife have become greatly beloved, and have done much to strengthen the ties developed between this country and Norway in the last war, of which the annual dispatch from Oslo to London of a huge Christmas tree for Trafalgar Square is so notable a symbol. M. and Mme. Prebensen are close friends of the Norwegian Royal Family, and entertained Crown Prince Olav at their Palace Green residence when he recently paid a private visit to London

My father giving the annual Christmas tree to London from Norway in Trafalgar Square, 1950

Chris and I hang paintings for Oslo show, 1960

With the portrait of Father, Galleria La Feluca, Rome 1955

Modeling my fashion designs on a Roman rooftop, 1963

London – The Norwegian Embassy

MAUNDAY MONEY

It was a lovely May day in 1947. The sun was shining in Oslo, Norway's capital. I had finished school and was ready to join my family in London. My father had been nominated Ambassador to the Court of Saint James in the fall of 1946. I threw a last loving look at my group of childhood friends on the pier, waving to each other for a long time, as the ship inched slowly south down the Oslo fjord. We rounded my beloved southern coast and crossed the North Sea. I sat at Captain Loveid's table encircled by old and new friends. Our destination was Newcastle-on-Tyne in England. From the ship Newcastle appeared a gray, dreary town, haggard with signs of heavy WWII bombardments. I assembled my luggage, disembarked and then boarded the rather dingy train for London, and was straight away disappointed with lunch in the dining car. It was so awful that I remember it to this day: a cup of watery cabbage soup and a tiny piece of hard meat, finished by a sad, tinned half pear. With a cost of only five shillings and sixpence, it's no wonder. Strict rationing still reigned in England and remained for quite some years.

In stark contrast, the English countryside was perfectly stunning. I began to get excited. A few hours later, I arrived at King's Cross station in London where my mother and father awaited. Mother looked very smart in a black cape and chic hat—definitely a new acquisition. I was impressed because, by comparison, Norway's shops offered so little this soon after the war. The railway station was dark and sooty. My first impression of London, like that of Newcastle, was definitely a little grim. Our driver brought around the 10-seater Cadillac that had belonged to King Haakon during the war— the same vehicle in which I later learned how to drive! London overwhelmed me at first. It was a turbulent myriad of people rushing everywhere amidst heavy traffic. What a contrast to my small country that had so long been occupied by the Germans!

On arrival at the embassy, a proper English Tea, expertly brewed including homemade scones, greeted me. It was a welcomed sight after the dismal train car lunch. Before dinner, mother took me for a walk around our neighborhood. Nothing but ruins and piles of rubble everywhere. The neighboring structure was an old bombed-out church whose stained-glass windows, oddly enough, remained intact. On moonlit nights, the colored windows created a romantic sight from my bedroom.

NORWEGIAN EMBASSY
LONDON.

Our brick, five story Norwegian Embassy was on a private, tree-lined street bordering Kensington Palace and its gardens. The enclave of ten houses opposite the palace was called Palace Green, and Kensington Palace Gardens occupied the rest of the street. Old fashioned street lamps blinked on the side-walks. Every evening an elderly lamplighter performed his rounds lighting each lamp post by hand. The London fog—or smog in those days—was often so thick the lamplighter and the lamps were barely visible.

Daily breakfast with my father in the dining room included reading the newspapers. After lunch we'd have coffee in the library. Every afternoon at 4:30, tea was served in the drawing room. If my brothers were home alone, tea was upstairs in the family sitting room.

One day, during one of the many times that Crown Prince Olav stayed with us, we returned from being out and were surprised to find that the crown prince had come home early. There sat the prince and my youngest brother, Chris, engrossed in their newspapers, each with a nursery mug of tea in their hands!

During our first few years in London, my two brothers, Peter Nicolai and Christopher—known as Nicken and Chris at home—attended St. David's School. It was the first time they had worn uniforms. Nicken then returned to Norway to continue his education, while Chris went to Westminster School. There, Chris earned two valued coins called Maunday Money. He gave me one as a gift for my charm bracelet. I so appreciate the coin because it forever reminds me of my very special brother and our lovely London years together.

Tall wrought iron gates closed off our private street at each end guarded by old uniformed veterans in top hats trimmed with gold braiding. When the guards were off at night, we had to get out of the car to open and close the gates ourselves. Imagine my surprise and delight when I came home from a party one evening to find the famous, romantic French actor, Gerard Philippe, holding the gate open for me. Then, with a very chevaleresque wave of his hand, he ushered me in! He was there as a guest of the Princess of Berar.

The princess was one of my best friends and lived a few doors down at number 6 Palace Green. Princess Hadice Hayriye Ayshe Durrushehvar, also known as Durru Shehvar, was the daughter of Abdul Mejid Efendi of Turkey, son of Sultan Abdulaziz and the last heir apparent to the Ottoman throne. In 1924, the family was exiled to France. The princess was sought out by the Shah of Persia and King Fuad I of Egypt as a bride for their respective heirs, Mohammed Reza and Farouk. Prince Azam Jah VII (1907-1970)—the eldest son of The Nizam of Hyderabad, Osman Ali Khan, Asif Jah VII—proposed to her. In 1931, she was made to marry him in Nice, France because Nizam was the richest man in the world. Every year his subjects gave him his weight in jewels. Princess Durru Shehvar was only 15 years old and begged her father to let her finish two more years of school, but the Nizam was adamant.

The princess' father was raised by a branch of the Ottoman Empire, and was deeply interested in modernizing reforms. He believed in education for women, including his daughter. Durru Shehvar became a popular public figure after her arrival in Hyderabad—a state the size of France. Hyderabad was not only the richest, but was also acknowledged by the British Raj to be foremost in the glittering Indian royal protocol. Durru Shehvar believed that women should earn their living, and she helped to remove the practice of purdah. In the 1940s, she became the first woman to inaugurate an airport in Hyderabad. In addition to establishing the Osmania General Hospital, the Princess set up the Durru Shehvar Children's and General Hospital for women and children in the old city of Hyderabad. She had two sons, Prince Mukarram Jah (b.1933) and Prince Muffakham Jah (b. 1936). The latter became a friend of my brother, Chris. The old Nizam allowed Durru Shehvar to oversee their upbringing, and the two princes were educated in Britain. They both went to Harrow, as did King Hussein of Jordan and King Feisal of Iraq, our other neighbors in Palace Green. King Feisal was small, but possessed a majestic bearing. We became friends during the years he went to Harrow. I was extremely upset when, later in 1958, he was assassinated on the steps of the Baghdad Palace. He was only 23 and just gotten engaged.

Hyderabad House was a red brick mansion filled with treasures, including some large paintings by Princess Durru Shehvar's father—a very gifted and well-known painter. Durru Shehvar was one of the most imposing women I have known, as well as one of the most loyal friends I've ever had. King Haakon always told me her beauty exceeded the beauty of all who attended the 1937 Coronation of King George VI. Among the many wonderful gifts Durru Shehvar gave me over the years on her visits—not only in Italy, but also in the USA—were a pair of fabulous pearl earrings, a beautiful pendant of flat diamonds and a gold sari for my 40th birthday. She also gave me a gold coin from Hyderabad, which I put on my bracelet. It has been among my most treasured charms!

Our private street was certainly one of the loveliest in London. It was tree-lined and ran alongside Kensington Palace. We called it home for the twelve years father served as ambassador. As the French say, "*L'adresse le plus chic de Londres!*" The French Embassy and the Indian High Commission were on Kensington Palace Gardens along with five Russian embassy houses. The Philippine, the Dutch, the Jordan and the Israeli Embassies, as well as Hyderabad House and our embassy resided in Palace Green. All these mansions had been private houses located on a street known as Millionaires' Row. The Royal Iraqi Embassy was right across the road from us. Princess Zeid—who was married to the uncle of the young King Feisal—took it upon herself to be my private art teacher. She was a famous painter as well as ambassadress.

In the early years, Sundays were set aside for pleasant family drives in the Cadillac. We would admire the landscapes, small town and villages, and stop for tea at beautiful clubs and country inns. In fact, tea was the only good meal during those first years of stringent food rationing.

After a wonderful summer trip to Italy in 1947, we returned to London to prepare for the most important social event of the post-war years—the wedding of Princess Elizabeth to Philip Mountbatten, Prince of Greece. King Haakon had decided to attend the royal wedding. During his stay in London, we gave several dinners and luncheons in his honor at the embassy. To my delight, His Majesty included me in all the events! Embassies were privileged to import goods from abroad, so invitations to our parties were highly coveted. It was such a thrill to meet the famous leading men of England, including both noblemen and politicians. Among them were Winston Churchill and the Duke of Hamilton and Brandon.

One day at lunch, His Majesty turned to me and said, "Would you like to come with me to the royal wedding reception?" "Your Majesty, would I!" I exclaimed. I knew that famous guests would attend from around the world and that they'd be wearing spectacular jewels, having emptied bank vaults and coffers for the exciting event.

As "The King and I" walked around together at the glittering evening reception, I realized I was gazing at the wonders of the world. At times my mouth actually fell open, and King Haakon would gently remind me to close it! One lady wore a large bunch of grapes on her shoulder made entirely of cabochon emeralds. The Indian Maharajahs were garbed in breast plates of rubies, sapphires and diamonds over their white silk suits. We simultaneously admired the tiara of a young, beautiful duchess when she turned to us and quietly said, "It was my grandmother's belt!" Whereupon King Haakon whispered, "Imagine what her grandmother wore on her head!"

One of the fabulously bejeweled ladies was the Nepalese ambassador's wife, The Rani Shankher. Her sari was woven from pure gold thread with rows upon rows of exquisite pearls. A huge diamond brooch in the shape of a bow fastened the sari on her shoulder. The bow was made up of diamonds that were almost as big as the Kohinoor diamond, with equally large rubies. Later that month, at a party at St. James Palace to view the wedding gifts, the Nepalese ambassador asked me to come to see his wife. He said she had dressed European for once. I found her in a long skirt woven out of real silver thread, as well as a fitted black velvet jacket with emerald buttons trailing down the front! That was what they called European! Rather than her gem-studded ensemble, however, she was more excited about her new Swiss watch. That was really what she had wanted to show me!

While at Princess Elizabeth and Prince Phillip's wedding reception held at Buckingham Palace, King Haakon introduced me to both royalty and statesmen. One of them was General Smuts of South Africa, whose presence and personality was extraordinary. We talked to King Peter of Yugoslavia; his two brothers became very good friends of mine a few years later. Prince Bernhard of the Netherlands—the father of the next monarch—was in the company of Albert, the present Belgian King's father. They came over to pay their respects to King Haakon. I was enchanted, of course. The fantastic Buckingham Palace celebration impressed me deeply with its gleaming colors and gala uniforms. King Haakon made it so easy for me to "enter" society. It was a time when England was still an empire. For me it was an extremely memorable and fabulous evening. I was only 18 years old!

After Crown Prince Olav stayed with us in London one year in the 50s, I returned to Oslo for a doctor appointment. While there, I planned to attend a friend's wedding. When His Royal Highness heard that I was coming to Norway, he invited me for lunch at *Skaugum*, his home outside town. He suggested I meet him at the palace so we could drive out together. All went according to plan until we got to the *Skaugum* gates at the bottom of the hill. It was winter and the roads were slippery. The crown prince turned to me and said, "Evelyn, you must change the gears, as I have to salute the guards when we approach the icy road." We pulled it off perfectly! Lunch was lovely, and Princess Astrid was at home. King Haakon joined us for coffee after lunch and entertained us with interesting stories and the best jokes.

Another time, the king later showed a memorable act of kindness to me during an especially difficult period in my early years in London. We were at a party and everybody was standing. He saw me struggle to stand due to my leg paralysis, and said to me, "Evelyn, just sit down on the sofa behind my back. Nobody will see you there or judge you for a lack of deference."

Early the following summer, King George and Queen Elizabeth gave a garden party as their first post-war presentation event at Buckingham Palace. Since WWII had only recently ended, Buckingham Palace had not yet returned to working order. The Diplomatic Corps were being introduced one couple at a time, after which each couple walked across a long stretch of lawn to be presented to the king and queen. I, on the other hand—in my first pair of high heels, as well as my new hat from Paulette in Paris—had to walk alone. The wide lawn had been a potato field during the war, and still had numerous lumps and bumps. It was a long, uneven path. When I approached the royal couple I observed that His Majesty was not a very tall man, and the queen was not much taller. I managed my royal curtsey to Her Majesty with no trouble. But, when I curtsied to King George VI, I had great difficulty getting back up. You can imagine how grateful I was when His Majesty pulled me up with his strong navy handgrip. Never having forgotten his kindness, I was greatly saddened when he died at such a young age a few years later. All the ladies at the royal garden party wore flowered dresses and picture hats. Suddenly, we saw the strangest sight. A black African prince was wearing a raffia crown, pearl embroidered slippers and a heavily embroidered coat, under which he wore a home knitted, brown wool turtleneck sweater—all this during a London heat wave!

A few years later at another garden party, I happened to be left alone in the tea tent with Queen Mary. I cannot remember exactly why I found myself in that position. Her brother, the Earl of Athlone and his wife, Princess Alice, were neighbors and had been one of our first guests at the embassy. They were among the royal couples living at Kensington Palace. Sometimes I would run into Princess Alice in Palace Green and she would ask me to accompany her to Barker's Department Store at the bottom of our street! She was charming and looked like a beautiful Meissen figure. I felt huge next to her, but was utterly delighted nonetheless. At a certain moment at the Buckingham Palace tea party, I do remember asking the formidable Queen Mary how she could stand so erect for hours. Obviously, I was having problems! "Well, Evelyn," she replied. "First of all I have 80 years of experience, and secondly, I have very comfortable shoes!" She was known for those flat-soled shoes, which almost looked like boats. She was a magnificent and impressive lady and must have been a great example to her granddaughter, Queen Elizabeth II. Years later, at Queen Elizabeth II's Diamond Jubilee, aware that no bride ever remembers the details of their own wedding, I sent her, via her Lady in Waiting, a page from my scrapbook recounting Her Majesty's wedding day. The Queen sent me a lovely thank you note that I have cherished ever since.

BUCKINGHAM PALACE

16th October, 2012

Dear Evelyn,

     The Queen wishes me to write and thank you so much for your letter and for your kind message on the occasion of her Diamond Jubilee.

     Her Majesty well remembers your late father, who was Norwegian Ambassador here in London for many years, and she was very touched by your kind thought in enclosing extracts from your diary, describing the events leading up to her wedding in 1947 when you were living with him in London.

     Your description of the Reception before the Royal Wedding at which, with your father, you accompanied the late King Haakon, brought back many memories to The Queen and she was most amused to read your account of the wonderful clothes and jewels on display that evening. Indeed it had been as you say, "the first magnificent event" after the end of the War, and your vivid description of the occasion has given Her Majesty much pleasure.

     I am to thank you for your kindness in writing to The Queen, in this her special year, and to tell you how glad Her Majesty was to hear of you again. The Queen has been deeply touched by the response to her Jubilee and I am to tell you that letters such as yours have been a great encouragement to her throughout her long reign.

With Her Majesty's best wishes,

Yours sincerely,

Susan Hussey.
Lady-in-Waiting

Mrs Evelyn Harrison

Among my parents' circle of friends in London, Notti and Marie Bohn figured first on the list. Notti was Norwegian and Marie was French. They had a daughter, Monique, who was two years older than me, and I was awe-struck by Monique's sophistication. At 17, when I arrived from Norway, my English was far from perfect. So I was very grateful when Marie and Monique helped my mother with the guest list for the first dinner party given for my English Society debut at 18! Twenty-two young guests were invited to our black-tie affair and, the better part of them remained my friends for life. The newspaper, *The Evening Standard,* telephoned me the day before the party. It was my very first experience with the British gossip media. The reporter asked me what I was going to wear. I was brought up in Norway to believe that one was written up in the papers at birth, marriage and death. So, I answered very diplomatically—or, so I thought—and said, "I don't know." The journalist asked me a couple of other silly questions, to which I answered just as vaguely. At this point he got annoyed. As a result, the following piece was printed in the evening paper:

At this moment Miss Prebensen does not know which of her many robes she will wear, but thinks it is going to be a pale blue afternoon frock, as anything very elaborate would not do.

I was mortified. First of all I did not have many choices about what to wear right after the war. Secondly, I never wore pale blue, nor had I ever worn an afternoon frock in my life and my English was not good enough to know what the word "elaborate" meant. On top of that, it was a black-tie dinner and the article made me sound like a complete country bumpkin. Totally crushed, I ran up to father's office. His only answer was, "Well, I guess you learned your first lesson about how to treat the media."

The embassy dinner-party was, thank God, a great success. The Tommy Kinsman's trio played, and we danced in the large drawing room. In those days the Scottish reels were very popular. Princess Elizabeth and Princess Margaret had brought them to London. The guests at our party included Earl Haig (son of the famous war hero), Caroline Thynne (daughter of the Marquess of Bath), Grizel Ogilvie (daughter of the Earl of Airlie), Elizabeth Lumley (daughter of the Earl of Scarborough), Tom Fairfax, Carl-Gustav Bielke of the Swedish Embassy, Charles Stourton (son of Lord Mowbray), Lord Dunboyne, Susana MacEachen (daughter of the Ambassador from Uruguay), Derek Stanley-Smith, Miriam Fitzalan-Howard, Mark Gilbey, David Yorke, Patrick Forbes, Rudolf Krefting, Veronica Stourton, Anne Maxwell (who a year later married the heir to the Duke of Norfolk), Gina Fox, Rupert Buchanan-Jardine (of the family of Hong Kong opium trade fame), David Scott and Paul Asquith. I mention their names and families because most of them became really great life-long friends. When the band played "God save the King" at two in the morning, everybody was still on the dance floor! For me, the event was a wonderful introduction to London and commenced twelve marvelous years rich in experiences and lasting friendships.

One of my friends from that first party was Patrick Forbes, a talented author. He spent years working in Epernay, France, and wrote a wonderful book called *Champagne*. Here is a sample of his writing:

Once at the Norwegian Embassy in London, I saw champagne shown off to as great an advantage as in the Georgian jugs at Castle Howard. It was a Christmas party arranged by the Ambassador's daughter. About twenty tables for four were placed in the dining room, each decorated with traditional Norwegian Christmas ornaments. These included apples from which sprang, at rakish angles, long, thin, porcelain white candles which were of a special kind that do not drip, and their flames hovered a couple of inches over the champagne glasses. The lights were turned out, and in the darkened room the flickering candlelight glowed through the crystal, transforming the champagne into a pool of dancing golden bubbles. One could study the wine – and marvel at its vitality and its infectious gaiety—with greater ease than in any 'salon de degustation' that I know in Rheims or Epernay."[1]

I think I fell in love with Carl-Gustaf the night of our dinner party. He was a very good-looking Swede with extra long eyelashes, which I have to admit I thought a waste on a man. He was an attaché at the Swedish Embassy which made it easy for me to include him at our embassy parties.

Once they were abroad and moving in diplomatic circles, I found that Swedes and Norwegians got on extremely well!

During the war, Notti Bohn provided the exiled Norwegian government with a weekend residence. His *Stonedene* was a rambling cottage in Hampshire not far from Hazlemere. The large living room overlooked the lawns, a swimming pool and the tennis court. After the war, the Bohns often had weekend house parties, and their Miss Hansen cooked excellent Norwegian fare. Some of her culinary specialties still make my mouth water. She made the most fantastic *croquembouche*, with fresh strawberries—the best I have tasted anywhere. Marie Bohn and her Pekingese stepped about and ran events. They both walked in the same fashion. We played croquet on the lawn (no lumps and bumps there) and tennis on the court beyond the pond and flower garden. And Carl-Gustav was in attendance. One evening, he and I drove over to the Crown Inn in Chiddingfold, which dates from 1282. On the way we stopped at Lord Tennyson's old place, *Allworth*, which we called the Dream Castle. A drink at the Crown Inn was just up our alley. Back at *Stonedene* we had long lovely evenings where we danced, played games to the early hours, and strolled on the moonlit lawn. I shall not forget how the sun glittered on the red and golden leaves in the valley the next morning. In a very merry mood we beat each other in croquet after church, walked to Waggoners Wells and teased each other mercilessly. Being in love, I wished it would never end. One day Carl-Gustaf was transferred to Warszawa, Poland. There were terrible times in Warsaw then, and he went into a deep depression. He broke off our relationship for a million stupid reasons. I was sad for a while, but my father was glad because he saw a dark side of Carl-Gustav to which I had been totally blind. He was all of 26 and I was only a teenager. In the following years, however, I got to know his family quite well. I heard he married much later, but the union only lasted six months! So, Daddy was right. The night I received Carl-Gustav's last letter, the Amsterdam Concertgebauw, conducted by the famous Bruno Walter, performed at Royal Albert Hall. That concert began a personal tradition of attending live music performances. I went not only when I was happy, but also whenever tragic events occurred. I felt it filled something inside me.

The "Season" brought Ascot races, balls, as well as cocktail and garden parties. Men still wore white tie and tails. One lived life as it had been pre-war. Although rationing was still in effect, the embassies could import food from abroad, so their dinners were very popular. I have been reminded of that many times. Formal dinners were *de rigueur*. "A small dinner party is a pleasant and civilized pretext for intelligent and audible conversation. Balls, to my mind, are a bore, cocktail parties an unspeakable curse and night clubs the nadir as a form of social intercourse." This was dear Brigadier Norman Gwatkin's remark, his ruby red face shone like a beacon. He was part of the Lord Chamberlain's office. Red-faced, ex-guard with a proud moustache, Norman had a permanent mischievous glint in his eye and a diabolic chuckle that was easy to hear above the din of any gathering. It was always a joy to run into him.

During the 1948 Olympic Games, the Norwegian royal family, including Crown Prince Olav, Crown Princess Martha, Princesses Ragnhild and Astrid, and young Prince Harald came to stay with us at the embassy. Also in tow were a lady-in-waiting, an equerry, plus a governess and the crown princess' personal maid! The embassy did not have enough bedrooms for everyone, so my two brothers were sent to Boy Scout Camp, and I was moved down to my mother's quarters. The governess and the personal maid were the only ones who refused to share rooms. Crown Prince and Crown Princess stayed in the main guestroom and bath. The two princesses occupied my rooms. Prince Harald and his governess shared a guestroom. The lady-in-waiting and the equerry, who were fortunately married to each other, took my brothers' bedroom and bath. We worked hard to prepare the embassy for our guests. The building had taken a beating during the war. Bombs exploded all around the embassy. Imagine our shock when we found that a huge piece of the ceiling plaster had fallen on the bed of the heir to the throne—just three days after his departure! Harald was charming, though not much older than ten. Mother once said she was so glad to know him so well at this age, and that she would remember that when he became King. "I will never become King," was Prince Harald's answer. "But we have to count on politics the way they run today," Mother said. Then Harald smilingly explained, "That is not what I mean. But you see they get so old in my family!"

The night before the guests arrived, my father wanted us to taste two different champagnes to decide which one to use for the festivities. I was feeling no pain after a couple of glasses of the fizzy stuff, so I went upstairs to wash my hair. When I turned upside down, however, all the bubbles went to my head, and I almost saw pink elephants. I ended up crawling on all fours with wet hair from the bathroom to my bed, at which point I saw my family in the doorway doubled-up in laughter. What cruelty!

That year we had a tremendously hot summer. No one in London had air conditioning. Every afternoon we tried to cool off in the great hall, the coolest room in the house. To keep everybody happy we served big baskets of fresh fruit—luxuries that had not yet found their way to Norway.

Every day we went to see the Olympic Games, a routine I loved. One wonderful advantage of hosting our royal guests was that we had a motorcycle escort wherever we went—as well as the best seats at the Olympics events. We went to track and equestrian races, and, not to forget, the great soccer games between the Danes and the Italians with Princess Margharetha and Prince Georg of Denmark and then celebrated a Danish win at Quaglino's. We saw *Bless the Bride* and the new musical, *Annie Get Your Gun*, with Princess Ragnhild and Princess Astrid. At one cocktail party for the Shah of Iran, the Shah talked to Princess Ragnhild and Astrid of nothing but German fighter planes. I was not impressed, nor were the Norwegian princesses!

Finally, the night of our much-anticipated royal dinner-dance and my coming out party arrived. We expected 60 people. It was a starless, warm summer night. The candle-lit garden threw romantic flickering lights on masses of flowers everywhere. Many of the royal families of Europe were in London for the Games and most of them were related to our royal family. They were all invited to the dinner-dance. Princess Margaret represented the British Royal Family. Prince Jean of Luxembourg brought his two sisters,

Marie-Adelaide and Elizabeth, and his cousin, Francoise de Bourbon-Parme. Prince Axel and Princess Margaretha and their son, Prince Georg joined us from Denmark. Princess Margaretha was our beloved Norwegian Crown Princess Martha's sister. Princess Margaret arrived in a lovely white crinoline evening dress, Crown Princess Martha wore a magnificent creation by Carven, and Princess Ragnhild and Astrid were in pale blue and light green. It was grand gala still in white tie and tails. My mother set out her magnificent Meissen china, which she had bought in Saint Petersburg, Russia around the time of my birth. She decorated the tables with pink and yellow rosebuds that matched the china. There were lovely colors of sweet peas and purple violets. It was stunning. Two mahogany tables were pushed together in a T-shape along with four additional small tables. The band played sambas, waltzes and even reels in the drawing room. Since it was so hot, people danced in the grand hall as well. Crown Princess Martha held court from the grand staircase in the large hall because it was the only cool place in the house. Princess Margaret was dancing with Prince Georg of Denmark when she came to me and complained about the heat. I said very quietly with an angelic smile, "I am so sorry, but I am not responsible for the English weather." Georg, who was a great friend of mine, winked to me above her head. In spite of the heat, nobody wanted to leave, including Princess Margaret. The band didn't play "God Save the King" until 2:30 in the morning, proving the party was a great success! What a wonderful group of friends!

It was during this heat wave when the opening of the Olympic Games occurred; the poor guardsmen in their bearskin hats must have suffered greatly. The evening reception for the Shah of Persia was a glittering assembly of the world's most important people. Caviar and champagne flowed. One evening we dined on crawfish with Trygve Lie, the United Nations secretary. While it was a favorite dish for all of us, my father hated the shelling process. So Crown Princess Martha willingly did the work for him! She was one of the greatest experts I have ever seen. For her many other attributes there was nobody I admired more. The crown princess was always thinking of other people. She had more charm, poise and kindness than anyone I have known.

I still remember the way she talked and how she gave of herself to the world. Those who had the privilege of knowing her will never forget her. When she became ill years later, I was asked to visit her in the hospital. She died in 1954 and we felt the world had lost one of its great citizens and Norway one of its greatest treasures.

The Royal Norwegian Yacht, the *Norge,* was in Torquay to see the Olympic sailing and regatta events. We were invited to spend the day on the yacht. Prince Georg of Denmark was on board, too. I was chatting with him on deck, when he suddenly noticed Morse signals coming from the British Royal Yacht. Princess Elizabeth and Prince Philip were approaching via ship to pay a visit to their cousins on the *Norge!* We hurried to tell everyone. Crown Princess Martha asked for a comb and, by chance, I happened to have one in my pocket. Everyone got a bit flustered with the unexpected honor. When Princess Elizabeth stood on our deck, she saw all the small crafts surrounding her yacht. Obviously amused, she called out, "Look people. I am over here!" We had a splendid day. As a typical Norwegian, I adore sailing and am always happiest on a deck at sea. When the crown prince returned from Torquay, we all went to a huge ball at the Savoy. After a successful two weeks, the very sad day of departure arrived on a visit most likely never to be recaptured.

As an ambassadorial tradition, each year Father presented an enormous Christmas tree from Norway to England. It was placed in Trafalgar Square. I remember one particularly cold winter when my father and the London mayor performed the tree-lighting ceremony. I was wearing a pair of chic green suede boots from Paris. According to the local papers, I was the envy of all the women in Trafalgar Square that day! The photograph was captioned, "Foot note!"

In 1954, the newspaper published a wonderful caricature of Father giving the traditional tree. The article read like this:

H.E. Mons. Per Preben Prebensen, GCVO and CBE, has been Norwegian Ambassador in London since 1946 and on the departure, now impending of H.E. Mons. Massigli, will become Doyen of the Diplomatic Corps here. During their years in this country M. Prebensen and his wife have become greatly beloved,

and have done much to strengthen the ties developed between this country and
Norway in the last war, of which the annual dispatch from Oslo to London of a
huge Christmas tree for Trafalgar Square is so notably a symbol. M. and Mme.
Prebensen are close friends of the Norwegian Royal Family and entertained Crown
Prince Olav at their Palace Green residence when he recently paid a private visit
to London.[2]

Soon after I had arrived in England, I went sailing on the Isle of Wight
with my good friend, Paul Methuen. He was one of the first people I had met
in London. His family had a summer house at Seaview. This diamond-shaped
piece of land off Britain's south coast was a different world. I sensed it as soon
as I stepped off the boat onto the pier at Ryde. In 1845, Queen Victoria and
Prince Albert had bought *Osbourne House* as a summer home on the Isle of
Wight. The prince consort transformed the gray stone pile into an Italianate
Villa. At that time, Queen Victoria had written enthusiastically to Lord
Melbourne that the house offered a private beach free of mobs and followers.
The Queen died there in 1901 and, I believe *Osbourne House* is still in royal
possession. The Isle of Wight was a popular place with authors. In 1853,
Alfred Lord Tennyson bought *Faringford House* where he wrote *The Charge of*
the Light Brigade. His guests included famous names like Giuseppe Garibaldi,
Henry Longfellow, Sir John Millais and Charles Darwin. Charles Dickens
wrote part of *David Copperfield* at *Bonchurch* on the southern tip of the island
and William Thackeray took his holidays in the village. Baron Macaulay was
there while working on his lyric epic *The History of England.* Every summer, a
prestigious British yachting event called Cowes Week was held on the island,
along with a number of social events. I spent a weekend with Paul's family
and raced in one of the regattas. They did not care so much about Cowes as
long as Seaview could beat Bembridge, and vice versa. One day during the
race, we were about to win when something broke. Paul just shouted to me,
"Hold on to the mast!" We were first over the finish line!

In 1948, when Winston Churchill was no longer prime minister, he
went on an official visit to Norway. He had been a strong voice of both truth
and hope during the war for the Norwegians, who as a result, gave him a

hero's welcome. This seemed to touch him greatly. When he returned to London, my parents gave a luncheon in his honor. We were only eight at the table: The Crown Prince Olav and Crown Princess Martha of Norway, the Churchills, Prince Georg of Denmark, my parents and 19-year-old me. I listened through lunch and then ran upstairs to write down the conversation. Winston Churchill was such a very special person. Prince Georg asked provocative questions, and Clementine Churchill helped by asking, "Winston, do you remember?" For instance, Churchill was asked what he thought of de Gaulle. "Well," Churchill said, "I thought he was a great fool." "Oh," quipped mother, "I am glad we are all diplomats here." "I don't care if the whole world knows it, he was a great fool." Churchill continued, "Only once did he behave like a good boy. It was when Eisenhower and I did not tell him about D-Day, about the invasion of Normandy!" (I thought history proved that regrettable.) On occasion, de Gaulle could be so rude to Mrs. Churchill, saying abominable things in public at lunches, she would rise in rage. Churchill also mentioned how the English had collected the Germans' weapons, then marked and kept them in the Ruhr mines for their eventual use against Stalin! The year was 1949! Churchill seemed in favor of backing the Germans, fearing Stalin more, as one cannot fight two enemies at the same time. Obviously, Churchill did not understand what German occupation or concentration camps were like! Prince Georg—having gone to Germany in March of 1945 with his uncle, Prince Axel, and the Red Cross—pointed out, "I still hear in England that they do not believe that the camps ever existed! Just propaganda!"

We talked about Churchill's compensation for his books: a gold medal and a thousand pounds. Georg was the perfect person to have around because he was part of the Royal family and Danish Military Attache. He brought up the matter of King Leopold, to have Churchill's personal opinion in the matter. Of course, both Churchill and King Leopold's own ministers urged him to leave for England right in the beginning and continue the war from London, the way our Norwegian King Haakon did. Instead, King Leopold stayed behind in his chateau and married Princess de Rethy. Crown Princess

Martha, being the late Queen Astrid's sister, told how she had often stayed with King Leopold in former years, but never knew him well. Apparently, he was never on very friendly terms with his brother Prince Charles, not even in childhood. Then discussion turned to the difficulties of the succession to the throne, between Prince Baudoin, the king's eldest son and Prince Charles. Baudoin, who had been brought up in the loaded atmosphere under his father, had trouble being accepted. Churchill saw the problem more from the side of Prince Charles since he had served for seven or eight years in the British Navy, and declared, "Democracy is a society of fools, ruled by wise men!"

Churchill then mentioned how Attlee was always drawing the most beautiful doodles and circles. In that way he was not bored stiff in the socialist party. Yet, when asked about a matter, he would feign having listened, "Oh, yes, quite so, sir!" When the subject of the rotten French Constitution—Parliament being of the deputies, by the deputies, for the deputies—came up, someone pointed out that was probably the way the French rather liked it. Churchill retorted, "Divided we stand, united we fall!" Churchill continued that the French were through after WWI when "singing, they marched in battalions against the Germans and were shot down in thousands, the flowers of the nation, those brought up with the thought of revenge from 1870."

A few evenings later, we gave a dinner in honor of our Crown Prince and Crown Princess. Among the guests were Sir Winston Churchill; the Attlees, the Prime Minister; the Jowitts, the Lord Chancellor; the Tedders, head of the air force; the A.V. Alexanders, the Minister of Defense; the Lew Douglas', the American ambassador; Sir John Monck, Chief of Protocol and Christian Hauge, head of the Norwegian Resistance during the German occupation. Lord Tedder talked about Churchill and his relationship with General Smuts, when they were in North Africa. Smuts was the only man in the world who had Churchill under his thumb. "Though they are very fond of each other, it is the relationship between uncle and nephew, with Smuts definitely being the uncle," Lord Tedder said. In a conversation with Attlee, I mentioned how hard it must be to have to make speeches all the time. I told him I thought it must be the worst part of a politician's life. "It is not so bad for me," Attlee said. "Being only an average speaker, nobody expects very much. It is much worse for Winston. They always expect one hundred percent from him!" My brother, Nicken, was allowed to offer after-dinner cigars. When he approached Churchill, the great man said, "Thank you so much, but I prefer one of my own small ones!" Whereupon, Winston Churchill brought out a cigar of double length! We never forgot that!

Another time when Churchill came to dinner at the embassy, we had difficulty with the seating arrangements. At the time, in-between his Prime Minister periods, Churchill had no official rank except for being the head of the opposition. In fact, we had five VIPs for four seats with King Haakon as the host. We asked the protocol at the foreign office to figure out the proper seating, but they did not have the answer. Finally, my father went directly to King Haakon for his advice. His Majesty solved the problem by saying, "My friend, The Duke of Hamilton and Brandon, will not mind if you put Churchill in his place." The duke was very charming and I was lucky that he ended up sitting next to me further down the table. It was to the duke's property in Scotland that the infamous German Rudolf Hess flew during the first part of WWII to try to force England to surrender. Hess was sentenced to life imprisonment at the Nuremburg trials.

In 1951, King Haakon made a successful state visit. The stately cream and gold royal yacht, the *Norge* heaved to at Nore. A Thames pilot went aboard, and the trip upriver began with both the captain and the sailor king on the bridge. His maritime ability was a characteristic that endeared this tall, slim king to Norwegians and Brits alike. Norway had invited the young Danish Prince Carl—brother of the king of Denmark—to be their king in December 1905. He was 33 and the best looking captain of a Danish naval gunboat.

When he became king, he had an English wife, Maud (who was Edward VII's daughter) and a two-year-old son. In 1938, Queen Maud died in England. As a small girl, I remember the cold, dark November day when she was brought back to Oslo on a British gunboat. The king was still grieving when the war broke out. Afterward, he experienced days of flight and years of exile. His return to Norway in 1945, however, was a great triumph. And two years later on his 75th birthday, the people of Norway gave him the yacht, the *Norge*—which was quite symbolic. Above all, King Haakon was "the man of his people."

The daily papers wrote:

After having been given a banquet at Buckingham Palace, King Haakon returned the royal hospitality with a dinner at the embassy. The guests included the Queen, the Princess Elizabeth, the Princess Margaret, Princess Astrid, the Duke of Gloucester, the Archbishop of Canterbury, Winston Churchill, the Jowitts, the Attlees, the Clifton Browns, the Duchess of Northumberland, the Marquess of Salisbury, Lord Clarendon, Lord Eldon, Lord Fraser of North Cape, the Hartley Shawcross', the Lord Mayor, the Alan Lascelles, Vincent Bommen, Ingvald Smith-Kielland, the Norwegian Ambassador and Mme. Prebensen, and Mlle. Evelyn Prebensen. Sadly, His Majesty King George was too ill to attend.[3]

The following morning, the newspaper then wrote:

Yes, Last Night it was Beef on the menu! And then they published the two menus: At Buckingham Palace: Soup, Salmon, Chicken with Peas and New Potatoes, Ice Cream, Biscuits and Cheese. At the Embassy: Clear Soup, Lobster patties, Foie Gras in Artichokes, Filet of Beef with Asparagus tips, Gateau, Cheese Biscuits![4]

The sumptuous array of food was astonishing because in England, there was still wide-spread rationing.

The Bohns lived on Cadogan Square in a many-storied town house that boasted of spacious drawing rooms, a French *Art Deco* dining room, a bedroom floor and Monique's own amusing top floor. Notti's private office was located beyond the dining room and through the hall toward the back of the building. Many were the afternoons that I would pop in to see him on my way home from shopping. He always had a *quart de champagne* cooling and ready on the outside windowsill! I loved our chats.

In 1949, we celebrated Monique's 21st birthday with a dazzling party at Cadogan Square. The lovely townhouse was lit by candles and filled with amazing floral decorations. Small tables were placed all over the house, and a violinist moved among them. A late supper was served in the *Art Deco* dining room and we danced in the grand salon. The wide, elegantly swung staircase was the center of life.

We gave a dinner party for eight in Monique's honor at our embassy. The guests included Prince Georg, Elizabeth (Skip) Lumley, Jennifer Bevan (Princess Margaret's Lady in Waiting), Charles Stourton, Carl-Gustav Bielke of the Swedish Embassy and Count Ferdinand Stolberg. Ferdinand was the smoothest Viennese walzter with whom I'd ever danced. At the Dorchester, guests cleared the floor when he brought me out for the famous Vienna Waltz. To my delight and satisfaction, I was able to follow!

Marie Bohn died in 1952 leaving a great void, both for her family and for her many good friends around the world. After that, Notti and Monique (Marie's daughter) were always included in Sunday family suppers at our embassy. A year after Marie died, Monique planned her wedding to Count Alphonse Kinsky. My parents hosted her engagement party at our London Embassy, and the wedding took place in St. Joseph's church, *Grayshot*. The Apostolic Delegate officiated with Father Christie from Farm Street Church. The music was inspiring throughout the service and the little church was decorated with delphiniums, lilies, lilacs, peonies and other garden flowers. Sprays of white gladioli and white sweet peas alternated the ends of the pews up the aisle. The bride was given away by her father. They had one child bridesmaid, Charlotte Laurent-Athalin, who was the great grand-daughter of the late Marechal Foch. Monique also had two young pages dressed in white shirts, pale blue trousers and crimson cummerbunds. Notti held the wedding reception at *Stonedene*. Happily, it was a warm, sunny day and the guests were able to enjoy an enchanting luncheon in the garden. It was a truly international wedding. Alfie's family from Czechoslovakia and Germany attended, as well as Monique's French and Norwegian contingent. Of course, there were innumerable English friends. Bridesmaids and ushers came from many different countries, also. Monique was brilliant at organizing. The wedding cake was placed by the swimming pool, so that when the groom and bride cut it, the scene was reflected in the water. The couple then walked to the dance floor which had been laid on the lawn. Beside it stood a little tree, from which were hanging small transparent boxes that contained delightful mementos of the wedding day, ranging from toys for the children, to inscribed silver ashtrays for the servers. Monique then distributed the boxes to all her pages, ushers and bridesmaids. Bride and bridegroom opened the dancing, which continued all afternoon. Unfortunately, my legs had been wrapped from ankle to knee with bandages for my circulation problem. But once the dancing started, I couldn't resist joining them. Because of the heat, I unwrapped my legs, took the bandages off and kicked up my heels for a spin on the dance floor! Unfortunately, I really paid for it the next day with swollen legs, but it was well worth it. At the very end, two of my crazy Norwegian cousins found Notti's antique black bathing suits and jumped in the pool. The wonderful sun-drenched day was so memorable, held at a place that gave pleasure to many. Life in London would not have been the same without the Bohns and *Stonedene*.

The Bohns also had a place called *Heracle* in the South of France on the Mediterranean coast of the Var, not far from St. Tropez. When they first went to see it many years ago, I was told that they wondered how it would be in summer. They had seen it in January! That is how much the climate has changed. In the twenties my parents told me the hotels were closed in summer because of the heat. Unfortunately, I never saw *Heracle* because the house took a direct hit from the American bombs during WWII. But the property was still beautiful. One year, Notti, Monique and I stayed in a hotel nearby *Heracle*. It gave us the opportunity to take cooking lessons from the chefs. I also sketched in every village in the neighborhood—Gassin, Ramatuelle and, of course, St. Tropez.

The Suez Canal crisis developed while Anthony Eden was Prime Minister. Our Norwegian Prime Minister was on an official visit to London the week of the troubles. We were giving a big dinner in the Prime Minister's honor with Anthony Eden as one of the guests. In the middle of dinner, the telephone rang summoning all the politicians back to Parliament. I found several notes I had written about this event. One was dated September 7th stating that there was a pause in the meetings of the Suez conference and that French troops had arrived in Cyprus. Then I had one note from September 9th mentioning that Nasser had not accepted the suggestions of the Committee, and listing the supporting 18 countries present at the Suez conference. In fact, Anthony Eden ended up resigning as a result of the Suez affair!

While Eden was still Prime Minister—before his resignation—my mother and I saw him at the Diplomatic Evening Reception at Buckingham Palace. My father, who was Doyen of the Corps Diplomatique, was ill that night and Queen Elizabeth sent a message saying, "Bring Evelyn." It was marvelous to attend this private supper with mother. I, of course, was more than delighted. We joined a small group in one of the reception rooms, awaiting our summons to one of the Queen's smaller salons for supper. Waiting with us were the Archbishop of Canterbury and Mrs. Fisher, Anthony and Clarissa Eden and Lady Dorothy MacMillan (who was married to the then Lord Chancellor, Harold MacMillan). Lady Dorothy was daughter of the 9th Duke of Devonshire. At one point the American born Nancy Astor joined our small group. Viscountess Astor was the first woman to serve as a Member of Parliament in the House of Commons. She turned to Anthony Eden and said to him, "Anthony, you have just presented the most terrible budget. What poor taste for Clarissa to be seen in a million-dollar dress!" We all sort of half-politely laughed. Then Lady Astor continued, "Look at Dorothy. That is taste for you. She may have a new dress on, but it always looks 20 years old!" What a sharp tongue! I hardly knew where to turn. Of course, she was the same lady who once said to Churchill, "If I were your wife, I would poison your coffee." Quick as a flash, Churchill answered her, "And if I was your husband, I would drink it." On another occasion, Lady Astor said to Churchill, "Sir, you're drunk!" Whereupon Churchill replied, "Yes, Madam, I am. But in the morning I shall be sober, and you will still be ugly."

The evening of the Diplomatic party, the Queen was wearing her Coronation dress. It was magnificent. It had been embroidered in Canada and was extremely heavy. At one point Queen Elizabeth asked me to hold just one pleat. It must have weighed 20 pounds. She turned to me and said, "Can you now imagine the weight on my shoulders?" I have always had a tremendous admiration for Queen Elizabeth, from the very first time I met her, just before she got married. We remained in London for twelve years and my father was Doyen of the Diplomatic Corps for over six years. My father had difficulty standing, and Her Majesty's kindness was remarkable toward him throughout all the years he was in London. The Queen always made a point to ask him specifically to sit down whenever she entered a room.

During the 50s, it was generally accepted that Oliver Messel was the most brilliant artist and set designer. He lived at Pelham Place in a charming house. He was known for his excellent taste and talent. And once had a private showing of his designs and sketches for the "Queen of Spades." I will never forgive myself for not buying the sketch of the old countess in the opera. Oliver gave a great coming-out party for his niece, Susan Armstrong-Jones, at Pelham Place. It was the first time I got to know Tony, Susan's brother, and their mother, Anne Rosse—a very beautiful woman. Oliver and Anne's parents had a lovely place in Kent called *Nymans*. When Tony became engaged to Princess Margaret, they paid a visit to the beautiful Kent estate. Princess Margaret showed great interest in a special piece of furniture and told Oliver, who was there, how much she liked it. Oliver replied, "So do I, Ma'am, so do I." If Queen Mary admired some beautiful object, she was known to pretend that people gave it to her! Princess Margaret was just trying the same trick. Oliver and his loyal friend, the "Great Dane" (our pet name for him as he was a very great friend of my Danish aunt and uncle), came various times to dine privately at the embassy. Several times the Rosses came too. I was mesmerized by them all. Oliver was the fascinating artist, and his Danish friend was a man of wit and a wonderful sense of humor. It was great to be able to see them "en petite committee."

In 1949, Charles Stourton, heir to the Lord Mowbray, Segrave and Stourton (a hereditary title that goes back to 1283), gave a birthday party at the family country seat, *Allerton Park,* in Yorkshire. He invited a lovely group of friends up for the weekend. Among them were Charles' sister and her husband, Bee and Petre Crowder, Carla Gallarati-Scotti (niece of the Italian Ambassador), Prince Georg of Denmark, Skip Lumley, Iain Moncreiffe of that Ilk and his wife Dinan. As the Countess of Errol and Lord High Chief Constable of Scotland, Dinan was personally responsible for Their Majesties when they were in Scotland! She was Puffin to her friends. Jamie and Christian Rattray of Rattray Hall were there, as well as Carl-Gustav Bielke and Jane de Yarburghe-Bateson.

Allerton Park is one of two country estates in North England which has to be seen to be believed. To begin with, it has nine staircases; seven of which run from basement to loft. The Canadian Army used the place during the war. In order to manage the house after the war, the family had to put in sixteen new bathrooms! The first time I visited *Allerton*, I spent a weekend with Charles and his father, the 25th Lord Mowbray. They had no servants of any kind and Lady Mowbray was in bed. His Lordship insisted that we send the food up in dumbwaiters. The three of us had cooked on the Aga stove in the kitchen downstairs. At lunch we used one dining room and at dinner we used the larger one. Of course, his lordship insisted we still dressed for dinner, even if we did serve ourselves. Charles had an ancestor who had been the baron who forced King John to put his seal on the Magna Carta in 1215. Later in his life, Charles traveled to Washington D.C. to present one of the four copies of the Magna Carta held by the British Museum to the U.S. Congress. By the time of his 26th birthday, Charles hired a Hungarian family to work at *Allerton Park*. They were refugees from the communist regime. The irony, as it turned out, was that the Hungarian father was a well-known count and his family was almost more distinguished than the guests! The men in the house party quickly removed their shoes from the corridors (for the evening shoe-shining) and the daughter ended up sitting chatting on the beds with the girls. Unfortunately, after our enjoyable weekend, the noble servants' employment came to an abrupt end.

Jane de Yarburghe-Bateson—Lord Delamore's daughter—married Charles not long after. It was one of the most important weddings in the north of England. Four of the men at the weekend party were guard officers and turned up in their blazers. Charles was in the Grenadier Guards, Bill in the Irish Guards, and the two Moncreiffe cousins were in the Scots Guards. It was quite a sight among the foreigners. Iain used to say in his narrow-minded way, "The blacks start at Calais, and anything north of that are Eskimos!" In his view, anyone who didn't share his British ethnicity was considered beneath him. Once, when I stayed with the Moncreiffes in Perthshire, Iain called a neighbor and asked (referring to me), "May I bring an Eskimo for drinks?" Iain was so snobbish, or shall we say, insular, that even if people were royalty or high aristocracy, they could never measure up to the English or Scots! In spite of his unpleasant biases, he was still a good friend of mine. I was invited to stay with Puffin and Iain many times.

In 1962, when I lived in Rome, I went back to visit London. Charles was then Lord Mowbray, and he and Jane gave a dinner for me in their London apartment. During dinner the smog descended and nobody could leave, except on foot. This was still the time when nutty coal and open fireplaces were in use. The smog became so dense that visibility was reduced to one foot. (I believe nutty coal was abolished soon after.) We were forced to spend the night. Tall Derek Stanley-Smith slept on the sofa in the living room, and I was relegated to the bed in Charles's dressing room. The next morning, Nanny's face was a picture of shock when she found me in his Lordship's bed—even though he was not there. She was bringing his morning cup of tea! The entire city was still covered with a thick blanket of smog. I had to walk in my black dinner dress to lunch with the Guinness' on Cheyney Walk. Their butler, Mr. Proudfoot, however, was the epitome of diplomacy. True to his name he was a true English butler.

One Friday evening, after a hunt ball, we had been invited to spend the weekend with a friend who lived in an old mill in the country. It was an exceptionally cold night, so following the ball, we all retired to the kitchen for a toasty drink and hot water bottles. I couldn't sleep that night because of the cold. Prince Tomislav of Yugoslavia was among the guests at the house party. We had a great time at the Hunt Ball, and I was eager to see him at breakfast. But when I came down in the morning, he was not there. When he did appear, he brought me an urgent message to call home immediately. I became quite nervous wondering what on earth had happened because my parents were not expecting me home until Sunday evening. So I telephoned and my mother explained in Norwegian, that Tomislav had called that morning and told her he thought I would freeze to death if I stayed another night. In fact, he had had more than enough of it himself, and offered to drive me home! I made some official excuse and we left to arrive home in time for lunch in the warm embassy. That was the beginning of our very close friendship.

Prince Tomislav, or Tommy as he was called, had an apple farm in Sussex and his brother, Andy, had a pig farm. They were King Peter's brothers, and I had met them during Princess Elizabeth's wedding reception at Buckingham Palace. Their mother, Queen Marie—daughter of the beautiful Queen Marie of Romania—lived in London. Their father, The King of Jugoslavia, had been assassinated in 1934 in Marseilles. King Peter was too young to govern when it happened and Prince Paul, his cousin, acted as regent. During the war, King Peter and his family went into exile. They lived in Kent during World War II. The famous big bandleader, Glenn Miller resided nearby. I believe the boys had the entire Glenn Miller collection. Later on, the records spent a fair amount of time with me. Once, my brother Chris and I spent a weekend with Tommy at the apple farm. It got so cold that the orchard alarm was activated. To save the apple crop from frost, there were small paraffin lamps under each tree, which had to be lit individually by hand. It was quite a job, but because we went out and lit every lamp, we saved the crop. Each Christmas Tommy brought us cases of his best apples—Cox Pippins were my favorite.

The summers of 1954 and 1955 I traveled with father to Yugoslavia. Tommy gave me his cameras and I took hours of film for him of all the places his royal family had resided. The country was still under Tito's strict communistic rule. It was most interesting to investigate and acquaint myself with both the country and its people. In the end, Tommy was finally able to return to Serbia with his second wife, where he died a few years ago. He was married first to Margharita of Baden, a niece of the Duke of Edinburgh. I was in

Portugal when they got married, but my brother, Nicken attended to represent us. At the time of the 1956 Hungarian uprising, a Swedish friend and I served as Red Cross public relation officers between the British authorities and the Hungarian refugees—who were arriving in great numbers. Most of the refugees were just happy to have escaped. But there was a contingent of criminal prisoners that was more complicated to deal with. One Saturday morning, I was alone in our office when an unruly group arrived and demanded money and the use of long distance telephone calls. I was very happy when some Hungarian friends suddenly turned up to solve the situation.

As previously mentioned, one of my best friends during the London years was Durru Shehvar. After India's Prime Minister Ghandi took away the titles of all the Maharajahs, Princess Durru Shehvar became Mrs. Berar—or just Durru Shehvar. It made her feel like a hat shop, she said. With time her name was modified to Princess Berar. Her father succeeded as Caliph in 1922 and they lived in the Dolmabahce Palace in Istanbul. Although Durru Shehvar was shy, she dominated any room she entered. I have a striking profile photograph of her taken by Cecil Beaton. She was tall and grand, yet sensitive and cultured. We often used to go to receptions and cocktail parties together in London. I have kept letters and Christmas cards from her, all in her perfect calligraphic handwriting. She penned some charming fairy tales and was greatly interested in art and music. After I left England at the end of 1958, she came to stay with us yearly in Italy. Later on, she visited us in the States—both in Cincinnati and Palm Beach. She even bought a house in Palm Beach, which I redecorated for her, where she wintered for a few years until she found the trans-Atlantic crossing too tiring. Only when she died in 2006, did I realize she was fifteen years my senior.

One night in London, at a cocktail party, a good looking American film producer, Sheldon Reynolds, grew so interested in us that he invited us for dinner at the Milroy that evening. He had, however, forgotten he had already invited an English call girl to meet him at the same location! The acute embarrassment of this sophisticated producer, made us giggle any time we thought about it. Durru Shehvar had a great sense of humor.

When my father left London to serve as ambassador to Roma, innumerable friends gave parties for us. Among those hosts were the Duchess of Kent, Princess Marina and her daughter, Princess Alexandra. They had us for tea at Kensington Palace. I had not seen the duchess since one wonderful dinner party at the Austrian Embassy where I had been seated at a table for six with her and Noel Coward. It was widely known that Noel Coward loved the Duchess of Kent and as a result he was exceptionally amusing that evening. She commented on it to me even months later. The Duchess, too, had a great sense of humor. We were invited to another charming tea party—this time at 10 Downing Street. Harold MacMillan was the Prime Minister. I always thought he resembled my grandfather. His wife, Lady Dorothy—daughter of the 9th Duke of Devonshire—was one of my favorite English ladies. It was Lady Dorothy who was the object of Nancy Astor's remark at Buckingham Palace! I felt it a great honor to be invited to the MacMillans in the middle of their busy schedule, and at such a famous address. Harold Macmillan belonged to the dwindling ranks of the English known as Squirearchy. His country home was called *Birch Grove House*, and was near Hayward's Heath in Sussex. His father was Maurice Macmillan, a director of the famous Macmillan Publishing Company. His mother was an American—a fact he shared with Sir Winston Churchill. I knew their children. Maurice married the daughter of Lord Harlech, and one of the daughters married the well known Captain Julian Amery of WWII Balkan fame

On a corner of Belgrave Square stands the Spanish Embassy. A good friend of mine, Fernando de Priego—as First Secretary—had an elegant flat on top of the embassy building. He gave a wonderful farewell dinner for eight in my honor. In the middle of dinner, a very snobbish English girl turned up uninvited and blasted the host for having given a dinner without her and in honor of a foreigner! David Westmorland got up from the table and told the girl, "What right do you have entering a foreign embassy and telling someone who to invite?" Of all the stupidities, this beat most of what happened to me during my twelve years as an "Eskimo!"

The Portuguese Embassy was on another corner of Belgrave Square. Pedro, the ambassador had a wife who was not well, so she did not accompany him to London. Pedro became my devoted friend, as did his two daughters who were my age. He would often take me to premieres at theaters or cinemas. Many times I had to duck from the media because his neighbor, the Spanish Ambassador, usually brought his mistress. With the aid of his Pakistani colleague, the High Commissioner Ikramullah, Pedro had arranged the job for me in Portugal. They called me "The One Man Legation!"

In later years, after a decade in New York, my brother Nicken and family moved back to London. They lived on Hyde Park square for years. From there they moved to Brompton Road, but their happiest days were in Rushden, a village with thatched roof cottages north of London. After years of traveling up and down every weekend, they moved permanently to their thatched cottage. Before they moved from Hyde Park Square—having spent Christmas with the Fraissinets in Champagne, France—our family traveled to London to celebrate the New Year with the Prebensens. I believe it was the only time our family was together after Father died. My brother, Chris had a stint as a diplomat at the London Embassy. With two sons in England, mother left *Setergrenda*, her house in Tuscany, where it had become difficult for her to live alone. She spent a couple of years in London. While in London she had another robbery. When Chris moved back to Norway, mother followed and lived her last years in the town where she was born. I loved Barberry Cottage in Rushden with its cozy low ceilings, even if my tall brother hit his head quite often. They tended their garden beautifully, and Nicken loved his English roses. It was an English dream to sit on the sunny terrace and look out over the valley. When they gave up their apartment in town, the commute became a burden. After years of hard work and suffering lung cancer, it was time to retire. The business and the cottage were both sold, and they moved to the south of France permanently. My niece and nephew still live in England, but that is another long chapter.

After several happy years of remission in France, Nicken's lung cancer came back with a vengeance. He had received superb medical help in France.

I went over for a couple of long summers to give a helping hand. As the situation worsened, however, the family decided to bring their father back to England. They bought a cottage in the village of Dulverton in Somerset, next door to son Preben's property. Nicken did not leave the South of France until he celebrated his 50th wedding anniversary. He and Else gave an elegant lunch at *Bas St. Antoine* in Grasse. We were 16 among family and friends. They came from far and near. The sun was brilliant amid a vivid blue sky. It was all so beautiful. The food was the best I'd ever eaten; the champagne and wines, magnificent. Nicken, a remarkable host, was always thinking of his guests. The party was unforgettable and just his style! He ended his career on a fabulous note!

A couple of weeks later, Nicken's grandson, Oliver, came down to accompany him on his last trip back to England. Else and I, on the other hand, decided to bring their car to England. We took the auto train from Nice to Calais, passed through the tunnel and then drove the big car from Dover via Folkestone to Somerset. It took us almost 30 hours from Chateauneuf. We met Monsieur Gnot just below Per's house in the village. Monsieur Gnot then led us through a network of backstreets to avoid building projects on the way to the railway station in Nice where we left the car. After the necessary paperwork was completed, we went café-hopping and ordered everything from cappuccinos to sorbets. The train left Nice at 17:59 p.m. local time. We settled into our couchette for six and enjoyed a comfortable night with blankets and lots of pillows, munching cheese and apples and drinking champagne.

At 10 a.m. the next morning we reached Calais. It was a very slow train ride, and because of various security issues, our departure was delayed. The trip, however, sped up on highways M20, M25, M4, and then west to M5 at Bristol. From there we went southwest to Devon, west on local roads, then north towards Exmoor to the village of Dulverton. At long last we arrived at Preben and Annie's home. The stupendous position overlooked the valleys and dales of the Devon Downs. It was Sunday, and they were home with two of their three sons, Harry and Tom. Nicolai was still at school and Charlotte, the only daughter, in Colorado. Nicolai came home on the weekend. Huge rhododendrons grew everywhere. There was a water garden as well as water-falls and flowering terraces behind the house and around the swimming pool. My guest room and bathroom window overlooked those terraces. There was even a tennis court behind an old stone wall. Because of the Somerset, the West Country's wet climate, the lawns were the greenest and the vegetation the richest. The cottages, of course, had thatched roofs. Besides the children, the family included the old fat lady, their beloved dog, Daisy, and Otis, the blue Grand Danois of ten months, and the parrot in his cage in the kitchen. The parrot said "Good morning," echoed the telephone, sang songs, and ate toast with marmalade for breakfast. A brisk wind had risen. Even though it was July, I still wore Nicken's elegant pink cashmere sweater over a Courreges turtleneck. Several construction workers brought song and music through-out the day. A stream ran down the valley towards Dulverton. Otis was my loyal shadow when I walked around the garden. The innumerable sheep were bleating constantly.

While I wrote and waited for the boys to return from riding, I enjoyed a biscuit and a glass of red wine, and listened to the wind rustle through the large surrounding trees. Else and Nicken's charming white cottage was located behind the church, so to speak, at the edge of the village of Dulverton. It had been nicely renovated, and the furniture Else had sent from France suited it well. It was cozy, warm, tasteful and livable—as I hoped it would be for them both. If this was summer, I thought, what would their winter be like? We had a delicious lunch at the quaint pub in the village. Then we went shopping in the village. I passed ten sublime days there. When I returned to their house at Chateauneuf de Grasse and France, it was with a very heavy heart.

I knew I would never see my beloved Nicken again.

Ireland – The Emerald Isle

GREEN GIFT BOX

"The smell of the Liffey is one of the sights of Dublin," a famous "Irish Bull" once said. The river that runs through Dublin is not dramatic like the Seine, the Rhine or the Donau, but it is definitely linked to Ireland's stormy fate. Often, in the early morning, there is a unique atmosphere that hovers over the river. A heavy grey mist covers the murky water making the silhouette of the city barely visible. Seagulls shriek constantly. On such a morning as this, we drove across the O'Connell Bridge past the old Parliament and Trinity College on our way to St. Stephen's Green.

As far as I know, my father was the only diplomat who was accredited to the Republic of Ireland in 1950 while serving as the Norwegian Ambassador in London. The reason he alone received the post was because Norway's Foreign Secretary, Halvard Lange, happened to be a close friend of the then Irish Foreign Secretary, Sean MacBride. So, in spite of England and Ireland's cool relations, Father was appointed as minister—a clear exception to the rule.

Since my father was only in Ireland periodically, the Norwegian government used the delightfully Victorian Shelbourne Hotel as their official residence, as did several other diplomats missing a long term embassy. Its only drawback was that the rooms were so dark we could hardly see our own shadow. The corridors were crowded with diplomats and their entourages. Most nations would keep a permanent residence for their envoys. With the recent end of WWII, many countries had not organized their real estate yet. On my way to breakfast at my parents' suite I was amused to bump into the Argentinean ambassador's butler bustling down the corridor with His Excellency's pressed suits!

Whenever a special event occurred, Father would visit Ireland. After we first arrived in Dublin, he (as Norwegian minister) delivered his Letter of Credentials to the president of Ireland. A motorcycle arrived at the Shelbourne Hotel to escort him to *Aras un Uchtarain*, the president's Phoenix Park home. Police kept the crowds at bay. Father stepped out to accept the official salute. A fanfare sounded, and with a nod to the commanding officer, the procession commenced towards Phoenix Park. An honor guard awaited him outside the presidential residence. Of course, the heavens opened up in a torrential downpour at the exact moment my father was to inspect the guards. We forever teased him for having to dash through the parade in a decidedly undiplomatic hurry. The press photos mostly caught just his top hat!

That evening, the foreign secretary gave an impressive dinner at *Iveagh House*, which was once a Guinness family property. The guests were received at the top of an imposing staircase in this elegant mansion—a worthy background for the glittering assembly of guests.

After his official visit to the prime minister (the *Taoiseach* in old Irish), my father exited one of the government buildings on Merrion Street only to be held up by a herd of ambling cows. I chauffeured Father that day, and had a good laugh at the incongruous sight. I remember the prime minister as a calm, pleasant gentleman when I was introduced to him at the *Iveagh House* dinner. Similarly, while shopping with my mother on Grafton Street (Dublin's Bond Street), we once had to stand back for passing sheep.

Dublin seemed to me a city of great contrasts. I loved Ireland and returned once or twice, but have not been back for years. At the time, the country did not possess the sophisticated success it enjoyed in later years. I noticed that there was a great deal of poverty. The children, especially in the back streets, looked quite miserable. They were dirty, grey, and dressed in rags. All this was in stark contrast to the beautiful architecture that surrounded us.

Phoenix Park was at one end of Dublin. With Ireland's abundant rainfall, the park radiated every shade of green. At the other end of the city the road went off for Bray and boasted palm trees and charming glances of Sugarloaf Mountain and the Wicklow Hills.

Not only was the presidential residence situated in Phoenix Park, but also that of the Apostolic Nuncio, the permanent diplomatic representative of the Vatican, equivalent to an ambassador. The third important residence in the park was the United States Legation. In 1950, however, while we were there, the status of the office of a legation was raised to that of an embassy. The Irish gave a grand dinner in honor of the United States and Norway and their ambassadors. Present were the Apostolic Nuncio, and members of the Diplomatic Corps, members of the government and other Irish personalities. When President Kelly arrived they played the Irish national anthem. The American ambassador and Mrs. Garrett had a beautifully furnished embassy. Their well known collection of horse paintings was of special interest to me.

One afternoon, the president's wife, Mrs. Kelly, invited us to tea. It was a ladies' tea party in honor of my mother, and Mrs. Kelly very kindly included me. My twelve-year-old brother, who was with us in Ireland, on the other hand, had a wonderful visit to the famous Dublin Zoo.

The presidential residence—a long white building somewhat resembling the White House—had earlier been the summer residence of the British Viceroy. The presidential guards opened the stately gates for us, and we drove up to the regal entrance. Once inside, we were taken through a long corridor to one of the drawing rooms that had a lovely view of the park. Here, tea was served to a small and select group made up of a few younger Irish diplomats' wives and some friends. It was an extremely cordial environment, and we felt entirely at home. Of course, I appreciated everything, but my lasting impression was how much taller Mrs. Kelly was than her husband! The president came in very informally just before we left. He was small in stature with thin rimmed spectacles and a high, stiff, old fashioned collar. He brought his beloved miniature white poodle on his arm, and escorted us out to the car. He stayed to wave us off till we had disappeared around a curve. He was a delightful gentleman and honored us with the extraordinary gesture of seeing us out.

When we were not being royally wined and dined by everyone from the American ambassador to the foreign secretary, we enjoyed lunch or dinner at the Russell Hotel across the Green. The hotel had an excellent French restaurant where we even hosted an official luncheon. Although it was for men only, one of the official's wives turned up in all her fineries. Mother called me in a panic and said, "Come over quick!" I rushed from the Shelbourne to help the lady feel less conspicuous. We would not have dreamt of turning anyone away. She obviously realized there had been a misunderstanding, but we all had a lovely lunch nevertheless.

I found Ireland to be a captivating island, certainly an Emerald Isle. While it didn't rain constantly, it was often damp and cold. Where the weather was wanting, the people made up for it in their friendly and warm ways. I felt very welcome as a Norwegian, despite the local reputation of the Vikings.

One night we went to a private dinner at the home of the Irish Foreign Secretary and his wife, Mrs. Sean MacBride. They lived in a large house in Clonskea. A few beautiful antiques dressed the drawing room. Mr. MacBride's mother was the famous Maud Gonne MacBride, to whom the well-known poet William Yeats wrote so many of his poems. Yeats was hopelessly in love with Maud Gonne, I was told. Sean MacBride's father was among the sixteen men shot by the English in 1916 and Maud Gonne exiled many years in France. This was the same time that Eamon De Valera was spared because he was an American citizen. Dining with the MacBrides was an unforgettable experience in every way. Maud Gonne, tall and dressed entirely in black, came downstairs to join us. At 84, she was still a cavernous beauty (as someone described) and her magnificent eyes remained unchanged from her youth. She sat down next to me on the sofa and murmured, "Old age has no compensations." "How can you possibly say that?" I protested in youthful enthusiasm. "You have worked for Ireland's freedom all your life, and now it has been achieved and your son is Foreign Secretary. You don't count that?" Apparently, she liked my outburst because her son brought me her book,

Servant of the Queen (Queen meaning Ireland) the very next day. She had written a dedication to me on the front page. The book was about her love and fight for a free Ireland. Her fame has been enduring.

The MacBrides gave me a green malachite gift box which I put on my charm bracelet. To this day people are in awe by the fact that I really met Maud Gonne! She was beautiful and fascinating. Her husband had died for the cause of freedom, and her son, Sean McBride, was an outstanding man in his own right. In addition to his many accomplishments, he received the 1974 Nobel Peace Prize.

One weekend we headed west to Kildare, Limerick, Adare and Killarney, and drove round the famous ring of Kerry. Our rooms looked out over the lake and mountains to a fantastic sunset. Overwhelmed by the beauty, I fell asleep with Tennyson's poem playing in my mind: "The splendor falls on castle walls…" [1]

The next day we followed the road to Killorglin where hundreds of Kerry ponies, goats, sheep and cows were exchanged and sold. It was a peaceful Sunday morning, so we passed several people on their way to church, either on foot or donkey. The women wore large black shawls, and the people often walked many miles to get to the nearest place of worship. The road from Glencar to Glenross held one beautiful panorama after the other. The road on to Kells hung high over Dingle Bay. This was one of the most picturesque and famous places in Southern Ireland. It's also the birthplace of Daniel O'Connell—the Emancipator—who campaigned for Catholics to be permitted in Westminster Parliament, and helped repeal the union between Ireland and Great Britain.

Only a glimpse of the sea is visible on the way to Waterville. But, as a writer once said, "…Look where one will, there is the wild beauty of untamed nature." [2] The first sight of Parknasilla is that of a tropical garden, oddly placed on the west coast of Ireland; an exotic garden on the Atlantic Ocean. We passed Sneem with its strange church spire, Derryquin Castle, as well as the ruins of Dromore Castle—where once the strong and mighty O'Mahoneys dwelt. It is always sad to see beautiful constructions in ruins.

After a world war, one knew what it meant to lose a family seat or cottage. The road continued past Dunkerron Castle to Kenmare with its impressive vistas, hidden fairytale caves and waterfalls. To get back to Killarney we had to take a winding road. The sun was shining when we stopped at Ladies View, and we threw a last glance at Killarney's three lakes surrounded by mountains covered with yellow gorse. Suddenly, we came across a few gypsy wagons with donkeys, goats, and dogs, as well as a mass of dark-haired children. There was something spellbinding about these colorful, southern nomads.

These enthralling sights speak to the deep affection I have for Ireland. But I also found it was the coldest place I'd ever known, especially the Dunraven Arms Hotel where we stayed on the way home from Kilarney. I hardly slept I was so cold and often felt I wouldn't survive the freezing temperatures. Ireland's frigid climate wreaked havoc with my Morbus Raynaud Syndrome. Still, the glory of its countryside outweighed the agony of my painful condition. More than things or places, my unforgettable impressions of Ireland are of the diverse people—from presidents to common donkey-riding people—who were so enchanting, and always willing to go well out of their way to demonstrate kindness.

We left Dublin the same way we arrived: by ship. We stared back at the town and the coastline that spanned Sugarloaf Mountain to the Wicklow Hills. It disappeared behind us in a grey mist. A half moon was high as we passed another ship in the night. Someone on board was singing:

"If you ever go across the sea to Ireland…

Then maybe at the closing of your day,

You will sit and watch the moon rise over Claddagh

And see the sun go down on Galway Bay."[3]

Denmark – Hamlet's Country

GOLD ENVELOPE

At the close of the summer of 1948, we drove from England to Norway across northern Europe. We took a ferry to Belgium, visited my father's old friend, Christopher Smith (our ambassador in Bruxelles), admired the statue of Mannikin Pis on his corner of the old city, and rolled northward to Holland. It seemed like the whole country was riding bicycles. By the time we drove along the tree-lined highways toward the German border, it was quite late. We spent the night in Holland. Even with a diplomatic permit, we still had to get through north Germany in one day. Three years after the war, both the country and economic infrastructure was still in ruins.

Because I was born in Russia, there was a slight delay when we crossed the German border. The problem was solved when one of the six Germans in uniform came up with the bright idea that accidents do happen to diplomats! We had to pack our own petrol and food. A petrol station attendant in Hamburg very kindly helped us with our heavy jerry cans. He could not take our money, but was happy to be paid in American cigarettes! After a full day's drive, we passed through Flensburg and finally traversed the Danish border. Our first night was spent in Aabenraa, where we had a delicious meal, especially considering that it was so soon after the war.

Denmark has always been a country brimming with storybook qualities. And never was that more evident than on the island of Fyn. Castle turrets popped up among lovely beech trees, sailboat masts tinkled a tune as they bobbed in the coastal breezes, and abundant crops blanketed the fields. These same images fueled the imagination of the renowned Hans Christian Andersen who was born there two hundred years prior. The Danes refer to Fyn as the garden of their country. That is why there are still about ninety inhabited castles and manor houses. This island is very fertile, and many of the estates have working farms.

Claus Ahlefeldt, my old friend Viggo Ahlefeldt's cousin, had opened his castle to the public at Egeskov Slot. Today, tourism brings in as much income as the estates' farms and logged acreage! Egeskov Slot is magnificent sitting in the middle of a lake. In 1554, it took a whole forest to build this castle on pilings, just like Venice. The castle's kitchen garden is one of Europe's most renowned. I have been told that it is only rivaled by that of the *Chateau de Villandry* in the Loire valley.

From Fyn we drove on to Copenhagen. The mermaid in the harbor bid us welcome. The Hotel Angleterre was still there, as was the Tivoli Garden. The Stroeget's shops were lit. Uncle Gus and Aunt Mitte had a chic penthouse apartment on a gaveled rooftop with a kitchen window that overlooked the port. The deep windowsill held fresh herbs for their delicious Fyn cooking. They had sent us food parcels to Norway right through the war! Their enchanting country house was at Espergaerde, on north Sjelland, near Helsingor and Hamlet's castle. World-class designer and friend, Bjorn Wienblad, had designed their patio table. Each family member's name was written on the table top, including place settings for their two adorable cocker spaniels! My aunt and her siblings were very musically gifted. They all played the piano and the house was continually filled with laughter, music and song. I loved that house with all its beautiful adornments. It was with great sadness that we received the news of its demolition. A new highway was to pass through their dining room! Some call it progress, but progress has ruined so many of my beloved childhood houses. Now, they only exist in my mind. Whenever I wear the gold wishbone charm that Gus gave me many, many years ago, I remember their lovely home.

I met Niels, my favorite Dane, in London. We quickly became great friends. His father had been an admiral in the Danish Navy and was Naval Attache' in London. Then, one day, Niels came by to say that his father had been transferred to Washington. As soon as his parents went to America, Niels joined them. He took out first papers in the States and was therefore called up right away for military service in the Korean War. He never wanted to be in the infantry, so through his father's connections, he was allowed to join the U.S. Marine Corps, even though he was still a Dane. A stream of letters made it possible for me to follow his training at Camp Le Jeune, and later, his journey to the Far East. Niels sent me gifts from every port they visited. The last package came from Tokyo with a gold love letter for my charm bracelet. He had asked me to marry him on his return from the Far East!

Arriving in Korea, he requested duty at the front. In one of his last letters he paraphrased Shakespeare's Henry IV: "We owe God a death; may it come this year or the next."[1] Niels died a hero's death in 1952, when he returned a second time to a radio station to save friends. I heard the news of his death the following day in London, while reading the morning newspaper. Because of his father's important post, the report of Niels' death made the front page of *The Times*. It was not an easy way to receive such devastating news. His wish was to be buried with his fellow U.S Marines at Washington D.C.'s Arlington National Cemetery.

Years later, on my way home to London, following doctor visits in Stockholm, I passed a few days in Copenhagen with some of my closest friends I have ever known. George Luden was the first Dutch Ambassador to Norway after the war. I also adored his two very handsome sons, Jan and Sam, who both died too young. The Ludens went from Norway to their embassy in Warsaw, Poland, only to return as Ambassador to Copenhagen a couple of years later. After weeks of painful treatments in Sweden, it was heavenly to be taken care of by Moeksie and Poeti in the comfortable Dutch embassy on Amaliegade.

In subsequent years, they included me in their vacations to France and Italy. Moeksie and I would spend lovely days painting. Poeti would make sure he planned always to be near a golf course. There was a course in Rapallo, so we stayed nearby at my favorite *Albergo Splendido* in Portofino. In France, there was a golf course near Nice, so we stayed in *Eze-sur-Mer*, an old white villa on the Mediterranean. During my year in Sicily, the Ludens even drove down to see me while I was in Taormina. In February, they took me to see the temples in Agrigento. Oddly enough, we found thick snow on the ground underneath the blossoming almond trees. The hotel there was as cold as a refrigerator. In the evenings we would play cards in the corridor because it was the warmest spot, sipping cognac to keep from freezing to death. Despite the extreme cold, we saw the almond blossoms around the temples, admired Piazza Armerina's famous frescoes, and looked at the splendors of a bygone Siracusa. Moeksie and Poeti then brought me north and treated me to a "Roman Holiday." Rome was much warmer!

A year later, my cousins invited me to go to the Far East on a Norwegian cargo ship. We were away for several months. As I traveled, from Hong Kong to the Philippines and even in Tokyo, one coincidence after another occurred as I met various people who had seen Niels on his way to Korea. Although these events happened over 60 years ago, I'll never forget them because the gold love letter charm on my bracelet reminds me every day!

Italy – La Bella Italia
A PAIR OF SKIS

In 1947, during my first summer in England, I escaped southward in search of sunshine in the country of my dreams—*Italia!* Our plane flew over the green forests of France and over the reddish-brown Alps. We sailed over deep valleys, the ragged coast of Corsica, the clear blue Mediterranean, and finally, landed in Roma. It made a deep impression on me that we had breakfasted in London, lunched in Marseilles, and made tea time in Rome—all in one day. What a contrast to the 11th and 12th century pilgrims who traveled a full year to get to the Holy Land and back!

We arrived at the Ciampino Airport outside the city. Since the war had only recently ended, the runways were still noisy, military landing strips, made of metal. A dilapidated black and green taxi drove us to our hotel via the old Appian Way, over the same huge cobble stones upon which Hannibal had arrived. The construction of this road had begun in 312 B.C. and was finished in 96 B.C. I got to know it, of course, quite well almost ten years later when we settled in the area! We drove by the Terme di Caracalla, the Coliseum, the Forum and the Palazzo Venezia, from which Mussolini delivered his propaganda speeches. It was a very hot day, and I admired the guards at the Vittorio Emanuele Monument where one can find the Italian graves of the Unknown Soldier. They stood like statues in the baking sun while passers-by shuffled along in the shade of the house walls. From Piazza Venezia, the

Corso goes in a straight line to the Piazza del Popolo, the original measurement of an English mile. It is always teeming with people and life.

Our taxi ride ended at the Hassler Hotel in the center of Rome. It is beautifully situated on top of the Spanish Steps next to Trinita dei Monti and the French Academy. The view from our room was breathtaking. We looked out over a sea of rooftop gardens and church cupolas, which extended as far as the eye could see. Below us, the Piazza di Spagna lay with its famous Bernini Fountain. We used to hang out of our windows at night and admire the full moon shining over the Eternal City. My father's old friend from the embassy used to say, "At the height of a sweltering summer, a tranquil terrace or tucked-away garden makes it possible to while away the days pleasantly with a Campari soda."

Everywhere in Roma one can find the most fabulous singing fountains, which are an inspiring sight, especially in summer! The fountains range from the most humble to hugely magnificent, like the Fontana dei Najadi on Piazza Esedra next to the new railway station. Behind our hotel was the Monte Pincio; one of the seven hills on which Roma was built. Having been in war-torn England, it cheered me to see that Rome, because it had been declared an "open" city, had escaped the war's destruction.

My mother had always loved Rome (the Eternal City), and she was very eager to show it to me. To visit it is like taking a plunge into the past. Rome's history spans 28 centuries. The richness of its history is still palpable. Rome started as a small city, grew to command the whole of Italy, and then spread in all directions across the Mediterranean and the Alps to leave its stamp on the world. The countries that made up the Roman Empire, such as England and Germany, Tunis, Algiers, Morocco, the Middle East, the coasts of Turkey and the Balkan Peninsula, are all full of Roman theaters, gates, baths, fortifications and villas. Renaissance Rome was built on top of ancient monuments, and often constructed with the same materials. For instance, in the 17th century, the bronze tiles and friezes of the Pantheon were melted down to become Bernini's Baldacchino in the Basilica of San Pietro. As the largest church in Rome, we decided to start at San Pietro and work our way to the smallest one, the Santa Maria in Cosmedin.

The Santa Maria conjures up images of Audrey Hepburn and Gregory Peck in *Roman Holiday*, especially the part when she thought for a moment he had lost his hand when he put it into the statue at the entrance to the church, the Bocca della Verita (the mouth of truth). I prayed and thanked God in every church for allowing me to experience this sacred city. Our first Roman evening found us dining at Tre Scalini, a trattoria on my beloved Piazza Navona. We then wandered back through the narrow provincial streets, and breathed in the special ambience of the city. The summer nights drew hundreds of people of all ages, accompanied by music and song, into the streets and piazzas until late at night.

The capital is a microcosm of Italy's history. It was the ancient fortress of the original city-state, like the Acropolis at Athens. When the city grew to be the hub of a huge empire, Rome became the nerve center. A walk through Rome was like a trip to the past. At every corner there stood a column dating back to Julius Caesar, a wall which saw St. Peter and St. Paul pass by, a façade painted by Michelangelo, or a church by Bernini. My mother guided me to the best exhibits in the most renowned museums. We started with her favorite Bernini sculptures at the Galleria Borghese, and then continued to the Vatican to see Michelangelo's Sistine Chapel.

These were some of my first Roman experiences: I watched a priest pace the back terrace of his church, reading his prayer book. Five cats settled on a sunny spot on the roof while church bells chimed. A melodious voice sang a sentimental song, and a woman emptied a water bottle from a roof terrace, its contents splashing down the lower floor's balcony, and then sprinkling the heads of the courtyard workers. Sometimes the late night walks would exhaust us. So we'd take a carozza (a horse-drawn vehicle) that would clip-clop home over the cobblestones. We were fortunate to have visited Rome during a full moon. Under a starry sky we stole a last glance at the Coliseum. The week of sightseeing passed too quickly. Before we left we threw our *soldino in La Fontana di Tre*vi and prayed *to* return. I had fallen completely in love with the Eternal City, and strongly sensed that it would play an important part in my life. My intuitions came true. For since that first visit, I returned innumerable times, and eventually resided there. The memories of the first visit, of course, are the sweetest.

We left Rome by train and headed to Rapallo, a town on the Riviera south of Genova. It was an extremely hot day. First class in 1947 meant wooden seats. Two Americans sat opposite us, one of them was exceedingly large, and he mopped his face constantly, poor man. The space between our seats and theirs was so miniscule that we had to take turns changing positions. After a ten hour journey, we finally arrived at the Italian Riviera! Our first week was spent at the Hotel Bristol in Rapallo. The hotel was situated right on the main coastal highway, and the noise was terrible. The buses made the worst racket as they screeched and hooted around every twist and turn of the road. It was more than we could stand.

The day before we moved on, I was sitting quietly on the hotel terrace reading a book. Suddenly, a young woman came out on the second floor balcony just above my head and shouted in Spanish to her aides (two fat Argentinean colonels), "Who does that girl think she is not getting up when I come out on the balcony?" The woman shouting was Evita Peron and apparently her complaint was about me! "Who does *she* think she is?" I said to myself. The twenty-five year old Eva Peron was on her way to see the Pope. I was not impressed. Later that night, her Argentinean colonels came over to us in the restaurant later and apologized for Evita's outburst.

The next day we left for Portofino, located at the western tip of the Gulf of Tigullio. It had long been a destination for the rich and famous. Baron von Mumm had first discovered this quaint fishing village around the turn of the 20th century. But in spite of the stunning mountain top villas, Portofino retains the spirit of a coastal village. The Splendido is "an eccentric grande dame" among hotels, and was the private villa of a Genovese family in 1901. It sits high above the port with a spectacular terrace framed by palm trees. Again, the view from our room was magnificent. The blue Mediterranean Sea stretched to infinity. In front of us lay the peninsula including the famous *Castello Brown*, where they later filmed *Enchanted April*. Brooke Astor and her second husband rented the *Castello* for ten years. She beautifully describes their long vacations in her book, *Footprints*. For centuries, Portofino could only be reached by boat or foot. In 1918, however, that all changed when an engineering marvel of a road was completed. It is a treacherous, narrow, winding road with breathtaking views around every turn. Portofino was the perfect place to spend the summer, and it has become my top vacation destination. I've returned often just to sketch and paint. While there, I made many new acquaintances. We would spend long days at the beach at Paraggi, or sail our Norwegian friend, Consul Ekland's, old sailboat. One day out on the water, a whale surfaced, spouting only one hundred meters away. It was indeed a rare sight on the Mediterranean. In the evenings, we would watch outdoor films at the Hotel Miramare in Santa Margherita. Sometimes we'd go dancing at the bar at *Capo di Nordest*, an old coastal castle ruin, escorted by charming Italian cousins or a friend's brother. Another favorite pastime was to sit at a breezy café, sip Camparis, and watch life around the port. We admired the sleek sailboats lazing in the sun. One popular port of call in Portofino was the Pitosforo, a restaurant perched right above the dock. They served excellent regional cuisine including simple dishes like ravioli in a walnut sauce, baked sea bass and clams, paired with clear white wines from the local Cinque Terre vineyards.

Later, during the many years I lived in Tuscany, we would always stop at Portofino on our way back from ski trips, and often bring Alexandra to the seaside town to quell her seasonal ailments. It was always wonderful to wake up on a winter morning to a sunshiny breakfast on a terrace under orange trees. One year we joined a friend on his yacht in Portofino's harbor and had lunch at the Pitosforo. It was raining cats and dogs outside, and only one other table in the restaurant was occupied. When somebody announced that there was a telephone call for Mr. Harrison, my husband got up, and so did the other Mr. Harrison—who just happened to be the famous actor, Rex Harrison. As it turned out, the call was for us! Rex seemed slightly miffed.

As mentioned previously, I adored my first Italian visit in 1947, and was forever eager to return. One such time occurred in 1950 when one of the Italian diplomats I knew in London invited me to pass a few months in northern Italy. Carla Gallarati-Scotti—the ambassador's niece—had stayed with us in London that spring, and we had become very good friends. The same year I had spent the summer in Norway seeing doctors for my circulatory condition. One early autumn morning I flew out from Oslo to Copenhagen, with stops in Prague and Vienna, and around eleven p.m. finally arrived in Milano. During the trip I talked to my grandmother's furrier. A group of jolly Italians came to meet him at the airport, but nobody had turned up for me. Some kind Italians waited with me for a while and then suggested they take me to downtown Milano. We all piled into their tiny car and drove the main highway. Suddenly, I caught a glimpse of my friends in a small station wagon headed toward the airport. After a lot of hooting and screeching of brakes, we managed to get their attention, which seemed quite a miracle. Imagine something like that happening in today's traffic!

Carla and her Gallarati-Scotti cousins drove me to her home, the beautiful *Villa Gallarati-Scotti* at Oreno di Vimercate. When I sent my mother a postcard of the villa, she thought it resembled *Schoenbrunn Schloss*—a palace in Austria—until she noticed the cross on the third floor window, which happened to be my room! My bags were unpacked for me, and my evening dress was ironed. I did not have to lift a finger. Carla's father, who had been mayor of Milano, was an exceptionally interesting gentleman. And her mother was an equally lovely Venetian lady. Both were extraordinarily kind and hospitable to me. Life in the country in Lombardy continued as it had for generations. The family spent the summer together at their country villa. The Venetian grandmother—the Contessa Soranza—joined them. She was another very gracious Venetian lady.

The *Villa Gallarati-Scotti* was surrounded by a large park of magnificent old trees. Roses grew en masse on each side of the two wings of the empire-style building. A quaint trail went through the park up to the Nettuno—a fabulous baroque fountain. At the *Villa Borromeo* on the other side of the park, life moved at the same old-fashioned pace. The families gathered at lunchtime. Only the old 84 year-old grandmother preferred her lunch upstairs, and came down only once a day. She was always dressed in black wearing some beautiful pieces of jewelry. She had a majestic air about her as she sat with her needlepoint. The old family butler rarely cracked a smile. I saw him smile one day at lunch when the gray parrot—which had been brought down to be shown off to an old professor—did "big-big" on the terrine in the middle of the table!

FONTANA D' NETTUNO

The butler served lunch and dinner at the large round table in the spacious dining room. When there were lunch guests at the villa, we would take coffee at the "Nettuno," the "follie" in the park. Visitors would arrive by horse and carriage. The younger generation would walk up the trail. In front of the follie stood a beautiful fountain, hence its name. It was calming to sit and listen to the tinkling of the water, while slowly sipping coffee. Most evenings before dinner we met in the mother's boudoir to say the rosary together. I loved the warm family atmosphere and miss the tradition and life in the old country houses.

One afternoon Contessa Ida, Carla and I went to the Sioli's villa for tea, *Il Buzzero* in Gorgonzola. Marisa Sioli was one of Carla's best friends. Other friends joined to play tennis. The following morning, a horse and carriage with a distinguished looking groom showed up to take us to Vimercate, the neighboring village of Oreno. From there we took the antiquated tram car to Milano, where we enjoyed a fantastic day shopping, with tempting bargains everywhere. We then lunched with Carla's sister and brother-in-law, Cecilia and Dody, in their lovely modern apartment in Palazzo Visconti. One of Dody's best friends, Giorgio Savini, joined us for lunch. He was tall and good looking with grey-streaked hair at only age 35. He was sharp-witted, amusing and a bit of a flirt. After lunch, Carla's cousin, Gianca, took us sightseeing in

Milano. We saw Da Vinci's, "The Last Supper," the *Palazzo Sforza*, as well as the cathedral, gardens, houses and monuments. I was immensely impressed. Later, we took afternoon tea with cousin Illa, Gianca's sister, and a good friend from London. Newly married, she looked radiant and was busy remodeling the two top floors of Palazzo Gerli. Gianca invited us to dinner at the old *Palazzo Gallarati-Scotti* on Via Manzoni. His brother, Lodo, joined us. The palace was enormous. Rows of salons brimmed with valuable family treasures. Following WWII, parts of the palace had been converted to offices and flats, both for family and friends. As we left, I stumbled on the top of the wide and rough stone stairs and immediately realized I was bleeding badly. A deep cut on my heel had left dark spots on the staircase. Perhaps it will be believed to be the family ghost in a hundred years time! We entered the house, and with a hero's courage, Gianca poured half a bottle of iodine over the wound. I went pale green, but the men looked even worse. Brandy was served to revive us all.

One evening the Siolis gave a dinner with Gianca, Anna, her brother, Beppe Belgiojoso and Carlo Gropello present. Their hospitality was so well-known that young people would always visit. We danced till late, and spent the night at *Il Buzzero* so we could play tennis with Giuseppe and Fernando Gnecchi the next day.

Bellagio is situated at the northern end of Lake Como's peninsula. Some of the most magnificent villas grace the point. *Villa Melzi* belonged to the Duke Gallarati-Scotti, the ambassador to London, whose daughters, Illa and Jepha, were among my best friends. The villa next door belonged to the Gerlis. Illa, whom I had seen in Milano, married "the boy next door," and the Gerlis invited us for the weekend. The two villas were among the most beautiful I have ever seen.

The *Villa Melzi* was a Napoleonic gift to the Duca di Melzi. At the entrance of the villa hung a fabulous painting of an African gentleman by Rubens, an example of just one of the invaluable treasures. The popular gardens are open to the public at azalea and rhododendron time. The first piece of art I noticed on arriving at Villa Gerli, on the other hand, was no less than a reclining statue by the world-famous sculptor, Canova. Our beautiful bedrooms had a magnificent view of Lake Como on one side, and mountains on the other. The houseguests included Carla's cousins with whom we had a wonderful time. We were not allowed to go out at night without chaperones, so cousins were perfect for the job!

After we returned to Oreno, we went to lunch at the villa next door. *Villa Borromeo* was the childhood home of Gian Vico Borromeo, my godmother Egidia's husband. His mother was born Gallarati-Scotti. There was a connecting door in the wall between the two magnificent villas.

Another weekend, we stayed with the Borromeo cousins who owned the fabulous islands in the Lago Maggiore. There are three islands, Isola Bella, Isola Madre and Isola Pescatore. Isola Bella resembles a palace out of fairytales. The gardens descend into nine terraces towards the lake. Prince Carlo Borromeo began designing the gardens in 1630. Forty years later his son, Vitaliano Borromeo, completed them—with the help of the famous architect, Barca. The island floats like some mysterious apparition. Pines and cypresses frame the statues, obelisks, and the balustrades of this extraordinary, man-made phenomenon. White peacocks parade among the basins and flowering bushes. Terraces border the waters of the lake, decorated with boxwood in arabesque designs. I was totally enchanted by this garden. Montesquieu, the French poet affirmed, "On peut dire qu'on ne quitte ce lieu qu'avec regret." (One could only say one leaves this place with regret). In great contrast to the magnificent Isola Bella and Lago Maggiore, was the Lago d'Orta, which I also loved. My friend, Albert Rothschild, had taken a farmhouse and remodeled it most attractively. The walls were so thick he arranged a terrarium in the middle of a double window. The domed dining room had been covered with real copper dust from his sister's copper mines in Chile. We had many happy house parties and wonderful holidays with Albert on his lake.

Carla brought me to the Dorias for a weekend at their lovely *Villa Doria* in Piedmont. We were there to celebrate the old Marchesa's birthday. The handsome mansion was set against a background of mountains and splendid tall trees. Six of her son, Oberto's friends—plus his sister, Lola—went up in two cars. Since it was not too far from the ski resort of Sestriere, Alberto Zambeletti (of pharmaceutical fame), went a little crazy on the way home from a dinner party one evening. He wanted to show me where he had broken his leg skiing the previous winter. He drove his Fiat 500, the "Balila," or "Topolino" as we called it. The tiny Italian car delivered quite an experience on night mountain roads!

The Crespi family, who owned the Milanese newspaper, the *Corriere della Sera*, had a fantastic party in honor of their daughter, Giulia Maria. It was given at their country estate *Il Biffo*. The large property had many entrances. Party guests came from a variety of countries, some of whom were good friends from England. The party lacked nothing—the food, drink and music were all excellent. The Italian girls were extremely elegant. I wore a new creation I had had made in Milano and felt on top of my form. After the dance, however, the notorious Lombardy fog had descended, and we were forced to inch back to Oreno at a snail's pace.

One day, Carla's Venetian grandmother said to me, "You can't possibly visit Italy without seeing Venice!" She arranged to open her palace on San Polo for us. Soon after, Carla and Marisa took me by train from Milano to Venice. As we exited the railway station, the view stunned me. We had arrived right on the Canal Grande where the old gondolier guide, Domenico—who had taken Carla's mother to her first dance—was waiting for us. He punted us in great style through the myriad of canals, telling us that gondolas first appeared in Venetian waters in 1095. And by the year 1500, ten thousand gondolas covered the canals, all of them opulently gilded and covered with *felze*—the cabin roofs aristocratic Venetians still display in their palazzos like a coat of arms. Domenico took us right up to the entrance of the *Palazzo Soranza*. On the landing, four smiling servants served as our welcoming committee—all dressed to kill.

Venice has a varied and extraordinary representation of European architecture. It is an unbelievable living museum of humanity. Its scores of galleries and churches testify to the most colorful and festive paintings that Europe has ever produced. With artists such as Bellini, Giorgione, Titian and Tintoretto, Veronese, Tiepolo, Canaletto and Guardi, Venetian painting is one of the greatest pages in the history of European art. For a week we went sightseeing to our hearts' content.

We often stopped at Piazza San Marco or Harry's Bar for a famous Bellini. (The bar—small, paneled and cozy—is one of the most celebrated in the world. It never changes.) Every time I paid a visit to that bar, it left me in a special frame of mind. One patron once aptly said, "Great restaurants reflect the history of their setting. I do not think it fanciful to recognize many profound Venetian traits in the personality of Harry's Bar; the diligence and the craftsmanship, the Slavic strength and the Italian grace, the touch of gravity and the talent for display." After a visit to Harry's, we had the energy to take a long walk. We covered most of the bridges like the Rialto and the Accademia, and made sure not to miss the well-known Bridge of Sighs. Only in Venice can one can cross a street, and even stop to talk in the middle of it, without the being hit by a vehicle! Carla and I were usually under strict supervision and could only go out at night if invited by family! Otherwise, we had dinner in the palazzo or our bedroom, served by the cook and white-gloved butler! The rest of the palace was closed for the summer.

The vaporettos (or water taxis) transported us to some of the innumerable islands in the laguna. The story goes that Venetian merchants would save their money, then escape to an island for peace and tranquility. Hence, Giudecca, a northern nearby island, was settled. The island was actually named by Jewish people living abroad. Famous for its gardens it became a favorite spot for the Venetian nobility. As a result of Jacopo de Barbari's city plan in 1500, beautiful villas dot the varied shores of Venice. Many noble Venetians chose the Island of Murano as their ideal refuge. At the end of the Quattrocento, splendid dwellings were constructed alongside the glass blowing foundries. Back then in 1500, Murano was one of the richest centers of the region with a population of 30,000. Only a few traces of the era's Paolo Veronese frescos remain in one of the villas. Except for the Palazzo Da Mula, little is left of this ancient era. The island of Murano is known for its exquisite glass, where the industry started around 1289. Murano chandeliers have become especially famous. A glass museum was founded in 1861 at the Palazzo Giustiniani, the former home of the Bishop of Torcello. I have often returned to Venice to purchase wonderful glassware. However, my first trip impressed me the most.

Torcello was the main refuge for those terrorized by the Barbarian invasions. The island used to be the most important in the Laguna. Flooded by the waters of the rivers, and in competition with the Rialto, little by little the island was abandoned and today Torcello has less than 100 inhabitants. The cathedral on the island is a Byzantine construction dating to 639 AD. The campanile was added in the eleventh century. Next to the cathedral is the church of Santa Fosca, a great witness to the lost city. It was reconstructed in 1100 AD on a much older foundation. It is of a very harmonious architecture, the art of Ravenna. Low in the water it has the most romantic setting. I used to think it a great wedding spot. The best restaurant in Venice is located there in Torcello, and has an indescribably beautiful view.

The first thing we noticed about Burano was its color. It's no wonder that the island is a favorite with painters. The men walk about the piazzas in the evenings, while the women tat lace. The Burano School of Lace dates from 1872 to 1972. It reopened a few years later, employing six local instructors who taught students the 1700 year-old patterns—hoping to revive a nearly lost art form. This island of farmers and fishermen once held many convents including the most famous, Santa Caterina. Cypresses bordered the island of San Francesco del Deserto surrounding the convent. In 1228, the Franciscan Fathers were given the place by Jacopo Michiel, and were responsible for the island's profound atmosphere of silence and peace. Legend says that in 1220, San Francesco of Assisi—upon his return from Soria with his companion, Illuminato—had shipwrecked on the island aboard a Venetian ship due to a storm. San Francesco built a hut and remained on the island for a time performing miracles. His walking stick, planted in the salt earth, seeded and grew. Even today the Franciscan Fathers remember the venerated plant.

The Lido is a long island that separates the city from the sea. Many great poets like Goethe, Byron, Shelley or De Musset and George Sand loved the Lido for the solitude of its deserted beaches. We too went out to the Lido, of course, which has the longest and one of the best known beaches for swimming in the world. Now there are long, tree-lined lanes, luxurious hotels, villas, as well as rows and rows of cabanas that line the beach. My host's staff served us hot lunch in front of the family cabana. We enjoyed the fine sand in view of a grand hotel occupied by elegant people. Those were the good old days of wonderful Venetian living. Ruskin, the famous English writer, lived for a long time on the Zattere—the sunny passegiata, or promenade—which faces the shipping lane with the island of Giudecca on the other side. The *Clary Palazzo* is situated on the Zattere. The palace's owners—Prince and Princess Alfy Clary—had escaped the communist regime in what was then Czechoslovakia. Having lost everything at home, they relocated to Venice and took up residence on the top floor of their palazzo and lived on the rent from the "piani nobili," or the main floors. The Clarys were the handsomest couple I knew. They were cousins of some close friends of mine, the Kinskys, who also had escaped from Czechoslovakia. Barbara Cerratti and her family lived on the main floor of the palace. They also owned a delightful house in Asolo in the Dolomite Mountains. Eleonora Duse—the famous Italian actress—once lived in Asolo, as did the writer, Freya Stark. Even Harry's Bar has a country inn in Asolo. Ever since my first visit, I have loved Venice. It was nothing less than dreamy to sail on the Laguna and watch many "red sails in the sunset." Every corner, every villa and every canal of that amiable town is worthy of being drawn or painted—which I heartily did.

One year, I visited Venice in the winter after skiing in Cortina d'Ampezzo. Snow covered the city of Venice and the gondolas looked like black swans cloaked in white ermine capes. After we spent an evening at the Teatro La Fenice with the Valmaranas, we walked through the snow-covered calle, carrying our shoe bags. The Valmaranas—who have been my cherished friends for many years—had a palazzo on the Gran Canale. But their *Palladian Villa Capra* outside Vicenza is much better known. Called *La Rotonda,* it is the most popular of the Palladian villas. It was built for Paolo Americo, a cleric, who was Apostolic Referenda to Popes Pius IV and Pius V. Inspired by the noblest example of Roman architecture and crowned by a dome like a sacred temple, the villa still possesses a quintessential Venetian character. It tops a small hill, creating stunning views—thanks to its four equal prospects—of the surrounding landscape. I loved to visit *La Rotonda.* The old hunting lodge was the Valmarana family's summer residence.

La Rotonda

Lodovico Valmarana, the oldest son, also inherited another country estate from his aunt, called *Saonara*. I spent some lovely times there, too, with the family. I was given the opportunity to sketch Lodovico's young Grimani nieces, as well as *Saonara* and its landscape.

Alessandro, another Valmarana son, was a great friend of mine in London, where he worked for Pirelli. His boss was Guido Barricalla, and I often went to the resort, the Cortina d'Ampezzo to stay with the Barricallas at their chalet. Pia Barricalla and her daughter, Pilla, were both among my best friends during the London years. In 1956, I was invited to Cortina for the Winter Olympics. Pia Barricalla shared an acquaintance with the Italian Olympic Committee President, Paolo Thaon de Revel. And I knew a Norwegian member of the International Olympic committee. Since he had not brought his wife, he frequently invited me to join him in the Royal Box. Pia and I felt quite honored, and had a tremendous amount of fun. Parties were non-stop. Cars were prohibited—an inconvenience arranged by the '"big guns."

In addition to the Cortina chalet, the Barricallas had an inviting property at Lazise on the Lago di Garda. Stendhal called the Garda Lake the most beautiful landscape in the world. Nineteen centuries ago Catullus, the great Roman poet, had a villa at Sirmione. It has a microclimate because the Dolomites and the Alps block the icy northern winds. Hot sulphur bubbles at its southern end. Although it shares the same latitude as Montreal and Maine, Garda lemons have been on the tables of Europe for hundreds of years. Lucrezia Borgia ordered them for the court at Ferrara and these lemons went to Tsar Nicholas II as well as to the Austro-Hungarian emperor. Today, the same old olive trees stand gnarled and ancient. A friend of ours had the most enchanting garden on the Sirmione peninsula overlooking the lake. She grew wonderful roses that climbed up the old olive trees! Large lemon groves still grow along the border of the lake. The area had long attracted illustrious people. Both Virgil and Dante visited Lago di Garda, as well as Catullus. Mussolini had even chosen the Gardone Riviera area for his mistress, Clara Petacci, and gave her the *Villa Fiordaliso*. We also visited the villa of Gabriele D'Annunzio, the famous Italian writer, who had been in the area since 1921.

Rome was routinely on my itinerary when I was sent south to recuperate from the cold winters. I was always welcome at the table of the Borghese family and even at the *Palazzo Taverna*. I roamed the streets and piazzas, read my mail on the Aventino, sketched on the Palatino, saw operas at the Terme di Caracalla, and revisited my favorite galleries and museums.

After my year in Oreno in 1950, I also visited Rome on my way to winter in Sicily, and devoted a whole chapter on that outstanding island.

When my father retired from twelve years of service in Great Britain—however sorry he was to leave his London post—he asked to be sent to Italy. My mother yearned for sunshine. These were the last years of Father's career, and he asked me to secure a residence for the embassy. I left London on the train with Pia and Pilla Barricalla. They were also going to Rome for the grand ball of Princess Palavicini held in her magnificent palazzo near the Quirinale. It proved to be a most splendid Roman event.

Before I arrived in Italy, the Norwegian Prime Minister and the Foreign Secretary had recently been to Rome. They were also looking to purchase a house as an embassy residence for my parents. They found one in the Copi De section. It was the ugliest thing you'd ever seen, but I didn't want to disparage the prime minister's suggestion. Then, a thought crossed my mind. I went there at several different hours of the day and realized it must have been about the only house in Rome that got little or no sunshine. I immediately telephoned my father in London and told him that the very reason for his leaving his beloved London was nonexistent. Mother would see no sunshine.

He spoke to the government while I continued to look at houses. I saw a house belonging to a film star that had closets larger than the living room—not exactly father's style. Another morning, I was shown a house on the Via Appia Antica, and immediately fell for it. It was only for rent, but that worked in my favor. It was owned by a very nice Sicilian who spent years in the States. That was an added benefit, too. It was a long yellow building with extremely wide front steps and wide French doors. The vast garden was perfectly beautiful with huge Pins Parasols or umbrella pines. Climbing roses grew up to a height of 60 feet and then cascaded down. The villa had an Olympic-size swimming pool, which I decided was ideal for summer luncheon parties! After we moved in, our garden became the desired destination on a hot Roman summer day. Everybody loved to come to lunch with us at the Appia Antica. Many a diplomatic or political discussion took place in the cool water of our swimming pool. Father, being a very old-fashioned man, found it a bit strange to suggest the ladies undress on arrival. After a refreshing swim, an excellent lunch and delightful wines were served in the shade of the grand, old trees. We celebrated my 30th birthday with a swimming pool luncheon. Although we were a small country, whenever we had parties, all the prominent people who were invited would attend. This delighted my father. Among the gathering of amusing friends, were William and Sonny Reinhardt, the American ambassador and his wife. The villa had a couple of open living rooms, a library and a sunken dining room with a vaulted ceiling. The bedrooms were all upstairs with fabulous views of the surrounding countryside—the Roman Campania. Above the living room was a large glassed-in terrace—which I used as my studio—that provided an even better view of the sublime scenery. What a wonderful property it was! Grapes and figs grew in the garden and the blue wisteria climbed up the walls. The driveway passed under a rose- covered archway that was attached to the gatehouse. The embassy was situated on the Via Appia Antica just across from the villa of Carlo Ponti and Sofia Loren. In fact, we had an infinite amount of illustrious neighbors.

I was so inspired while I lived at the Appia Antica, that I painted a great deal there and held several art shows. The timing of my displays coincided with the release of the film *La Dolce Vita*. My first show was at the Galleria "La Feluca." A feluca is a hat that ambassadors wore with their diplomatic uniforms. Father had never had an artist in his family and was a bit confused, but quite proud at the same time—especially when 13 ambassadors turned up for my opening. I received some good reviews and was later written up in two Italian encyclopedias of artists! My very inspirational art teacher in London, Princess Zeid—a renowned painter—had a charming house at Forio on the island of Ischia. Prince Zeid, her husband, had been the Iraqi ambassador in London while we were there and was our nearest neighbor across on Kensington Palace Garden. The first time I visited Princess Zeid at Ischia, she completely altered my style of painting. We continued to discuss it over lunch at Harry's Bar on Ischia. Harry, by the way, happened to be a transplanted American who served the best fresh, cold tomato sauce over his spaghetti on the island of Ischia.

Over the next few days we continued to discuss painting—and every other subject—in the cool of her vast living room. By the time she finally sent me off on the boat to Naples, I was thoroughly inspired. As the boat left the pier, I stood and waved to my good friend in somewhat of a mesmerized state, and I saw what looked like a blue Madonna in the oily surface of the Mediterranean. When I returned to Rome, I painted what I had seen in the water. It became one of my most arresting works, I have been told, and a series of paintings on the theme of the blue Madonna sold very well. I had another successful show in Oslo, at Gallery Per, where a number of paintings and drawings were also sold, boosting my courage immensely. Then, in 1961, Albert Rothschild arranged for a show in New York.

A pilot friend lent me his apartment in Rome while he was flying for Alitalia. He was part of the four-member Italian military air show team called the Azzurri. Not only were they good pilots, but excellent skiers as well. We would often ski together. I had the same black, blue and white Norwegian sweaters made for all of us. Six of us would storm down the slopes at Terminillo, a ski area outside of Rome. Many summers these friends, my brother and I would sail to Porto Ercole, a fisherman's village on the south side of the Argentario. The peninsula claimed the distinction of having been charted by Leonardo da Vinci, whose original map hangs in the Vatican Museum. The low hills that embrace the harbor of Porto Ercole are dotted with forts dating back to the Spanish sovereignty. I had the wonderful treat of staying at the lower fort which belonged to Giulia Borghese Cornaggia, one of my best Roman friends. The old town is suspended like a ship's prow above the old port. Its flagstone streets are linked by shallow flights of steps that descend from the parish church to Piazza Santa Barbara. In the early days one could sail in and anchor in the old harbor of Porto Ercole. Boys slept onboard and girls rented space in fishermen's houses.

Once many years later, we rented a house near Porto Santo Stefano on the north side of the Argentario. The Princess of Berar came to stay with us. The first morning, I heard a strange sound from the living room. It was the princess mopping the floor! My husband almost had a heart attack when he saw the very dignified Princess of Berar cleaning!

I loved the Mediterranean and spent many weekends on Capri, as well. In the early days, I always stayed with my Roman friends at the Pensione Weber in the Marina Piccola. Blue wisterias almost completely covered the entrance. The free and airy atmosphere of island life was intoxicating. I understood so well why the famous Swedish doctor and writer, Alex Munthe, had chosen to live a long time in his beloved Anacapri.

Portrait of me by Hugo Caballero, 1963

Sicily – The Kingdom of the Sun

GOLD ELEPHANT

Goethe once wrote, "To have seen Italy without having seen Sicily is not to have seen Italy at all, for Sicily is the clue to everything. If Italy possesses a magical charm that lures foreigners to her shores and keeps her natives at home, then Sicily—a paradigm of all that is good and bad in Italy—has an almost limitless power to captivate."[1] With these lines in mind, in November 1950, I was ready for my new adventure.

I arrived at the pier in Naples with my luggage ready to leave for Sicily, as was the ship. The first mate greeted me at the top of the gangway and helped me find my cabin. He carried my luggage into the cabin and then did not make a move to leave. I immediately realized his game, and feigned having left something on deck. As soon as he was outside in the corridor, I swiftly went back into my cabin and immediately locked the door behind me. I had just been through a similar "romantic interlude" in the afternoon in a movie house in Naples, when I had to change places twice in a dark movie theater to avoid "the wandering hand syndrome." I did not want to repeat the experience with admiring Neapolitans, so I remained in my cabin foregoing supper.

Early the next morning, we docked in Palermo, Sicily's capital. The city cradles its harbor against a mountainous backdrop, and derives its name from Panormus, which is Greek for "sheltered harbor."

Sicily seemed to me a place of contrasts. The islands of Italy had a combination of each essential element. Fire (Etna, Sicily's famous volcano),

Water (the seas surrounding the islands), Earth (the Afro-Mediterranean) as well as the air of mystique, which proved irresistible. A friend and a scion of one of Sicily's oldest families once said to me, "Here is both the nourishing sea and the savage sun. And it has always been like that; the beauty and the beast, and that is how we have survived a dozen invasions. There are mountains, the Mafia, solitary Greek temples, Spanish baroque buildings, Moorish vermillion cupolas, golden Byzantine churches, stern Norman forts and cloistered pleasure gardens. There are markets where North Africa and the Mediterranean meet. Here there is breathtaking beauty and extraordinary opulence, contrasted with great poverty. Here there is extraordinary food and exuberant people, but the Mafia too, which now lack any charm it might have possessed when it was founded in the Middle Ages." [2]

Arriving in Palermo, friends of the Gallarati-Scottis—also my best friends in Milano—met me at the dock. They brought me to the palace *Ajuta mi Cristo* (Help me, Christ!). It was a thirteenth or fourteenth-century stone palace. It had never been heated! At night I would say to myself, "Ajuta mi Cristo" when I went to bed. In spite of the furs and blankets, the room was frigid. At sunrise, I would throw open the shutters to thaw.

Friends had arranged that I be a paying guest of a White Russian family. Baron Boltho and his family were refugees from one of the Baltic States at the time of the Russian Revolution. The streets around their palazzo were dirty, narrow and over-populated. Laundry hung from every window. Barefoot children, stray dogs, as well as constant shouting completed the picture. The women hauled baskets up and down from the markets in the streets below. The men on the corners earned very little, and cheated more than they worked. The Bolthos had another paying guest, an English girl, who immediately offered to take me sightseeing. She showed me the San Giovanni degli Eremiti Church, which became my favorite place to sketch. With its Arabic domes, cloisters and garden it really was a "Sanctuary of Imagination and Light." We drove to the Monastery Monreale with its magnificent world-famous cloisters. We walked to the Quattro Canti Fountains, on the corner of Via Maqueda and the Corso, and saw the statues of the Four Seasons and the Four Kings of Sicily. There, also stands the Four Patronesses of Palermo: Christina, Ninfa, Olivia and Agata.

The impact of the WWII American invasion was still evident in the capital. We came across bombed-out squares and city blocks of blackened buildings along the once prosperous harbor front; all this amid Byzantine cathedrals, narrow crooked vias and street markets. Many of the city's beautiful palaces became casualties of the 1943 bombings, and several families I met had lost their beautiful homes during the Allied landing in Sicily.

A lovely girl named Graziella celebrated her 18th birthday the day after I arrived in Palermo. Her debutante party—given in the family palazzo that was still intact—was the grand ball of the season. Paintings in heavily gilded frames adorned the walls, and Venetian chandeliers hung from the high ceilings. It was an impressive setting for a splendid party, matched by the prominent guests. Strikingly beautiful girls in elegant dresses, including every generation of the Palermo first families, were present. My friendly welcoming committee came to fetch me at the *Ajuta me Cristo* palace and escorted me to the party. At one point during the evening, four very tall boys came across the room to greet me and said, "Mamma ti aspetta per colazione domani a l'una." (Mamma expects you for lunch tomorrow at one o'clock). I duly thanked them, but after they had left, I turned to my new friends to ask who they were. "The Paterno boys," was the reply. I remembered then that a friend of mine in London had written to her aunt Giovanna Paterno in Palermo. Since the aunt had never answered, this invitation was quite unexpected. The following day at one o'clock, I walked through the magnificent gardens of the *Villa Trabia* with my new friend, Bice. The property was situated in the middle of town, next to the Excelsior Hotel. The villa belonged to Raimondo and Galvano Lanza di Trabia, the nephews of Princess Paterno. Since the downtown Paterno palace had been destroyed by bombs, the family was all living together. The old butler, who had been with the family for years, opened the front door and showed us into a small sitting room. "Scusate, but nobody is at home yet," he said. "They should arrive soon," he added encouragingly. After about half an hour, Miss Russell, the old governess who had been with Princess Paterno's mother, the famous Princess Trabia, came downstairs. Despite having been with the family for over 50 years, she spoke hardly any Italian. She was, on the other hand, the reason the whole family spoke fluent English. Ten minutes after she joined us, Pirzio, a shepherd dog entered and greeted us. Then, little by little, five of the six boys turned up.

At half past two, their mother, Princess Paterno, arrived. Although we had waited so long, she managed to make the moment amazingly special. She had an infinite grace and elegance about her that I loved from the moment I saw her. Giovanna Paterno told me she would be my Fairy Godmother, and she remained so till the day she died. She was a true matriarch. This was demonstrated when I stayed there later. For, it was customary that, every time one of us had been out in the evening, we would have to see Fairy Godmother before we went to bed—even if it was four o'clock in the morning. Monsignor Pottino, of the famous film, *The Leopard* and who was also great friend of the Paternos, joined us for lunch. It was an unforgettable introduction to a very special family. The table conversation centered around the upcoming wedding of their Borghese cousin in Rome. While still in London, I had received an invitation to that wedding, but as I had already travelled to Palermo, I had not thought of attending the grand occasion. Then the Princess exclaimed, "But how could you possibly stay in Palermo without us?" She had only known me for one half hour! This was the beginning of an extraordinary life-long friendship. After lunch, one of the sons was sent to secure a ticket for the ship that brought us to Naples. One of the other sons was sent to call the hotel in Rome to keep an extra room, and yet another one to inform the Borghese family in Rome that I was coming. The night ferry from Palermo to Naples, however, was completely booked that day and so I shared a cabin with my newfound Fairy Godmother.

The next morning, bright and early, we all sat on our suitcases at the Naples Railway station, waiting for our train to Rome, munching on some wonderful, Neapolitan delicacy with our morning coffees. On our arrival in Rome we checked into the Hotel Regina, a very respectable old hotel on the Via Veneto where generations of noblemen had always stayed. Suddenly,

I felt very much part of the "old school" in Italy. Pepito, the third of Fairy Godmother's six boys had been in Rome for some time and was given the honor of picking me up at the hotel and escorting me to the festivities. He was the most charming of the boys and we immediately became lifelong friends. The next four days turned out to be just fabulous. Adopted by the Paterno family and being included by friends and cousins was like living a dream. The wedding celebrations continued for over three days. The actual ceremony took place in the magnificent Borghese Chapel. Both the wedding reception and the family luncheon were given in their own palazzo on the Tiber River. Chateaubriand, the Brazilian media magnate, was one witness and the other witness was Vittorio Orlando, who was one of the signers of the 1919 Versailles Peace Treaty. Orlando was a senator and although he was 92 years old, he could not leave his parliament for any length of time. Pepito introduced us at the reception given for 2,000 people before the wedding. Vittorio Orlando had short, wiry, white hair and intense eyes. He was a Palermitano and a great friend of the Paternos. We were having a very interesting conversation, when, after a little while, Prince Borghese, the father of the bride, came to take Orlando to speak with some more important guests. When I met Orlando two days later at the bridal luncheon for 40 people, I expected to be reintroduced. However, not only did he remember me, he continued the conversation where we had left off two days earlier! I had never been so impressed. Senator Orlando later came to stay at Villa Trabia in Palermo while I was there. I listened to his many stories during our long walks in the park. But, after only a week, he returned to his beloved Parliament.

When we came back to Palermo after the wedding, I realized I could no longer tolerate the freezing palace *Ajuta mi Cristo*. So, I moved to Taormina, a resort town on the east coast of Sicily, between Messina and Catania. Taormina is Greek, Arab, Spanish and Norman; that is to say, Sicilian. It clings to the mountainside on the Greek side of the island and has a gorgeous view of the famous volcano, Etna, as well as the dramatic coastline toward Catania and Siracusa. More than the Neapolitan guitar, the area's music is of flutes and pastoral bagpipes. At Christmas, in fact, the bagpiper goes from house to house—through the narrowest of streets—and plays in front of one little presepio after another.

Hellenic and neo-pagan architecture dominated the area. There were closed-in gardens protected by high walls, decidedly like a monastery. The grandest hotel, San Domenico, was an old convent. Steep serpentine donkey paths wind up and down the hillsides covered with orange and olive trees. Today luxury cars sweep around the curves. Mount Etna watches over the whole landscape and once in a while makes its presence known by erupting and sending streams of boiling lava down the mountainsides. The best view in Taormina was from the ruins of the Greek theater, and so I moved next door into the Hotel Timeo. My sun-drenched room faced the view, and every morning was spectacular. Because of Taormina's unusual beauty, I painted and sketched at both the mountains and beach.

I met an elderly American lady from San Francisco named Mrs. Ophuls at the hotel. She was the widow of a German doctor of pathology and looked it. She carried herself straight as an arrow, always wore a small hat with a veil and AAA shoes. She decided to be my chaperone. At first I thought this would be very restrictive, but then I realized the great advantage for both of us. It enabled me to accept any invitation without being criticized by the local population and Mrs. O. could enjoy invitations that would otherwise have not come her way. Mrs. O. had traveled extensively and possessed a great background and old-fashioned charm.

One day Lord Maugham, Somerset Maugham's older brother, arrived at the hotel and joined our little group. He was about 84 years-old and had been Lord Chancellor in 1939! At a later time in London, after I had returned from Sicily, my father had a luncheon at the embassy, and I asked whether I could invite a couple of my friends. When my father mentioned there would be no other young people present, I told him one of my friends was Lord Maugham! My father had no more objections. Charles Hambro, the British banker and friend of my father, had given me an introduction to a Mr. Campbell. Everyone called him Mr. Campobello in Taormina. His friend was Miles Wood, the British actor. They gave special cocktail parties where they served a drink they called Goat's Milk (Latte di Capra). Don't ask me what strange concoction they served. I am afraid I stuck to wine. Miles and Mr. Campbell had been together for 25 years and they celebrated it one night at the San Domenico Hotel, the old Monastery.

I learned that the monastic orders in the old Sicilia had luxurious buildings with great artistic details and art. Until the 1800s, Taormina had not been a tourist attraction because it existed in the shadow of the great Dominican Monastery. Today, the San Domenico is one of the great hotels of Southern Europe. I was repeatedly invited by a charming Sicilian couple to a house on the beach below Taormina. The waves broke gently against the rocks and over the clean sand, and the sea ranged from deep blue to turquoise. I spent many sunny days sketching the local fishermen and their colorful boats in that lovely spot. Because it was difficult to make the steep climb back to Taormina, one of my friends would always give me a lift up the hill on his Vespa. Doctor Gaylord Hauser—a tall and handsome friend of the Swedish film actress, Greta Garbo—became another good friend of mine. Gaylord also had a house on the beach, and I often went there for dinner. I was fascinated because as one of the first great experts on nutrition, he took care of many of the actresses in his day.

Christmas of 1950, I was invited up to *Castello di Maniace*, the enormous property of Peter Bridport, the Duke of Bronte. Lord Nelson, Peter's ancestor, had been given this large castello, as well as the title of Duke of Bronte, by the King of Naples in appreciation for one of the admiral's great victories. The property was in the middle of Sicily, but only a little more than an hour's drive from Taormina. *Castello di Maniace* had been a very handsome monastery with a striking view of the mountains and Etna. Sheila and Peter Bridgeport had put in central heating, but no electric light in the castle. In the evenings, two servants came in with huge candlelit candelabras. It was all very romantic. Sheila, Peter, Alexander (their four year old son), their nanny and I were joined for Christmas by an old family friend, Bobby Pratt-Barlow, who himself owned a charming house above Taormina. Because of Alexander, we loyally kept it a traditional British Christmas, complete with mince pies!

In fact, I passed one of the coziest English Christmases right in the middle of the "Kingdom of the Sun," the title of John Norwich's famous book on Sicily. John, son of Duff Cooper and the beautiful Lady Diana Duff Cooper, is a wonderful writer. In winter the famous Etna is snowcapped as it sends its smoke out over the rocky landscape and out to sea.

In addition to sketching and painting, I wanted to do something more important with my time in Taormina, so I opted to help a local doctor in the hospital children's ward. At first the parents were suspicious of a foreigner, and I was not permitted to go near the little ones. So, I decided to read to them, and within a few weeks I was allowed to really help, both in the hospital and on the doctor's rounds. It was an enlightening experience in more ways than one. The poverty was extreme in many cases. The families lived in one room houses co-existing with the animals, even when they were sick. It was a dismal picture. The bleakness of their future was discouraging, but the families' gratitude was touching.

One of the antique stores on Corso Umberto belonged to the two Panarello brothers. Their shop was filled with heavy Sicilian ceramic platters, old marionettes, embroidered pieces, oil paintings, carved Madonnas and altar triptychs. Since we daily did the "passegiata" with the old chaperone, I became good friends with the Panarellos. They would invite us to musical evenings where they served fresh almonds, salty olives, tangerines, and lots of wine. Over the years all sorts of people had come by their shop including Andre Gide, Jean Cocteau, Truman Capote and John Huston. They all had dedicated a drawing or something to Carlo and his wife, Mirella. Why did we stop there on the Corso? Because there was always time to "chiaccherare" or chat! Almost half a century later, my sister-in-law, Anne, was in Taormina and went by chance into the Panarello's antique store where she bought a lamp. She asked if she could leave the item for a couple of hours. When the brothers saw her name written on the lamp, they asked if she knew an Evelyn Prebensen. When Anne identified herself as my sister-in-law, they loaded her with gifts to bring back to me. Friendships like that are precious.

In the early spring, I got a call from my Fairy Godmother that two of her boys were leaving home. One son was going to study in the north of Italy, while the other one was going as far as Canada. She asked if I would please come over to Palermo for their departures. The early morning I waited to go by bus from Taormina to Catania, to then catch a flight to Palermo, the driver never appeared. Then we saw him come out onto a balcony at the other end of the square, shouting, "Un bambino, un bambino!" His wife had just given birth to a baby boy—the greatest joy any Italian can experience. The driver finally came down to the bus, carrying big bottles of wine. He wanted everyone to drink to the little boy's health. It was 6:30 in the morning, and I was getting nervous that I might miss my plane. So I approached the happy father when he boarded the bus and told him my story. I heard him ask the other passengers, "What about taking the Signorina to her airplane, I will take all of you to your destinations afterwards?" They all agreed and like one big happy family, they saw me off at the airport!

While I was staying at the villa in Palermo, Pietro, the eldest of the boys, was producing the film, Car*ozza d'Oro* with the fabulous Italian actress, Anna Magnani. I met her at dinner around 2 in the morning! I was quite taken with the fire in her black eyes and her sharp wit and sense of humor. Anna Magnani had made a film called *Volcano* at the same time that Rosselini was making *Stromboli* with Ingrid Bergman. The drama was that Roberto Rosselini had left "La Magnani" for the Swedish superstar, whom he later married.

One day, cousin Raimondo had to fly to Rome. Back then, the airport was still in downtown Palermo. Another lunch was running late. So what did Rudy, the military valet do? He called up the airport to inform the pilot to hold the Roman flight because Prince Raimondo had not yet finished eating his spaghetti! Those were the days!

I was also staying at the *Villa Trabia* during the "Giro di Sicilia" (the Sicilian car race). The famous industrial family, Marzotto, from Vicenza produced four brothers to race that year. One of them, Paolo, won the race. Raimondo had arranged for me to return to Taormina the following day with Paolo. Both Paolo and his brother, Vittorio, came by in the morning to pick me up. Vittorio was in one of the race cars and asked with whom I preferred to ride. Paolo was driving a sedan and, frankly, I thought that might be the safer of the two options. Little did I know then what was in store for me! Paolo insisted on showing me how he had taken the curves and won the race the night before. I reminded him that when he raced—unlike that moment—there was no oncoming traffic. I really began to get nervous when it started to rain. Paolo slowed down a little, but as we reached the mountains above Milazzo, he suddenly shouted, "Look behind us!" A heavy truck had appeared down a side road. It stopped, blocking the main road and several men jumped out. They had machine guns and started to shoot in our direction. Fortunately, the road was full of twists and turns and the bandits were not shooting well enough to hit us. Our car continued at full speed towards Messina. I was so shocked that I remained silent for about five minutes. Then I turned to Paolo and asked, "What the hell was all that about?" "Well," he answered, squirming, "I am from Vicenza, the north of Italy. When I got a telephone call this morning about paying a few million for a free passage to Taormina, I just refused, thinking I could out-drive them." We were lucky to have eluded our pursuers because the rain had slowed us down. Paolo was shaken as well by the episode, so we stopped at a bar for a large cognac! My mother was arriving by train that evening to spend a few weeks with me in Taormina. We arrived just in time to pick her up at the station. The following day we had lunch at the *Villa Marzotto*. Everyone was very relieved we had not been captured, detained somewhere in the hills, and held as ransom for the Marzotto fortune. My mother was certainly glad we were safe and sound because we'd heard that many Sicilian and Italian friends had been involved in kidnapping incidents.

Mother had always adored Italy, and stayed with me in Taormina for a month. She took a villa in the hills, and I was able to return some of the wonderful hospitality which had been shown me by everyone through the winter. We entertained on a wide terrace with a splendid view of the Etna, the coast winding its way south and the magnificent part of the Mediterranean which rolls towards Greece.

One of the many friendships I made in Sicily was with Madeleine Bielke. She later invited me to visit them at *Sturefors Castle*, her home in Sweden. She happened to be the sister-in-law of my Swedish boy friend during his stay as a diplomat in London. The world is very small.

Albert Rothschild invited mother and me one day to Siracusa. He had a house above the Greek Theater. Siracusa had been the most powerful city-state in all of Magna Graecia, outshining Athens and Carthage, as well as Rome and Alexandria. Albert took us sightseeing. Siracusa was probably the most southern example of Baroque architecture and was truly awe- inspiring. Their patron saint, Santa Lucia's shrine in the Duomo was Syracusa's richest chapel. The site of the Duomo had been a place of worship for over 25 centuries. The cathedral was the first Christian church in western Greece. The translucent representation of the Santa Lucia was carved by the Florentine sculptor, Gregorio Tedeschi around 1630. I became even more interested in the history of Syracuse when I worked there on anchors of antiquity. I helped Professor Lionel Casson publish an article on the topic for *Underwater Archeology*. These anchors were the very earliest, originating with the Phoenicians.

Years later, in 1955, I was summoned to Palermo again when Raimondo died. I flew in on the day of another "Giro di Sicilia." The airport porters knew I'd come because of Raimondo and immediately dropped what they were doing in order to accompany me to a waiting car. The Sicilian prince had been part of everyone's life in Sicily—he was their hero! He had been a leader in soccer and car-racing organizations, and had introduced many things to the island, including baseball. I was invited to have tea in town with Raimondo's mother and brother, Galvano, at Villa Trabia, which brought back scores of memories. The police had blocked the roads due to the car race, so I was driven out to the *Villa Trabia* in Bagheria late in the evening. This *Villa Trabia* is one of a group of impressive 18th-century villas in this small town 15 kilometers outside of Palermo. In spite of the sad occasion, the birds twittered, the sun shone, the bougainvillea blossomed among palms and pines. Big yellow lemons hung on the trees.

I continued going to Bagheria to see my Fairy Godmother and her wonderful family as long as she was alive. But I never again went back to *Villa Trabia* in Palermo.

Sweden – Never Take No for an Answer

GOLD 5 KRONOR COIN

WWII brought harsh conditions to Norway. The results of long term food shortages and freezing temperatures left me with Morbus Raynaud Disease and a complicated circulatory condition. My veins were constricted, risking the loss of my extremities. The doctors predicted possible amputation.

A few years after the war, I felt it was time to leave Oslo and its medical team. I was tired of being tested on and getting very few results. Once in 1945, the doctors performed an experimental procedure and rubbed nitro-glycerin cream on my knee. Within minutes, I felt like throwing myself off the balcony. The pain plunged me into such a dark depression that I begged my family to stay close until the effect subsided. My muscles weakened, my nerves hurt like hell, and I felt like 105 at the age of 17! I had lost patience with my neurosurgeon who, with each trial treatment, would say one of two things: 1) "You are going to die within three to six months if you don't do this;" or 2) "Now you must admit you are well!" My answer to these stupid statements was, "How can I admit anything when I'm still in excruciating pain, can't live a normal life, or play any of my favorite sports?" In Moscow, I was given my first pair of skis at age one and a half, and have been a skier ever since. I also played tennis and, of course, loved equestrian activities. I was told I was allergic to the cold, although I had figured that out by myself! The doctors then advised me to go south for the winter—which I did.

Late summer of 1945, after five long years of war, my father became the Permanent Secretary for Foreign Affairs. I had grown significantly from age ten to fifteen, so we all desperately needed new clothes and shoes, as well as housewares and material to upgrade curtains and furnishings for social representation. Germany's occupation of Norway had weighed heavily and difficult.

I awoke after a pleasant night on a sleeper train to see an unscathed and opulent Stockholm. It was almost unbelievable. The great Venice of the North was full of lights, food and flowers. I was only 16 years old—which was a while ago! So, let me take you back to the Charlottenberg station on the Norwegian-Swedish border. There I got my first look at how different life was on the Swedish side. They sold open-faced sandwiches with three slices of salami on each piece of bread! After the meager rations in Norway, it was a dream to be able to buy both candy and chocolates. Exhausted from all these new impressions, we boarded our comfortable sleeper and fell into a deep slumber.

The next day, the first sight of shop window displays made me exclaim in awe, "Are all these goods really for sale?" During the final years of the war, we had grown accustomed to seeing only artificial items in the store windows. We had come to Stockholm to shop, and it was fantastic. Mother and I were left to our own "work" while Father was back working in Oslo. In between purchases at fabulous shops like Nordiska Kompagniet, we sat outside the Grand Hotel while the sun glittered on the shiny windowpanes of the royal palace across the water. Boats drifted up and down the Strommen in front of us. Then, we walked from the top of Kungsgatan—one of the city's main streets full of elegant shops—over Stureplan and out Strandvagen. Djurgaarden Park was bursting in fall colors.

We enjoyed delicious meals with friends at restaurants including the K B (Konstnaerbolaget) where so many exiled Norwegians had been during the war. We also ate at Lilla Paris, Branda Tomten, Riche and the Cecil. At the latter, a strolling violinist came over to our table and played just for me.

I was only a teenager and had never experienced anything like that before. I blushed.

One evening, we dined at Gyldna Freden, one of Stockholm's oldest and most famous restaurants. It had thick, chunky walls and domed ceilings. A narrow stairway led down to a room of small tables with checkered tablecloths. The feeling of bygone days remained with us long after we had left our fantastic dinner. We sauntered back to our hotel over the century-old cobblestones of Gamla Stan, the oldest part of town.

After my father joined us, we lunched with him at the Grand Hotel. It was the only place one could buy plain milk chocolate bars in packages of 20. It amazed me that chocolate was the only thing in short supply in Stockholm that year!

On our last night in Sweden, Ambassador Esmarch invited us to dinner at the Strand Hotel. I can still remember the Smoergaardsbord menu: chicken and fabulous ice cream cookies for dessert! We drank an exclusive red Bordeaux wine. I was even given a large box of chocolates, which I brought home and shared with the rest of the family.

The last day was a rush beyond compare. My personal treasures consisted of a red tulle evening dress; a white and gray checkered coat; a red, white and blue tartan dress; and a red wool skirt with two coordinating white and striped woolen shirts. I also got a pair of brown shoes and black shoes, which I desperately needed because my feet had grown a bit from age 10 to 15. These were actual leather, something that really fit. During the war, only shoes made of fish skins or paper were available—very uncomfortable! I remember going to school in old rubber boots inherited from older cousins. It became a fad among the teenagers! After years of wearing dresses made from old curtains and sheets, like Scarlet in *Gone with the Wind*, I felt like the most fashionable person in the world in my new Swedish wardrobe. Besides clothing, we bought new curtains, linens, glassware, a dinner service and even furniture. In so many ways, I've always considered Stockholm one of the most beautiful cities I have known.

Six years passed before I rode that same night train again to Stockholm. In spite of not being able to obtain my medical records, I finally escaped the Norwegian doctor's so-called care. As I boarded the sleeper, I remembered having taken that famous train trip before!

By this time, my father had been nominated Ambassador to the Court of St. James in London. England's winter climate quickly proved to be even worse for my health. So, in 1950, I was sent to Sicily for six months.

In Taormina, I met Madeleine Bielke, the sister-in-law of my old Swedish boyfriend, Carl Gustav, from early London days. Madeleine suffered back trouble and swore by her Swedish doctor, Professor Birger Enocksson in Stockholm. She invited me to come to Sweden and stay at their castle, *Sturefors Slot*. I was encouraged by her recommendation of a good doctor. After the rail trip across Sweden, I spent a day in Stockholm and then sat shivering on the local train to Katrineholm where at 4:19 p.m. we arrived. It had been raining cats and dogs and storming violently. I was not looking forward to a 70-minute wait for another local train to Norrkoping. I changed trains again before finally arriving at 7 p.m. in Linkoping. I had had lots of time to think about both the past and my future. I happily anticipated the help of a doctor, but was a bit anxious to meet my ex- boyfriend's mother.

When Madeleine met me at the station in Sweden, everything brightened. As I mentioned, she was the sister-in-law to Carl-Gustav, my old boy friend. Unfortunately, I would miss Carl-Gustav, because he had just left for the USA on the Swedish-America line from Gothenburg. Had I arrived just two days earlier, our paths would have crossed again. According to Madeleine, he had been very disappointed and sent his love. Five years had passed, after all, since he left London. Catharina and Marianne, two of his sisters, were both charming and bore a distinct family resemblance. I had, I understood, been an item of conversation since I met Madeleine in Sicily. Carl-Gustav's mother, Countess Bielke, had accompanied him to Gothenburg. Consequently, she would only return the following evening. I was curious to meet her. She lived in the widow's villa next door to *Sturefors Slot*. The following morning broke with a real storm, but the place still looked magnificent. A large lake framed the stately 1660 castle, classical in its beauty including two wings. Surrounding it were formal gardens and a park, and a castle bell chimed every half-hour. The wooden stairs and corridor floors creaked. My room, with its pale gray-flowered wallpaper and airy white curtains was located one of the wings, and had been tastefully restored in the 1930s by Carl-Gustav's parents. The bathroom, belying its 17th-century beginnings, was entirely modern.

Breakfast of hot coffee, toast and pepparkakor (Swedish ginger snaps) was served in a gracious room overlooking the lake. After the morning meal, we took a walk in the park, and admired the regal trees and bright flowers. On the garden side of the house, pools of water and flowers led down from a gracious temple-shaped white gazebo. The views in every direction were breathtaking. The *Fide comis* or most formal part of the castle contained priceless pieces of furniture, as well as a library of 17th and 18th-century books. Family portraits looked down from the walls. The rooms breathed tradition and history.

STUREFORS SLOTT

Madeleine and I played tennis while the others went to Stockholm. The very talented Marianne studied painting at the Arts Academy in Stockholm. When the girls returned with the countess that evening, they brought a handsome young Austrian for the weekend. His name was Hansi Rosenberg. He was very charming and had a sparkling sense of humor. I could see him looming up in Catharina's future. In fact, they eventually married and moved to Karnten in Austria.

Every morning I walked to enchanting corners of the garden. Days were passed playing on the tennis court, relaxing at the bath house, or roaming through the countryside. We all met for lunch, but then we were off again. A little cool juice in the afternoon, and always tennis before dinner. Eric, the marvelous old butler, served the evening meal at 6 p.m., after which we chatted and played canasta until bedtime.

Through the years, Carl-Gustav had always portrayed the countess as rather formidable, so I had been nervous to meet her. Our meeting, however, went off splendidly as she quickly asked me to just call her Tante Brita, which is Swedish for Aunt Brita. I loved her on sight, and admired her so for her many accomplishments, especially her work on Sturefors Slot.

She had been widowed as early as 1940, I believe. Easy she was not, but I decided that God must have a big sense of humor to have put me in that unusual situation. Carl-Gustav had said she would never accept a Norwegian daughter-in-law! Instead, she ended up with a Norwegian son-in-law! I felt wholly accepted into their family life. As my command of the Swedish language grew, they kidded me about my Norwegian accent, and I teased them back about their Swedish one.

The trips through the woods on the property were indescribably captivating. Nobody would hear about my leaving, so I delayed my return to Stockholm a few days, which provided me with another amusing weekend.

This visit was the first in a three-year period of care under Professor Emocksson. Every year when I went for treatments in Stockholm, I was invited to spend my weekends at *Sturefors Slot*. Since most of them had been the professor's patients too, they were extremely supportive. The professor was experimenting with a new sort of treatment involving intravenous injections to dilate the veins. He was over-worked and over-booked. But, with an introduction from Tante Brita, he did see me and found me a very interesting patient! Over the next three years, he worked on me a month at a time, daily, three times a year. The painful treatments were performed at night, because he had no other time. Even so, I sometimes waited up to six hours in the reception room for my appointment. I shall never forget that dismal room.

The first year, to please my father, I stayed at the Norwegian Embassy. But because of my late-night returns from the doctor, this arrangement grew inconvenient. So, I moved into the Hotel Stockholm, a small hotel closer to the doctor. In Stockholm, it was cold enough to keep roasted chicken, Wasa bread and Ramlosa mineral water on my window sill.

Fortunately, my friends at *Sturefors* had themselves gone through the treatments and therefore understood the utter exhaustion. The weekends with breakfast in bed, the lovely walks in the park and the warmth of their wonderful friendships were a huge help.

The second year I returned to Stockholm, I had the good fortune of being invited to stay with my marvelous friend, Gunvor Hagglof. She was not only one of the nicest human beings I have ever met, but she was also beautiful. She taught me so much. Gunvor had been in a wheelchair since she was a newlywed at age 19. She had spent a weekend in the country and was walking along a road with friends, when the son of the house accidentally ran her down with his car. One of her ribs went through her spinal cord. She became paralyzed from the waist down, and was relegated to a wheelchair for life. Always home when I returned from my visits to the professor, Gunvor made me feel grateful I still had my two legs, even if they were problematic and painful.

Years later, Gunvor came to visit Rome with her husband. We stowed her wheelchair in the trunk of the car, and spent a day sightseeing together. At the Coliseum, I found a spot where I could drive the car in through an arch so that Gunvor could see the arena and the Christian cross where the martyrs had fallen. She was so impressed she asked me to go home, paint the cross and give her a print of it. I did paint the cross for her, and it became one of my best-known pictures. In fact, when Father went to the hospital for the last time, he secretly brought that painting with him for comfort. That made me very happy, even if it meant the picture was absent from my scheduled 1961 New York exhibit. I treasure the painting to this day.

The third year I went to see Dr. Enocksson, I stayed with the Thiels. I had met Ingeborg Thiel at Peter and Bibi Johnsen's wedding in Denmark. The bride and groom were both good friends of mine. They had met when Bibi was staying with me, and I gave a party for her in London. Ingeborg Thiel, also a good friend of Peter's, instantly became my best friend. From that day, I always had somewhere to stay in Stockholm. Her husband, Sten Thiel was a wonderful person. He headed up the Swedish Boy Scouts. Once, when my leg pains were especially bad, my brother Chris came to stay with the Thiels, too. I shall never forget how family and friends made it possible for me to get through those years.

Recently, I found a note that I had written to a dear friend while I stayed in Stockholm with the Thiels:

It is a gray and cold winter day. The clock ticks away the minutes. Cars and buses rush past as if they were racing against time. The thoughts do the same, even if deep down they only seek one important thing—Harmony. Pain seems like a physical lack of harmony. The search continues, to try and understand life and the problems that every day brings. The trees reach their bare, black branches up towards the icy blue sky. Darkness has already started to cover the city. Days are very short at this time of the year in the north. Inside my room it is quiet and peaceful. From outside comes the noise of the metropolis. An airplane flies low over the rooftops. The trams whine. Motorcycles race by. Car engines rev. People run to the bus stops. The telephone at the taxi-stop across the road keeps ringing. Soon I have to join the chaos out there.

Henrik Ibsen wrote:

Det er viljen som det gjelder, viljen frigjoer eller feller, viljen hel I alt det spredte, I det tunge som det lette." Translated, this means: "I learned that one can overcome anything if you believe in the motto: "'Never take no for an answer.'"

France – Beauty, Culture and Love

GOLD RABBIT

Someone once told me, "The French guard their culture as Americans guard Fort Knox, and their citadel is the Institut de France." Therefore, I made it a practice to read as much French literature as I could and admire as much French art as possible. I have loved and been loved in return by unforgettable French friends. Ever since the very first summer that mother and I passed through the south of Europe, France and the Fraissinet family have played a large role in our lives. My mother first met Edith Fraissinet in 1922 during Oxford's commencement week. They became fast friends for life. The following summer my mother went to stay at *Bellavista*, the villa of Edith's grandmother (Mrs. Colgate) in Geneva, Switzerland. They spent a wonderful summer together and kept in contact throughout the following years. Both my mother and Edith married, and respectively had three children—one girl and two boys. During WWII, my mother heard that Marc Fraissinet, Edith's French husband, was a prisoner of war in Germany until the war ended. Edith and her children survived in the southern part of France. After the war, they all lived in Marseilles.

In 1947, after mother and I spent the summer in Italy, we decided to visit the Fraissinets in France on our way home. We had a narrow escape with the trains. Our train from Genoa took us to Ventimiglia on the French-Italian border. With an hour layover, my mother stepped down on the platform to buy something. Suddenly, the train started to move, and I shouted, "I am not leaving our luggage!"

"Oh, I am sure they are only changing tracks," Mother said. "Well, I am not going to take any chances," I repeated. At the very last minute mother jumped onto the caboose. Thank goodness, she made it because the train never stopped until well past the French border. Even though we arrived in Marseilles two hours earlier than expected, we were no less warmly welcomed. The apartment on Rue Sylvabelle was decidedly chic. Edith's husband, Marc was very charming. His mother was Italian—a great combination. Gerard, Nicole and Jacques-Marie, their three children also became my lifelong friends. We spent a heavenly week from moonlight dinners at the Cassis Port (when it was still a small fishing village), to wonderful mountaintop drives where the Cecily family entertained us royally. We tasted bouillabaisse and Pernod in the Vieux Port, and we took a boat out to *Chateau d'If,* the infamous prison. We visited *Mazargues,* Edith's other grandmother's lovely property, which had been used to harbor Vietnamese refugees. Unfortunately, very little was left of the property's former beauty.

Before we left for London, it was determined that I would return to Marseilles the following year to learn French. We left the sunny south with heavy hearts and flew home to London from Marignane Airport. Our southern European summer had been thoroughly delightful. The flight was uneventful, which could not be said for my return trip home the following year. I had my ticket for Marseilles to Paris and then to London. One paid a hefty price for overweight luggage in those days, so Marc was offering to bring my extra suitcases north by train, and I was to pick up the luggage when I changed planes in Paris.

It sounded perfect, but once in Paris the airline could not find my suitcases. They then forgot to warn me the flight was taking off without me. My luggage was recovered, but consequently I was late for my flight. Since it was the airline's fault, they put me on a jeep and raced out to the moving aircraft. The crew opened the door just long enough for me to be heaved on board along with my suitcases. I landed on all fours, which the Air France stewards found frightfully amusing. They quickly strapped me into a seat. Once in the air, I was offered champagne and peaches, and a seat in the cockpit to view the crossing of the channel! The visibility was perfect and I had a wonderful flight. Times certainly have changed; it would never happen today! Can you imagine someone driving out on the tarmac today to board a late passenger?

Occasionally I took my French lessons on horseback through Cezanne's beautiful rolling landscape outside Aix-en-Provence. It was inspiring, but sometimes hazardous. Once I badly scratched my leg and Francois, Cecily's father—a doctor—produced a horse-sized hypodermic needle. Gerard kindly nursed me through the ordeal.

Apart from taking a couple of flying lessons—which abruptly ended once my father found out—I had all the time in the world to sketch while learning French. That spring of 1948 in Marseilles, General de Gaulle visited neighbors of ours on Rue Sylvabelle. We heard him make his famous speech, the one that kept him home under the shadow of the Croix de Lorraine in Champagne for the next fourteen years! I remembered de Gaulle's speech later that year in London, when Churchill made disparaging remarks about the French general in our embassy dining room.

After Monique Bohn's fabulous 21st birthday party at Cadogan Square in London, her father, Notti, invited me to go skiing at Val d'Isere. The group included Monique, Jean de Rochetailler and Florian de Kergolay, my friend, Anne's brother. Stas, a Polish friend, saw us off at Victoria Station with two large bouquets of tulips. The flowers survived the long train journey and revived their beauty with the aid of an English copper penny once we arrived in Val d'Isere. We changed trains in Paris and were greeted by the Norwegian ambassadorial Rolls Royce. Ambassador Rolf Andvord, his chauffeur and a footman on the box, brought us in the grandest luxury across Paris, from Gare du Nord to Gare de Lyon. Rolf Andvord, Notti Bohn and my father were long-time friends. From Paris, however, we traveled by ordinary couchette with all the other skiers.

Val d'Isere was high and beautiful, but there was hardly any snow at the higher altitudes. I had not skied for a while, but kept up well with the other three. Then disaster struck because a root caught my ski and I had a bad fall. Of course, it happened on top of the mountain during lunch hour when ski lifts were not running. The ambulance couldn't scale the mountain either, so we sat there freezing in a sharp wind for two hours. A kind Frenchman stopped and offered me a sip of cognac from his flask. Finally, help came and they took me away on a stretcher. On arrival at the hotel, I was revived with a hot red wine toddy. The following few days when the others went skiing, I was carried over to Bar du Soleil and heaved up onto the piano, where I remained as a mascot late into the evenings. That week I learned a lot more French and several new French songs!

Two years later, I went back to Paris to continue my French lessons. I stayed with a Vicomte Lyonnais on Avenue Victor Hugo as an exchange student, and their son came to stay with us at our London Embassy. Since my Oslo doctors had prescribed a vegetarian diet, all the Vicomtesse served me for lunch was one huge artichoke. It took years before I could look at an artichoke again! My cousin Nick joked that he would give me a silver artichoke so I would never forget. The dining room and elegant salons in the Avenue Victor Hugo apartment faced the street. There was only one bathroom and one washroom that didn't have hot water. My nicely furnished room was small, but pleasant. Fortunately, for me, my cousin Nick was in town and the Vicomtesse did allow me to go out with him. He was very good looking, and together we explored the "Culture, Beauty and Love" that Paris offered.

My American friend, Elizabeth Miller invited me to a party on le 14 Juillet, Bastille Day. She had a delightful penthouse and rooftop terrace at Quay d'Orleans on Ile Saint-Louis. She lived there with her Indo-Chinese cook and a large black poodle. One living room window faced the left bank and viewed the Pantheon. Another window framed the Notre Dame and Ile de la Cite. That night the floodlit monuments glowed all over Paris. Sacre Coeur looked down over the city. The Eiffel Tower stretched skyward like a giant candlestick. A happy international group crowded the balcony. After the late-night fireworks when the guests had all left, Elizabeth, her boyfriend

Mike and I took a walk through Paris and picked up breakfast at Les Halles. It was the thing to do when the farmers brought their goods to market.

When Marc Fraissinet came on business from Marseilles, he took me to see Galerie Charpentier. An hour later, we went down to the left bank, met my cousin Nick at Café Flore, had a drink and watched the crowds ambling up and down the boulevard. Up on Montmartre, we had another drink at Place des Tertres and ended up dining at Lady Patachou. After dinner, the men were made to entertain us Mardi Gras style. Some had their ties cut off and others danced the can-can. Marc shot a wig off the head of a guest with a party gun. Nick had to ballet dance with his jacket turned inside out, and pants turned up and a flower crown. The hilarious antics of these otherwise stoic men set us laughing so hard we could hardly stand it!

Later that summer, Nick and I went to the south of France and camped with the whole Fraissinet family. As we drove Edith sang, "Les belles routes de France" while accompanying herself on ukulele. The campsites overlooked my favorite Mediterranean. We swam for hours, played tennis and ate at wonderful bistros. A great deal has changed on the Riviera over the past 50 years. However, I had a successful French summer. My cousin was totally charmed by the French Fraissinet daughter and a certain French gentleman was quite charmed by me!

Once again, my annoying health issues began to flare up again. I was getting tired of the doctors' treatments. Someone suggested a visit to Lourdes for healing. Several of my friends had made yearly trips bringing the sick— even on stretchers. Willing to try anything, my parents and my brother, Chris came with me. Arriving at Lourdes, I ignored the typical tourist spots, and at six in the morning went straight to early mass with Chris. To my amazement, unwell people filled both the church and the courtyard. The atmosphere was charged with hope. As a result, I too, left hopeful and encouraged. Even though pain continued to be my steady companion, after a few years I began to see improvement. As the Arabic saying goes, "Your pain is the breaking of the shell that encloses your understanding. Even as the stone of the fruit must break that its heart may stand in the sun, so must you know pain."

During our years in London, my parents and I visited Paris often. Crossing the Channel from Dover to Calais could be quite rough, so I was happy when my mother requested a cabin. From Calais to Paris, we boarded the luxury boat train, the *Golden Arrow*. It was quite a trip and the dream of taking only two hours these days seemed unimaginable. My mother visited her designers Dior and Jacques Fath and her milliner, Paulette. My father loved the Parisian restaurants, as did my future American husband, Billy. In fact, Billy told me two amusing stories.

One day at Taillevent, the sommelier asked Billy to try a wine. If he guessed correctly, he could have it at cost. The bottle was brought in. The first part was easy. It was a Bordeaux. Then Billy said, "It is either a great wine of a poor year or a lesser wine of a great year!" He got the bottle of wine at cost. The wine was a Chateau Ausone—the same wine we had served at our London wedding lunch.

Another time, Billy was in Beaune to buy some cases of wine at the famous winery of Louis Latour. Monsieur Latour wore a formal suit and an old-fashioned stiff-collared shirt. When he heard Billy was living in Italy where—according to him they only ate pasta—Monsieur hesitated selling his precious wines, but relented when Billy piped up, "We do have chicken on Sundays!"

The Fraissinets were always there when I needed them. I'll never forget the day when Billy and I returned from our USA honeymoon in 1964. We docked in Cherbourg after another wonderful Atlantic crossing on the *United States*—a fabulous ship. As a Norwegian, I shall never understand how she was put it in mothballs only a few years later. After all, the ship had won a blue ribbon for the quickest crossing of the Atlantic by an ocean liner.

We arrived in Paris without any trouble, but at the Hotel Vendome, the manager insisted he had no room for us because of the Auto Salon (car show). For once in my life, I had a written confirmation from the hotel. This time I actually agreed with Billy when he called the manager a frog as we stood in the lobby with 21 pieces of luggage. Nothing helped. It was obvious that this unknown mid-western couple was not important enough to concern the hotel. It was a new experience for me, so what did I do? I called my good friends, the Fraissinets. In no time, they came to our rescue. Marc's language to the hotel manager was very different from Billy's, but most effective. The hotel even agreed to store our luggage for a few days until we continued on the night train to Rome. Of course, we never returned to the Hotel Vendome again. Imagine if we had not had good friends in Paris!

The French spoken by a Fraissinet always seemed to improve my own French a degree or two. They infused beauty, a sense of humor and chic into their elegant speech. Every time I read these pages through, I am saddened that so many of my beloved Fraissinets have died. How lucky I was to have known them!

When I came on business from Rome years later, I again stayed with Marc and Edith. They had moved from Marseilles to Avenue d'Eylau in Paris. They also had a lovely country place east of Paris, near Colombe des deux Eglises. We went out there for the weekends. The charm of *Vauchon Villiers* was too much to miss. In my inner eye, I still see the black poodles playing with Marc on the lawn. After I married Billy, and we lived in Tuscany with our two daughters, Edith and Marc Fraissinet invited us for Christmas one year at *Vauchon Villiers,* their place in Champagne. Tickets had been booked on the Wagon-lits to Paris in good time before the holidays, but Alexandra fell ill. Having to reschedule, the only reservations available were for Christmas Eve. So we started off from Florence in an empty train. The galley gave us a very special Christmas dinner, even with a "Buche de Noel." After dinner, we offered the crew cognac, and they gave the children pannetone. To this day, I remember it as the most incredible Christmas Eve we have ever experienced.

Between Paris and the train for Troyes in Champagne, we had a couple of hours to kill. We went to Christmas morning mass at Saint-Nicholas-de-Champs, an ancient church near the train station. It was one of the most meaningful Christmas masses attended as a family. Although delayed, we arrived at the Fraissinets in time for Christmas Day lunch. Two silver Christmas trees flanked the stone fireplace in the dining room. The rest of the rooms were decorated in equally good taste. Billy and the children felt the same warmth from the Fraissinet family that I had felt—a feeling that remained all our lives. Those happy days spent together in the French countryside were unforgettable.

When we returned through Paris having spent a Happy New Year with all my family in London, we again boarded the wagon-lits. By chance, we caught the same crew as we had been with on Christmas Eve. They treated us like royalty and other riders on the train were asking, "Who are they?"

I visited the south of France often in my earlier days in London. At the time, travel in and out of St. Tropez—the town that ousted Spanish invaders in 1637—was smooth. Notti had a place on the coast in Var, which gave me wonderful opportunities to sketch in Ramatuelle, Cogolin or simply in St. Tropez itself.

Years later when I stayed with Nicken and Else in Chateauneuf de Grasse, I had a car and visited Nicole Fraissinet Rufenacht at her delightful summerhouse in Beauvallon. There she surrounded herself with grandchildren and children. From the main house, a long flight of wide stairs led to a wonderful in-door/out-door living room. It had a huge fireplace, playroom, and kitchen-dining room, flanked by a swimming pool. It was the most fabulous structure I'd known in my life! Flowers and large trees protected against the elements. From the house, one had a delightful view of the Mediterranean towards St. Tropez. Now—except for very early in the mornings—St. Tropez is accessible only by boat!

Nicken and Else had recently moved from London to Chateaneuf de Grasse in the south of France. They lived in a village "en pique" with a breath taking 180-degree view of the green landscape, the coast down below and the blue Mediterranean from Nice to Theoule. Chateauneuf is not far from Cannes, but is still off the beaten path. Houses climb up the hill and narrow roads wind their way to the upper village. Colorful flowers and trees complete the picture.

Alexandra and I went to stay in Chateuneuf in September of 1995. Nicken fetched us at the airport in Nice after a particularly hard rain. Under a slight cloud cover, we drove over the mountain through Tourette-sur-Loup and Vence to Saint-Paul-de-Vence for lunch at the Colombe d'Or. Nicken was introduced to Hotel St. Paul's delicious chicken with truffles. After lunch, we continued to Colle-sur-Loup and Else's antique shops before we returned home via fruit and grocery shopping in Valbonne. As always, we took a pre-dinner walk. An altogether pleasant evening was dampened when we got home to the frightening news that brother Chris had collapsed at the hospital in Bruxelles. He ended up with a pacemaker!

Friday brought the same lovely weather, and so we drove to Cannes to pick up some pants for Nicken and lunch at Ondine by the water's edge. As usual, they served fresh salads and moules. Then—surprise, surprise—it was shopping before drinks with Per Bjorn-Hansen at his amazing house. Saturday, the host went to the bakery, but the hostess did not want to be tempted by the fresh baguette and so Nicken and I had breakfast alone. The temperature was still super. Nicken had a control telephone call with Anne and checked in on Preben's rowing Oxford—direction Putney yesterday, about 20 miles.

In the late 90s, I flew to France from Palm Beach after undergoing a broken shoulder and poor medical care from the local sports medicine doctors. Nicken picked me up at Nice Airport and we took off for the "Arriere-Pays" (back-country), the area between the Mediterranean and the Alps Maritime. We passed through Villeneuve-Loubet where old friends, the Panisse Passis have a chateau on the Loup River. King Francois I stayed there during his negotiations with King Charles V, which led to the 1538 Treaty of Nice.

We then headed straight for Chateauneuf, one of the medieval towns surrounded by olive groves, vineyards and flowers. The village perches on a promontory and exudes an atmosphere of charm and solitude. Both the King and Queen of Belgium and the Grand Dukes of Luxemburg had hidden vacation paradises on the nearby hillsides. I had not seen these old friends for many years and it was such a joy to meet again at my brother's neighbor's house. Grand Duke Jean attended my coming-out party in London during the 1948 Olympic Games.

Besides the company of friends, Chateauneuf provided me with lots of artistic inspiration. A tall palm stood as a loyal guard on a terrace below my window. I called him "the Lone Sergeant" as he guarded my fabulous view. When Nicken and Else went off to Norway I took care of the house and the proud cat, Monsieur Grey. Their two town houses (which had been combined), sat on the old ramparts off a small square halfway up the village hill. I could not get over how spectacular a view they had of the valley and the Mediterranean coast. Their terraced garden was a pleasure to work in under the lovely southern sun.

In the village of Chateauneuf, I found wonderful help for my ailing shoulder from the local doctor Bodran and his rehab therapist, Eric. Each day to and from their offices, I would buy the morning's fresh bread and newspapers. Yves and Reine du Monceau de Bergendal, old friends of 50 years ago, lived next door, and families in the village extended warm hospitality in the absence of my brother and sister-in-law.

On the way home in September, I saw the Fraissinets and the Bourbon-Parmes in Paris. Pia and Michel still lived in Versailles and nothing was more divine than one of Michel's barbecues. We wandered up the Victor Hugo, crossed to the left bank of the Seine, paid a visit to the Ile Saint-Louis and lunched again on Place des Vosges with Jacques-Marie Fraissinet. All these excursions including dinner at a petit bistro and, for a splurge at Taillevent, made Paris amazing. France is a corner of the world that truly combines, as I have said before, love, culture and beauty.

Another year I arrived in Nice on a Saturday morning between rain showers. The following days continued rainy and quite cool. When the famous Provencal blue sky did arrive, the birds sang and the luscious green landscape continued all the way down to the Mediterranean. The Bay of Napoule and Theoule was clearly visible. My trip had started from West Palm Beach with a layover at J.F.K. and a plane full of lively passengers headed for the Cannes Film Festival. Again, I had come to spend some time with Nicken who was suffering from a recurrence of his lung cancer. Intense chemo treatments had taken their toll. I busied myself cooking and gardening and tried to keep smiling for the next six months.

While the rain pelted over the next few days, Else and I planned their move to England and decided what was going and what was to remain in France. We asked everybody to pray for good weather for the moving days, the house being in such an awkward position at the end of a very narrow street!

After a week of moving, I sat in the square of Opio one day drinking coffee on my way to the hairdresser. I was looking up at the old village where it sat like a crown overlooking the commercial center. The fog had just lifted. I was still in awe at how fabulous the French movers had been and I wished we could have the same help everywhere—outstandingly nice, polite and efficient workers. The sun was warm again and the profusion of roses only slightly damaged by the rain. We picked two gorgeous lemons off the fruit-laden tree in the corner, which was in competition with the pear tree on the lower terrace. The jasmine also was in bloom, soon to be accompanied by the confederate jasmine. There was a wide view of the Mediterranean from Antibes to Theoule.

When that lovely house sold, another chapter of my life closed. I have seen far too many chapters close in my life!

The Far East – The Dawn of Understanding
CHINESE GOOD LUCK CHARM

While still in Stockholm, Mother, Aunt Else and I were discussing my latest health episode over lunch. Due to my ghastly appearance, Aunt Else suggested I take a trip south and offered me the owner's cabin of her family's cargo ship. The line plowed the oceans of the world, so I was given a choice between South Africa, Australia or the Far East. I chose the latter without hesitation. Our ship, the *Tournai* was leaving Europe between Christmas 1953 and the New Year. We joined it in Marseilles. Baron d'Outhorne, our dear family friend, drove us to the port. Someone asked the baron, who was 92, what he would do if his driver's license was taken away. He answered, "Je prend un motocyclette!" or "I'll use a motorcycle!"

It was a dark, cold day in 1954 when mother and I boarded the 10,000-ton cargo ship of the Wilhelmsen Line. Our sitting room, next to the cabin and bathroom, featured pale blue curtains and paneled walls. Flowered cretonne covered the sofa and easy chairs. A large bouquet of red carnations and white lilacs from Uncle Niels served as his bon voyage wish. Three books rested on the table: *Prison and Chocolate Cake* by Madame Pandit's daughter, the sister of Nehru who was High Commissioner to London, *Old Men Forget* by Duff Cooper, and *East of Home* by Santa Rama Rau. These were gifts from my dear friend Patrick Forbes. In the last book, Patrick had inscribed: "To dearest Evie, in the fond hope that east of home she will find health, happiness and food for the spirit." Food for my soul I found, indeed, as well as artistic inspiration.

The noise of engines and crashing waves signaled that we were on our way to a place full of golden promises. Icy winds persisted as we steamed into the Genoa harbor. On land, we roamed Genoa's streets for hours and revisited piazzas and old, quaint corners. Like cats in a church cloister, we purred as the midday sun warmed us. The following day was New Year's Eve and we watched the famous Italian fireworks light up the sky. Then the ship's sirens and whistles summoned us back to the harbor.

The next morning we left Europe, with Corsica, Elba and Monte Cristo fading in the distance. We passed by my beloved Lipari Islands with Stromboli's smoke trailing from its craters. Of all the Aeolian Islands, Stromboli is one of the grandest and tragically beautiful. The rich color of its steep slopes varies from copper and burnt sienna to olive, moss green and pitch black. Small white houses in a distant tiny village stand out against the dark background. I understand why the Strombolesi felt a deep kinship with their cruel volcano. They consider him a sort of deity, and would say, "Today he is angry," or "Today he is peaceful." Devout fishermen would cross themselves before they embarked on their colorful boats. Another favorite Aolian island was Vulcano. One year, I went snorkeling there with Sam, a friend and fellow diplomat. The translucent water was perfect for watching underwater sea life. I created a whole series of paintings inspired by those dives. Several playful dolphins jumped high over the waves as we glided through the Strait of Messina.

I gave a longing gaze at the rugged coastline of my dear Sicily as we passed the lighthouse, Faro del Torre. We swerved slightly to avoid the ferry, *Scilla*, which was en route from Messina to Villa San Giovanni on the Italian coast. The Sicilians call the mainland, "Il Continente" (the continent). Greek mythology attributes the foundation of Messina to Orion, the great hunter, and Messina's curved harbor to Saturnus who dropped his scythe there. Poseidon, the lord of the ocean and friend of seamen, became its deity. But he and the other trusted gods proved faithless. After centuries of wars, plagues, tidal waves, earthquakes and fires, the earthquake of 1908 became the greatest disaster of them all. Eighty-thousand people perished. Mist enveloped my dearly loved island for a while until I caught sight of the well known white cone of Etna, the Sicilian volcano. Smoke towered from the crater and floated out towards the sea. As the Italian saying goes, "Con vento al mare, si po lavare," (You can wash clothes when the wind blows out to sea). The Greeks called Etna the "The Pedestal of Heaven."

Only twenty miles out, our ship passed Crete off the southeastern coast of Greece. As I met the captain with his arms full of envelopes and other important looking documents, he said, "The officials want all particulars about our cargo going through the Suez Canal to be sure we aren't carrying any explosives." "It is a good thing we don't have any then," I quipped. "Just three grenades—which are rather difficult to ignite." The captain gave a wry smile.

Our only stop in Africa was Port Said with its 174-foot high lighthouse. The colossal statue of Ferdinand de Lesseps stood proudly on the western breakwater at the north end of the Suez Canal. The Egyptians, however, knocked down the statue of de Lesseps when they took control of the canal a few years later.

As the *Tournai* slowly sailed southward, we viewed the interesting desert landscape. Both sides of the canal had small stations. We steamed in convoy down the Red Sea and reached Aden one o'clock in the morning. With all the work and bustle onboard, sleep was impossible. So we went up to watch life on deck. Aden's seaport was situated on the Saudi Arabian peninsula. Not far from the entrance to the Red Sea—about a one hundred miles east of the Strait of Bab-El Mandeb—our ship bunkered oil and water, and two massive black iron barges came alongside. The dock workers wore red headdresses with checkered and solid-colored kilts. In the morning, the deck astern had been turned into an oriental market. More small boats arrived to sell all kinds of sub-quality goods—most of it made in Japan.

In contrast to the grumbling bunch in Port Said, the Arabs in Aden were smiling cheerfully. My camera was useful for many amusing incidents.

An Oriental house on the way to Cape Aden fascinated me. Its white round frontage faced the sea and contrasted dramatically against the volcanic rock. A black clock tower rose in the pale blue sky next to it. As we continued our voyage eastward, the topography appeared parched. Just a few months later— after a nine-day crossing of the Indian Ocean—we would return to Aden to see the color of the area had changed to moss green. For the first time in seven years, Aden had received a day of torrential rainstorms.

Ships of every nation waited outside Aden for their harbor pilots. By this time, our fellow passengers consisted of two female missionaries and a British couple from Singapore. The husband had retired from the police in Johore at the age of 40, and started raising racehorses in Singapore! Dressed in baggy shorts and a short-sleeved open shirt, he shuffled along in worn-out slippers. His big belly was bloated from drinking, his face, pallid, save a monocle on a black velvet ribbon. He thought he was the cat's whiskers, and behaved accordingly. He was a man definitely to be avoided. Seagulls battled ruthlessly over food scraps we tossed. I wanted to make friends with these strong, screeching birds because of how gracefully they glided through the air.

At noon a launch appeared. "How are you, pilot?" Our captain said rather arrogantly as he shook hands with the Englishman coming onboard. "Very well, thank you. Though I must confess I would be no good as a pilot. I am the Norwegian Consul," the Englishman smiled. The consul had come to fetch mother and me for a luncheon with Governor Higginbottom. We were more than happy to leave for shore.

The governor's residence was out at Cape Aden. It faced the sea, just above the yacht club, where gaily-painted dinghies waited for the coming regatta on Sunday morning. Because of its favorable position, Aden became an important port on the way to Asia. The Romans had captured it in the year 24 B.C., the Portuguese attacked it in 1513, and the Turks seized it 15 years later. It was only in 1839 that it was captured by the British, made a free port and chosen as a main fueling station en route to the Far East. The old part of town was built in the crater of an extinct volcano, accessed by a narrow mountain pass. Goats roamed freely through the streets where Hindu

cows would suddenly block the passage. Because of a recent heavy rainfall—
the first the area had had in seven years—part of the bank had collapsed and
safes were clearly visible. Only a deep hole in the road and a heap of rubble
remained. Another curious fact was that the watercourses had not only been
filled, but were overflowing. This was unheard of in the history of Aden. The
Jewish houses were in ruins due to recent riots. But no amount of persua-
sion had succeeded in getting the rubble cleared away. Large groups of Arabs
lounged outside the shops. The women in Aden's streets were dressed in black
with red and green veils. Judging by the good looks of their children and hus-
bands, the women must have been very beautiful. The rain and the floods had
done great harm to the Italian salt pyramids on the beach. They had simply
vanished. The governor drove us out to the village of Sheik-ut-Mahn, where
streets and houses were still flooded from the rain. The market square, where
the camel caravans came in from the protectorate, was one big lake. The poor
camels looked unhappy as they rested at the water's edge.

Our drive back from Sheik-ut-Mahn to the government barracks was
delayed due to a funeral procession. All of the people in the procession were
men. A small boy of seven or eight with large black eyes, a mass of black
curls and an engaging smile, was scurrying after the procession in bare feet.
I couldn't help but smile at him. He caught up to the car and smiled back,
whispering, "Ma-as-Salama" (Go in Peace). We stopped the car and I thanked
him. His name was Ali-Zhalib, and I was enchanted by how he kept up the
conversation, until he ran off to join the funeral procession. We approached
the barracks amidst more flooding. The head of the governor's special Arab
guard was named Sadik, meaning friend. He was tall, extremely handsome,
and looked quite striking in his Arab kilt and headgear. At teatime we were
served some delicious honey, brought from the protectorate in a hard, round
yellow gourd. "By the way, I asked. "Who lives in the fascinating white house
next to the black tower?" I suddenly had remembered how interested I had
been by it. "Well, I once lived there myself," the governor grinned and continued to tell the history of the house. Intrigued by its secrets, I again sur-
veyed its wide entrance facing the sea and the lower level porch that was

once a harem. We had one more view of Somalia's shores on our way east. It took ten days to cross the Indian Ocean. As a child in Norway, the thought of going to America seemed as far away as the ends of the earth. At the time, it took ten days to cross by ship from Oslo to New York! In 1954, we found that those ten days were just a short span compared to our lengthy sea voyage across the Indian Ocean.

As we left the Arabian coast, we could feel the northeasterly monsoon. The wind became stronger towards evening. Huge foamy waves crested high. I was allowed on the bridge during the First Mate's watch. He taught me how to navigate by the stars. I often went up on the bridge at four or five in the morning to watch the Southern Cross and other stars. The sea was usually calm and the dark, starry sky was stunning. The whitecaps glowed brightly. During the voyage, the captain progressively grew jealous of Mother and me because of the attention we received from the consuls in each port. When he punished us by withholding fresh food and fruit, the first mate would sneak us some at his own expense!

We followed the coast of Ceylon (now known as Sri Lanka) and were soon south of the Dondra Head Lighthouse. Through binoculars I could see the sailing boats out on their early morning fishing trips. The voyage continued across the Bay of Bengal. Heavy rain showers and cool winds were a daily occurrence. Ten days gave me ample time to draw, paint and write. I was delighted, however, when we finally cruised down the Strait of Malacca between the island of Sumatra and the Malayan mainland. We experienced nearly 100% humidity; water was virtually running down the decks. "We've come such a long way just to find humidity," Mother sighed one morning. The *Tournai* passed the Fathom Lighthouse and then took another twelve hours to reach Singapore waters. Singapore is a microcosm of Asia, located only 85 miles from the Equator. As Noel Coward said, "Only mad dogs and Englishmen go out in the midday sun." That certainly described Singapore.

One morning on deck as I looked toward land, our captain approached and said, "I am afraid rain has held up our stop here for several days. I have just had a message from the agents saying we will have to wait in the outer harbor for at least two or three days." "Can one get a launch into town from here?" I asked. "A message has just come for you. The Norwegian Consul will be on board to fetch you at nine o'clock," the captain assured us. "Wonderful, then we will definitely not return to the ship until after dinner," Mother stated.

It was exciting to set foot on land again. Our ears were met with "Selamat Pagi!" (Good Morning in Malayan). Tanned Malayan boat men, Chinese women dressed in wide black trousers holding parasols, and trishaws made up my first impressions. Trishaws were bicycles with sidecars that had replaced the antiquated rickshaws. Only 40 percent of the people were actually Malayan. The Chinese made up another 40 percent and Indians the other 20 percent—each dressed in their native costume. The most colorful outfits were the Indian saris. The street scene resounding with trishaw bells, honking horns and the crunching of bullock carts. We walked up and down Change Alley. When we stopped so I could sketch the crowd, we quickly created an embarrassing traffic jam. All the market pedestrians gathered to watch. When they saw they were the subject of my sketch, they giggled with delight.

The next morning the sun shone again. Singapore—which was the crossroads of all the important shipping lines in the East—became a British Crown Colony in 1867. The Chinese, who made up four-fifths of the population, controlled a large percentage of the trade and commerce, and had amassed great fortunes. One of the rich, Chinese inhabitants had made an enormous fortune from a medicine called Tiger Balm. It was used by millions all over the East. He built two huge, grotesque gardens; one in Singapore and the other in Hong Kong. I threw one glance inside the gate and turned away. I did admire his world-renown jade collection, though, which consisted of magnificent pieces from the Han, Tsui, Tang, Song, Yuen Ming and Ching dynasties. Two large rooms were lined with jade objects ranging from the classic pale green, to amethyst, crystal, ruby, emerald, pink and lapis lazuli.

The celebrated Raffle's Hotel was the most popular gateway to the East, dating back to 1886. They used to call it, "The Grand Old Lady of the East." It was here that Somerset Maugham sat in a corner of the palm court among the palms and frangipanis, and wrote many of his tales about the colonials. Outside the hotel's entrance were wonderful traveling palms. Anthony Burgess, Joseph Conrad and Han Suyin have all written about their experiences in Malay, but it was Maugham who immortalized The Raffle's with his Malayan short stories.

In 1954, Singapore and Malay proper were under British dominion. From the long bridge which joined the island of Singapore to the mainland, we caught the first glimpse of Johore Bahru—which is now the capital of one of the Federated Malayan States. High on a green hill, with a splendid view of the strait of Johore Bahru, was the great white Mosque. Its soaring, imposing entrance etched a deep memory in our minds. The sun shone through the open windows casting strange, colored mosaics on the white marble floor. The sultan's palaces sat high up in the hills. "It was the Sultan of Johore who, in 1824, sold Singapore to the British East India Company," a friend had told me. Before the sultan reclaimed his palace, the high commissioner of Southeast Asia, Malcolm MacDonald, used to live at *Bukit Serene* near Johore Bahru. He very kindly invited us to a grand luncheon. I shall never forget, however, that I had to wear stockings, hat and gloves for the occasion as if we were back in England. We ate mutton chop with mint sauce and white pudding with red sauce. It was truly British to keep this up in that tropical humidity. The day was sweltering with not a breeze in the air. As soon as we left the formal party, I asked the Chinese driver to look straight ahead so I could relieve myself of stockings and gloves. It was like wearing steel armor.

Before we crossed back to Singapore, we drove slowly along the Johore Bahru waterfront. A black sailboat with large matching sails scarcely moved on the calm, placid waters. People walked leisurely along the promenade. Fishermen with wide shady hats that drooped to their shoulders waded a great distance out with their baskets afloat in front of them. When they filled their baskets with fish from their nets, the weight submerged the baskets, thus keeping the fish alive until the return to shore.

In August, 1957, Malaya gained its independence. The Union Jack was lowered for the last time and the Malayan flag was raised. It flutters atop the highest flagpole in the world at the corner of Padang, so I've been told. The

Federation of Malaya was founded in 1963. Two years later, Singapore left the federation to become an independent and extremely prosperous nation.

Later, we would return to Malaya on our way back to Europe, and visit Field Marshal and Lady Templer. Gerald was the British High Commissioner of Malaya and a great friends of ours. Fortunately, it was decided that the ship would call at Port Swettenham. The Templers sent a car to fetch us. We drove 30 miles through rubber plantations on winding roads that sometimes resembled the roads of Kent. On the way, we drove straight through a group of young Chinese communists. Their faces showed no emotion as they were being deported. Once in Kuala Lumpur, the Malayan capital, the driver took us on a verdant country lane. In gentle curves, it wound its way up the hillside. On top of the hill we passed a Palladian mansion. It was the former official residence of the governor of the strait settlements when he came on tours up-country from Singapore. We then arrived at an even more impressive, large white colonial mansion. *Carcosa* was set in a lush, expansive park. The splendid hall boasted a carved staircase and high-vaulted wooden ceilings. There were large wrap-around verandas and an impressive porte-cochere. It was built in 1897 for Sir Frank Swettenham who once was Britain's resident administrator. He helped rebuild Kuala Lumpur after a great fire destroyed most of the capital in 1881. He once said, "*Carcosa*, looks like a combination of the Italian words *cara* and *cosa*, and would mean "desirable dwelling," as indeed I found it."

The 1904 Palladian mansion, the *Seri Negara,* was the Templers' residence and featured large wrap-around verandas. The visitor's book—kept in a sentry box down the road—was brought each morning by the private secretary to review the entries and list prospective guests for future events. After changing out of our traveling clothes, tea was served on the terrace. To my great delight, Mary, then married to Viscount Montgomery's son, David, who was also on Templer's staff, turned up for tea. Later on, we saw a great deal of each other when she married a cousin of mine and moved to Norway.

Life was never dull, whether one accompanied Peggy Templer to visit the cook's new baby or took a trip with Gerald Templer in his jeep. The

Templers all over the country by jeep. I believe they wanted to thoroughly research the background and stage for their work. "I am so sorry, I cannot take you sightseeing." Peggy Templer said, "For safety's sake I am not allowed out without a police escort, which would draw too much attention to you. I am afraid you are better off without me." So on our own, we visited the tin mines and rubber plantations—Malaya's most important industries. We learned, however, that because America subsidized its own synthetic rubber industry, Malaya's economy suffered. Malaya's rubber commerce could not compete with the American prices.

Field Marshal Sir Gerald Templer succeeded Sir John Harding as Chief of the Imperial Staff. As High Commissioner and director of operations in Malaya, in only two years Gerald transformed a very bleak situation by his sheer competence and force of personality. He coordinated the suppression of a communist insurgence in Malaya. After nearly two years of increasing communist insurrection and guerilla action in the Federation of Malaya, then a British Colony, Sir Gerald Templer was sent there. According to official British story of the campaign, Templer "swept through Malaya like a whirl wind." History added that by the time he left at the end of 1954, "ultimate victory was assured." He pushed the guerrillas into the jungle and, through punitive actions, discouraged villagers from aiding the insurgents. We saw a crowded ship, full of very young Chinese being sent back to their mainland.

Gerald Templer—just two years younger than Father—was a wonderful friend of the family. He began his army career in the Royal Irish Fusiliers and saw active service in WWI. During WWII, he was the youngest lieutenant general—at age 44—in the British Army. He was badly injured in the Italian campaign in 1944. After the war, Sir Gerald was appointed Director of the Military Government in the British sector in Germany. He was knighted in 1949, and then in 1956, promoted to Field Marshal, Britain's highest military rank. He had a brilliant sense of humor, and I relished dining together, whether it was at our embassy or later in their home in Wilton Crescent in London.

Kuala Lampur began as a tin mining outpost a hundred years ago at the confluence of the Kelang and Gombak rivers. Although KL looks like a Muslim city at first with its arabesque arches and minarets, it has both a strong Chinese influence, as well as Hindu. Of course, when we were there, it had an overriding British imprint. The 1911 railway station, however, was a monument of Moorish magnificence with minarets, domes and cupolas. Someone told me that it was originally designed for a Moscow trade fair with snow gutters and a roof to withstand six-and-a-half feet of snow! So much for the English designing for the midday sun!

Sadly, our wonderful visit at the *Seri Negara* came to an end. We had to say goodbye to Peggy and Gerald Templer and rejoin our ship. They sent us down to the coast in his personal car. Heavy rain persisted until long after we were back on board. In the dense forest of rubber trees, the smell of wet leaves and humidity was overpowering. It was interesting, however, to know that the first rubber seedling was sent from Kew Gardens in London, 1870s. A few Malay boys hung around the pier. The raindrops dripped from the white turban of a tall Indian Sikh riding a trishaw. When we exited the launch, we could hardly have been more soaked than if we had swum out to the ship.

Our vessel left Port Swettenham and steamed up the coast. The Island of Penang, our next port of call, was known as the *Pearl of the Orient.* The naval adventurer, Captain Francis Light, took the island for the British East India Company and motivated his men to clear the jungle by loading his cannons with gold and silver coins and blasting the bounty into the island's soil! The city of Georgetown, which Captain Light named after the King, evoked the British colonial past. It was pastel-colored and sleepy the morning we arrived. But as somebody said, the colonial architectural was only part of Penang's fascination. Like all of Malaysia's settlements, it was "part pomp and circumstance and part trishaw-driving, rice-frying, incense-burning Piccadilly Bazaar." The Eastern and Oriental Hotel certainly belonged to the "pomp and circumstance" category and still drew one into the colonial prestige and grandeur era. She was one of Asia's Grand old Ladies, established in 1884, three years before the opening of Raffles. The E&O—as it was known—was advertised as "the premier hotel east of Suez, with the longest seafront in the world" (842 feet). It was a favorite with writers, actors and artists—from Rudyard Kipling to Douglas Fairbanks, and Noel Coward to Somerset Maugham.

On our first morning in Penang, we disembarked and went over to the E&O to eat breakfast and read the morning newspaper. Imagine our horror when we read the first page news. Field Marshal Templer's car had been ambushed five minutes after we left it. They must have thought the Field Marshal himself was in it. He had a great deal of difficulties on his hands, what with sending back thousands of young Chinese communists to China and taking care of local terrorism. I had another cup of coffee as I gratefully acknowledged how lucky we had been to escape the ambush. We sat in silence for a while, letting the whirl of the overhead fans stir our imagination as we looked out over the Indian Ocean through the mist to the Kedah hills on the mainland.

It was St. Patrick's Day, and the E&O was having a gala dance. We sat in the airy hall, supplied with tall cool drinks. We could not help noticing the crowd surging in and out of the dining room. Men were dressed in black dinner jackets and their women in—of all things—velvet evening gowns. It was a scene out of a hunt ball in the English country side, except for the pink coats! The hotel kept the temperature so low that we had to go again outside to defrost.

The next day, we toured the island and learned much about the natural resources and forms of worship. Then returning for another long cold drink, we dined in style at the E&O, before we boarded the ship with its cuisine again, or lack thereof.

Continuing on our way east (at first north), we left Singapore and enjoyed good weather for a while. At one point we passed the Vietnamese coast to the west. The Spratly Islands were somewhere to our east. The China Sea gave us four extremely stormy days. Mountainous waves washed over the ship, even over the bridge. I stepped out for a second to take pictures, and then jumped back inside the wheelhouse. It was terrifying, yet fascinating to watch. Fortunately, we had been cruising long enough to avoid seasickness, proving we'd truly found our sea legs.

On the fourth day, having followed the severe, rocky coast of China, we approached Hong Kong. Wang Lai Lighthouse stood to port. We gave Red China a five mile berth, otherwise the Communists would shoot. The first junks, high astern with colorful sails, met us. "You know pirates still operate on these shores," A.B. said smiling. "Not long ago a Dutch ship was seized, and then robbed of its cargo in a small harbor on the Chinese mainland. Shortly afterwards, the ship was released, and no harm was done to the crew."

We looked around at China's high barren mountains, rocks and islets, and thought of the days when Hong Kong fortunes were founded on the opium trade and smuggling. Names like Jardine and Matheson from Maurice Collis' book *Foreign Mud* came to mind. We had just endured four days of the raging South China Sea. Hong Kong, in Chinese, Hiang-Kiang, the place of sweet lagoons, is an island situated in the estuary of the Canton River. As we came through the strait to enter Hong Kong harbor, a British Man of War sent by the governor came to salute my mother's arrival to the Crown Colony. It was a very proud moment for a Norwegian freighter. The captain's nose, however, was put out of joint even more.

Mother adored Hong Kong. Its name means *fragrant harbor*, which spoke of their history of incense factories and opium ships. Whatever the reason, the city was a product of 3000 years of Chinese culture and 100-plus years of British rule. Today, skyscraper-studded Hong Kong is the world's third largest financial center. The city boasts innumerable hotels, but my favorite—the Queen of Hong Kong hotels—was still The Peninsula. It opened in 1928, and has become the flagship of a chain that stretches all the way to New York City. The lobby will forever be the grand arena for tea-sippers, gawkers, gossips, spies *and* footsore shoppers—like my mother. Hong Kong was and is a shopper's Mecca. I was thankful we had journeyed by ship, when one evening, she impulsively bought a set of china with plates and bowls of all sizes—140 pieces in all!

A good friend of ours in Hong Kong was the seamen's Pastor Nielsen. He was an exceptional human being. He took us on countless sightseeing trips, both to Kowloon and the New Territory. One day, he brought us to a magnificent house high up on the Peak of Victoria Island. It belonged to Sir Robert Ho Tung, a very distinguished and handsome octogenarian with finely chiseled features and a wooly, soft white beard. He was dressed in the same fine silk that made hangings on the black teak chairs in the drawing room. We enjoyed a lovely tea party there. I still have twelve beautifully embroidered handkerchiefs that Sir Robert Ho Tung gave me more than half a century ago. He was a contemporary and good friend of George Bernard Shaw, and was the proud owner of a photograph taken of the two.

Flagstaff House is the oldest Western-style dwelling intact in Hong Kong. This Greek Revival structure was erected in 1846 as the residence of the Commander of British forces in the Crown Colony. It sits at the base of the gentle slopes of Victoria Peak. It was the Governor's Mansion. Governor Grantham gave a festive luncheon for us. When we drove in from the gates, I admired the fabulous dark red poinsettia hedge. We followed it in to the front door of the lovely white house with its deep, columned verandas on two floors. Grateful, we thanked the governor for his courteous welcome to the colony. Well-heeled people lived up on Victoria Peak. You either were a 100, 200 or 300-foot-man, I was told by the man sitting to my left.

To my right sat a very charming American naval officer. Our conversation was quite profound. At a certain moment he mentioned that on one of his troop transports to Korea he had met a young Scandinavian; a son of a Danish Naval Attaché in Washington. I turned pale as a cold shiver crept up my spine. What a small world it was! This man next to me had brought Niels, my own fiancé, to his last destination. The man turned to me with a preoccupied expression as he noticed my reaction. With a very soft voice, hardly audible, he said to me, "Could you be the Evelyn he talked about?" I nodded. Very kindly, like an old friend, he told me about his conversations with Niels. It was a strange sensation to feel as if I had been met by Niels's spirit on arrival in one of the ports he had touched on his way out.

The poinsettias saluted us after lunch. Down narrow streets to the harbor, the busy life of Chinese commerce changed the former picture. Big dark junks glided across the harbor. The wala walas darted among the larger crafts. Lithe Chinese girls hurried in high slit dresses. Coolies staggered under the weight of heavy laden bamboo poles. The star ferries plowed the waters between Kowloon mainland and Victoria Island. Flat-bottomed sampans were loaded with cargo and passengers.

One day we were invited to lunch at the giant floating restaurant in Aberdeen Harbor. From there I sketched some of the Chinese children on their sampans as well as family life onboard the junks. Pastor Nielsen told us that the New Territory was the only part of the Chinese mainland that we could visit in those days. It was an area of farmland between the teeming streets of Kowloon and the border of the People's Republic of China at Lo Wu. The scenery bubbled with small market towns, fishing villages and duck farms. Visions of crouched workers donning large straw hats drooping to their shoulders dotting the rice paddies remain vivid in my mind. East into the New Territory we found the Taoist Monastery of Ching Chung Koon, a serene collection of temples, gardens and moon gates. The monastery was also well known for its collection of tiny trees. Punsai art started during the Qin

Dynasty (221-206 b.c.). The art of growing tiny versions of great trees then moved to Japan several hundred years later and became known as "Bonsai." At Ching Chung Koon, petite, stunted pines, diminutive bending willows, miniature red maples and elfin elms were kept out in the open air. I was told that a tree was even planted for the Dowager Empress in the Quing Dynasty.

We left Hong Kong with the feeling that someday we would return. The 36-hour passage to the Philippines was rough due to remnants of a typhoon. In fact, when we arrived in the former capital Manila, we learned that the entire roof of the Manila Hotel had blown out to sea, never to be seen again. A Norwegian friend of mine was staying on the top floor when it happened!

We entered Manila Bay through a narrow strait leading to the Bataan Mainland and Corregidor. Stories of WWII's Bataan Death March (Japan's terrible march leading captive Americans to their prison camps) flashed in my mind. This was the country of jungles and swamps with the Bataan Mountains rising in the background. Manila and the new capital, Quezon City, are situated on Luzon, the biggest of roughly 2500 inhabited islands. There are more than 7000 islands in the Philippines, discovered by Magellan in 1521 and named for Philip II in 1565 when they became a Spanish Colony. From 1868 to 1946 the islands were under American control. As a friend then put it to me in 1954, "The Philippines have been 300 years in a Spanish convent and 40 years in Hollywood."

We had hardly docked when I was called to the gangway. Two hefty sailors carried an enormous basket of tropical fruit onboard. The array of fruit was a generous gift to me from the nieces and nephews of the Philippine Ambassador to London—our next-door neighbor. The whole group had come from the sugar-growing Island of Negros to welcome me. Malueca, one of the nieces, dressed in beige and white, looked cool and beautiful. I was more than touched. Greetings over, Miguel, a nephew, suggested a sightseeing trip. I enthusiastically accepted.

Intramuros, the old Spanish part of Manila, was completely destroyed during WWII. The only building left was the Church of San Agustin standing like a chapel in a churchyard. From there, we went to the Santo Tomas Catholic University, which was founded by Dominicans in 1611. My friends from Negros proudly announced it was 25 years older than Harvard. We returned to the sea at just the right moment to see my first magnificent sunset over Manila Bay. Never had I seen such flaming colors, such rich beauty of contrasting shades. The sky was transfigured into glory.

That evening, Malueca, Miguel and their friends asked me out for dinner and dancing. They were all remarkable dancers, and I had a great time. The next night we enjoyed before-dinner drinks with our consul in their garden. The heavy scent of tropical flowers wafted across the terrace. Gimlets were served. This cocktail consisted of lime, gin, water, a slice of orange, a red cherry and ice. Dinner started with cold mango. It was my first taste of this delicious golden-colored fruit. While at lunch the following day, some Europeans and Americans at the Army and Navy Club informed me that in no uncertain terms did one mix with the natives. In fact, I was told that an American official had invited the Minister of Finance in the Philippine government for lunch at the club; even the Minister was refused admittance! I could not believe my ears that here in 1954, such class bigotry still existed.

I had one more delightful evening dancing with the ambassador's cousins and having tea at Mrs. Igual's fantastic garden. She was a charming lady of Spanish descent and lived in a lovely, old Philippine house. It was one of the few houses which had survived the war. The outer walls had sliding panels that opened up to the garden. Spacious rooms on the first floor had a few lovely pieces of antique Spanish furniture. An ancient tall tree, encircled by a bamboo bar, stood in the middle of the lawn. Orchid plants hung from that bar's thatched roof. Mrs. Igual had 15 different shades of bougainvillea, 21 various colors of hibiscus and 20 kinds of canna lilies. I don't know how many different orchids. Proud and slender bamboo trees adorned the courtyard. The entire atmosphere was enchanting, and Mrs. Igual served us coffee and churros. As we got up to leave, Mrs. Igual broke off a wood rose and gave it to me. Its delicate color changed from cream to dark brown. It lasted for years and reminded me of the serene white butterfly orchids that covered an espalier of translucent pink cherry blossoms that decorated an archway.

As we skirted the Island of Negros, I sketched the many small outriggers with their blue striped sails. The following day we docked in Cebu, an island in the Visayan. Entering the harbor, our first unforgettable sight was of a ten thousand-ton freighter that had been lifted up on the dock by the recent typhoon! That morning I awoke feeling miserable. I had caught a high fever overnight before we reached Cebu. We were expected for lunch at Consul Jones, and he insisted that they bring me to his house. It was a wonderful frame house on stilts and with wrap-around verandas. This is the only architecture of any use, according to me, in that tropical heat. I was placed on a bed outside on the veranda with a ceiling fan keeping me as cool as possible. Silent Filipino servants brought me homemade chicken soup—the universal medicine. Even with a fever of 39 degrees Celsius, I recovered enough to join the others that afternoon. A friend of mine from Scotland had joined the party. We took a pleasant walk along the beach of the fine sand under the elegant swaying palms. I was told a wonderful story to cheer me up: "A Cebuonian dies and goes to Hell. In the morning the devil finds him trying to get out asking him where he thinks he is going. The Cebuonian then answers with chattering teeth, "I have to go back to Cebu to fetch a blanket!" I agreed with the Cebuonian whole-heartedly.

Despite everyone's kindness, I felt worse when they brought me back on board. I believe we went out to open sea between Samar and Luzon. I think we exited Devil's Gap or something, and then crossed a nasty bit of ocean northward to Japan. I was in bed, and missed the good times on the bridge. The first mate tried to bring me fresh fruit behind the captain's back.

I lost track of the passing days, but we finally arrived in Kobe, Japan, a prominent shipping port located at one end of the beautiful Inland Sea. First mate carried me ashore as if I was a bale of hay. I was so weak. Although unwell, I was not about to miss anything in Japan. The Japanese call their country Nihon, or Nippon, which is derived from the combination of nit-su-sun and lion rise. Kobe was our first port of call. The Brandts, our Consul in Kobe, had lived in Japan for the last 20-30 years, and we could not have found a more wonderful introduction to the country and its places of interest. Mrs. Brandt spoke fluent Japanese, which made everything so much more fascinating. They had a very comfortable car. They fed me February's first strawberries, which the Japanese pack in small camphor boxes, available from December to May

A two hour drive through beautiful country brought us to Kyoto—also called Heiankyo or City of Peace. In 794 A.D. Emperor Kammu moved his court from Nara, and in 1868 it was again moved by Emperor Meiji. He moved it to Tokyo, which was then called Edo. Kyoto was surrounded by mountains and traversed by two rivers, creating beautiful scenery. It is said to be the spiritual home of the Japanese people. The clear winter sunshine lights the beautiful gardens of the Heijan shrine. A characteristic bridge crossed its dreamy lake. I could picture those lovely grounds when the aged, graceful cherry trees (Sakura) wear their pink blossoms—Japan's national flower. The Nyjo Castle, a former palace of the Shoguns, was a very beautiful building with fine exterior dark wood carvings. Combined with the white chalk exterior walls, it was striking. The different rooflines were gracefully turned up at the corners. One legend tells they are designed as such to prevent the devils from climbing on to the houses. The last Shogun lived at Nyjo Castle until the restoration in 1863 when it was presented to the citizens of Kyoto as a Museum. The Shogun was actually a title reserved for generals who were sent to fight the aborigines, those strange people in the north of Japan. It was the title under which the Minamoto, Ashikajo and, lastly, the Tocugawa family exercised unlimited power.

The following day trip took us to Nara, the first capital of Japan. Nara had a vast urban park where hundreds of tame deer roam among the giant trees, unafraid of human visitors. About 1400 years prior, Buddhism was first brought to Japan from the Korean Peninsula, and signs of the Korean culture can still be seen in and around Nara. The Hortuzi Temple which was built just 50 years after the introduction of Buddhism, I believe, is the oldest wooden building in the world. Nara is also the home of the largest wooden structure in the world, the Tosaiji Temple which was built in 750 AD. It shelters Daibutu—a 500-ton bronze image called the Vairochana Buddha. He sat on an open lotus blossom in an attitude of calm reflection. We walked up the alley of 2000 stone lanterns. I could picture the magnificent scene when they were all lit up on a dark night.

I put on my new Mandarin coat for a dinner party. The Brandts lived high up on one of the surrounding hills. There were no real addresses in Japan, so we followed arrows with our host's name written on them after we left the main road. Smiling Japanese girls in red kimonos greeted us. The living room held a large bay window overlooking Kobe and the coastline. Exquisite black lacquer trays brought our dinner of Osnimous (clear soup with pink fish pudding), Onizarayaki (grilled lobster), Osashimi (sliced raw fish), Tori no kushiyaki (chicken brochette), Sawara Shioyaki (grilled fish), Yasai no Niawase (mixed vegetable, yellow and green), Gohan (rice), Ichigo (strawberries) and Yokan (a sweet pressed fruitcake). With it we drank warm sake, which is Japanese rice wine. To end the meal they served o-cha, or green tea in small fine cups. Next to me at table sat a Norwegian colonel, who had been head of the Norwegian Field Hospital in Korea for five months. As he told his stories from the time in Korea, I realized how ignorant I had been on the subject and its age-old culture. One little incident a week later in Tokyo, seemed to me significant. I was walking through the Imperial Hotel arcade and stopped in front of an antique shop. In the window was a beautiful, delicate celadon bowl which had immediately caught my eye; next to it a little card said: "From the Koryo Dynasty in Korea, 9th century A.D. to circa 1200 A.D." With a shock I realized that this date was about the time when Leif Erickson discovered America, a couple of centuries before Christopher Columbus!

After a few charming days with the Brandts, the ship continued first to Osaka and Nagoya, and then to Shimizu. Cold, overcast days broke to clear skies. Around ten o'clock at night *Tournai* sailed very slowly out of Shimizu Harbor. In all her snow covered splendor, the imposing silhouette of Fujiyama appeared in the romantic moonlight. The Queen of Volcanoes made a deep, inexplicable impression. The following morning brought a beautiful sunrise above the dark coastline when we dropped anchor outside Yokohama. The smoke lay dense over the busy port, which was playing an important role in the reconstruction of Japan. Snow lay on the roof tops, and winter still held a firm grip on the country. Our trip was halfway over, and the ship was leaving for North Chinese ports, where it was wiser not to have passengers.

As my mother and I were driven from Yokohama up to Tokyo, I realized that 80 percent of the town had been destroyed during the war. Rows and rows of low, gray wooden shacks mushroomed out of the piles of rubble and lined the streets for miles. In Tokyo, as in any other parts of Japan, there were no street numbers or street names. To overcome this difficulty in downtown Tokyo, the American occupation forces had named the streets 3rd Avenue or 15th Street in order to find their way home. We drove towards the part of town called Minato-ku. On the corner where we turned up the hill to the Dutch Embassy lay Minato Hoteru. "This is a landmark to remember, if you want to find your way home," our driver said as we passed the brightly colored Japanese Hotel. A moment later we swept up in front of the embassy.

We were staying with one of Mother's old school friends, Aimee, who happened to be married to the Dutch ambassador. The Japanese servants lined up outside to receive us. They bowed low with their hands on their knees and smiled. The two older men servants bowed even lower, and inhaled loudly. Apart from the family, the household consisted of A-rei-san, the butler, and Sa-rei-san and Emi-ku-san, the two maids. In the kitchen, the cook reigned over a different domain. I-wa-hori-san, the driver had been born at the embassy, as had his father before him. He was one of the finest, most gentle and loyal people I have ever met. His understanding of east-west differences helped me acquire a better knowledge of Japan and its inhabitants.

Tokyo had a unique flavor of its own. The Nicolai Cathedral, they say, might have come from Moscow, the detached palace, Asahusa from Fontainebleau, and the flashing neon lights from New York. Tokyo, however, was none of these cities. It combined the gaiety and colors of the Ginza—Tokyo's Broadway—with the wistful loneliness of its dark back alleys.

Among the diplomats who wined and dined us, were Blasco d'Ajeta, the Italian ambassador and his wife and daughter, who were friends from London. They gave a big ball in their beautiful embassy and introduced us to half the world. Imagine my surprise when seated next to me at the dinner table was a Dane. Imagine my further astonishment when he said, "I am the one who sent all of Niels' gifts to you!"

We saw less of the American occupation troops than I had expected, except for one night while at the military cinema. These US compounds were self-contained. I discovered that many of the GI wives had never been anywhere in Tokyo or had ever been inside a Japanese shop. I almost cried at the thought of what these women were missing—the fabulous art and architecture, so interesting and beautiful, not to mention the people!

Mrs. Aso was one of the first Japanese people I met in Tokyo. She was the lovely daughter of the then Prime Minister, Mr. Yoshida. Brought up in Europe, she had a greater understanding of the two cultures, and applied her knowledge with her own charm. People in the streets stumbled along on their "getas" as they click-clacked on the pavement. A "geta" is a kind of clog that was worn only out of doors. A y-shaped cord passed between the big and the second toe. This was a constant feature in all footwear. The Japanese wore a sort of sock, known as tabi, which had a separate division for the big toe. It reached just above the ankle and was fastened with hooks at the back. When people were indoors they removed their getas at the door and ran around in their tabi feet. In Japan, a woman's age is seen by the color of her kimono. Younger women wore light shades and older ones wore darker and more dignified colors. This point was very important even in the choice of linings for their kimonos. I found that kimonos were being worn, even in Tokyo itself, by women of all ages. An obi—a broad, stiff sash of about four yards of fabric—was worn with the kimono, often of a contrasting color.

In the center of town, around the Imperial Palace, some taller buildings remained. The beautiful, spacious grounds of the Imperial Palace were surrounded by a wide moat, lined with weeping willows, reflecting on the dark, limpid water. Not far from the Imperial Palace was the Nihombashi Bridge.

The bridge was regarded as the actual center of town, from which all distances of every part of Japan were measured. The bridge was first built in 1603, and then rebuilt 13 times. The last disastrous earthquake in 1923 destroyed it by fire, along with many other bridges in Tokyo. The present bridge was modern, completed in 1929. The Dutch embassy was situated on the site of an old shrine. Cemeteries surrounded us all over the hillside. Outside my window a 700-year-old tree towered against the pale sky. A stone lantern stood in the garden among pastel-colored bushes on the edge of a small oblong pond. Stone lanterns were originally placed in front of a shrine, temple or grave for lighting purposes. They were used as ornaments and were quite indispensable to Japanese landscaping design.

Parts of Tokyo had wide avenues, but most residential areas had narrow, winding lanes. In the center of the city, heavy traffic boomed at all hours of day and night. I noticed every kind of vehicle, from the longest American limousines to Japanese three-wheelers. Once in a while I caught the sight of a Jinrikisha or rickshaw, a human-powered vehicle. At one time, the geishas and rickshaws were the two chief tourist attractions. In 1954, however, the rickshaw was seen more often in other ports on the Asian continent rather than in the land of its invention, Japan.

On weekends we often drove down to their small Japanese summer-house at Oiso on the road to Odawara. It was foggy when we left Tokyo, but suddenly Mount Fujiyama appeared clear and white above the haze. The little house was situated in a forest of characteristic pine trees near the beach. Roaming the nearby hills one saw meditation caves. Here men sat meditating on a script, stripped to the waist. They believe that if one meditates in the sunshine more wisdom will soak in. Later when the sun disappeared we went inside the house. In the living room the only piece of furniture was a low table, over which lay a thick, pink blanket. Underneath was a box sunk into the floor, containing burning charcoal beneath a grating. We put our feet on the grating and tucked the blanket well round us. (This is what is called to sit in kotatsu.) The Japanese believed in keeping their heads cool. The other form of heating was the hibachi (fire brazier), which is a big pot of charcoal. When it was very cold, the Japanese wore heavily padded coats over their kimonos.

The beach offered a fantastic view of Fujiyama and of the sun setting like a red fire ball behind the clouds—looking like Japanese scrolls. "This is the road of the 53 famous Tokaya prints," I-wa-hori-san said, and I looked more intently at the passing landscape. Some new friends of mine were holding a ceremony on the building site of their new summer house near Oiso. In accordance with Japanese custom, an altar was erected. A Shinto priest in a long white garment and high black head gear performed the ceremony. Different offerings had been placed on the altar. The priest blessed the offerings in a loud, inarticulate voice. In answer to these strange sounds, three dogs started howling most embarrassingly, making it difficult to keep a straight face!

One day at a luncheon, I met Princess Chichibu for the first time. I had heard so much about her from friends in England. Her late husband was the emperor's brother. She came with her mother, Madame Matsudaira, wife of the one-time ambassador to London and several other important capitals, as well as the president of the Upper House. Princess Chichibu wore a pale blue kimono with a very handsome obi wound several times around her waist, tied in an intricate big bow in back. She combined simplicity with such great dignity. Her mother—a lady of brilliant intelligence and insightful human understanding—wore a dark green kimono. "I am so sorry that my house in Tokyo is not yet ready," Princess Chichibu said as she was leaving the luncheon party. "I would have liked to invite you to tea, but I have been living in the country near Fuji for many years." We were moved by the sweet and sincere way she expressed herself. That same evening the telephone rang from the imperial household. "Would you take tea with Princess Chichibu one day soon at her mother's house?" "Of course, with the great pleasure," was our reply.

We were also invited to lunch with her. We drove out to the country to her charming house and had a lovely time. Amazingly, we found out the princess did not own a car and had to walk to the train station to go into Tokyo.

The American occupation forces—after almost a decade—still prohibited any member of the Imperial family to have a car. After the war, when the Matsudaira house in Tokyo had been completely destroyed, Mrs. Matsudaira lived at the Imperial household. It was a small wooden house in a garden on one of the many hills of Tokyo. Princess Chichibu asked us many questions about her birthplace, London.

March 3rd was the Japanese Doll Festival. When the princess heard we were staying on in Tokyo, she wanted to show us her sister-in-law, Princess Takamatsu's outstanding collection of dolls. I had met Princess Takamatsu at Italian Embassy party. She was of the Tokugawa family—one of the greatest families in Japanese history. Ilyasu was the founder of this family and of the Tokugawa Shogunate. He died in 1616 at the age of 74 at Shizouka, but his body was later transferred to the famous Tosho-gu shrine at Nikko. One hundred miles north of Tokyo, the town was a gorgeous spot among snow-clad mountains.

The morning was sad and grey when I-wa-hori-san drove us to the station to catch the express train to Nikko, but the sky cleared gradually and the sun came out as we arrived at our destination. Nobody spoke English, but we managed to get a car to take us up the hill to the main shrine. The car stopped near the painted Pagoda. The first thing that struck me was the trees. Huge cryptomeira and camphor trees stood as they had for centuries; the former often reaching 100 feet high. We proceeded through the many finely carved and splendidly painted gates to the main shrine, passing the different red lacquer store rooms and the black and gold stable of Prince Ilyasu which dates from the 17th century. The detail of the wood carving was splendid, and held a distinct Buddhist influence. The decorations of the Toshu-gu shrine were gorgeous, and very different from the usual pure form of shrine architecture. Descending from the Toshu-gu shrine, between the gigantic trees, we went to the Hall of the Three Buddhas. This beautiful old building, again lacquer red, was set between withered old trees, a tiny lake and a waterfall. The shafts of sunlight glanced through the trees, across the limpid water. The stillness and the knowledge of centuries of dedication, gave the place an unearthly quality. "Be still my heart," wrote Tajore, "these great trees are prayers."

One of the most arresting and beautiful features in Nikko is the sacred bridge over the river. It is painted a lacquer red. Upstairs in one of the shops, I found a treasure I had been searching for, a real beautiful Kakemono—a famous wall hanging. On the trip back to Tokyo that evening, the flame-colored sunset behind the hills and the black silhouetted pine trees on the ridgeline made me even happier I'd bought the Kakemono. Our wonderful stay in Japan was drawing to a close and saying goodbye was difficult. When the car came to take us to the airport, the gracious servants had lined up to wish us a happy voyage. I felt sad to leave.

"Domo Arigato," I said, "for all I have learned here."

We flew from Tokyo to Hong Kong, and after a few days we were back on the ship. Here is a letter I wrote to my father as we left Hong Kong bound for home:

Dearest Puschka,

Finally, we are homeward bound. It is disappointing that after these raw, cold weeks of winter, it looks like we will have no warm- weather ports, only one day each in Manila and Singapore; then straight to Aden. Let us hope the captain is only bringing bad news on purpose and that we won't miss the trip up to see the Templers in Kuala Lumpur, the capital of Maluya. It was very nice to be welcomed back on board, we have been missed and they all say they have not seen a smile since Yokohama when the Prebensen ladies went ashore. Even the captain seemed in a better mood; may it last. We left Hong Kong at 6 this morning. When we looked out of the porthole after breakfast, we saw thick, brown woolen pants, pale green undershirts and underpants on a clothes line, all together a magnificent view. We have two female missionaries on board and they had put their wash out to dry! It reminded me of a tenement. This morning was very humid, but I got up early and went up on the bridge, as usual. First Mate had four-star positions prepared for me, and all was back to normal. The sunrise made everything light and hopeful. We are back in summer clothes and enjoy it hugely. We seem to have been away from the ship for much more than a month. Life on the bridge is lifesaving, even for a couple of hours. Breakfast is now being served in our suite, thank you; we were too tired of the captain's constant unpleasant remarks and bad temper. I am sorry to say, I think First Mate is getting the brunt of it but he insists he has broad shoulders. The "Swimming pool" will be put back after Manila. I have learnt an immense amount on this trip, about humanity and kindness. I have noticed the great power of smiles, especially in all the countries where we did not know the language. I have found so many of the things I have been searching for here in the Far East. It has proven not only to be a voyage in search of health, but a better mental outlook. I am sure, if you could, you would send me out here every six months! I cannot wait to see you and the two bandits and hear some lovely music again. Love You!

P.S. I have at least got to the "Dawn of Understanding."

Seven years later we were given another opportunity to return to the Far East. We carried memories as part of our luggage and hoped to rediscover my "Dawn of Understanding" in the East again. Just after my father's funeral in Rome in 1961, Scandinavian Airlines invited mother to cut the ribbon and officially open their new route from Tehran to Calcutta. I was delighted to take mother away for a few days. There were too many problems, legal and otherwise facing us suddenly. The SAS director, Johannes Nielsen, brought us to the airport and saw us well on board the aircraft. The flight from Rome to Tehran was crowded so we had to fly economy. The dinner, however, was first class and we toasted the trip with a good bottle of champagne. Snow covered the mountains in Tehran; the air was cool and crisp. It was midnight, local time, and the moon was shining bright. Very few passengers continued the flight to Calcutta. We flew first class. Apart from a stop in Karachi, Pakistan, we had a very comfortable night. The sun was up by the time we reached Calcutta. From Calcutta we flew straight to Bangkok in time for lunch.

Gill and Helge Vindenes from our Norwegian Embassy came to meet the plane and arrange our papers. Helge then went to fetch our luggage, only to find none of our suitcases! Being special guests of the airline, we had been treated royally, that is to say, we only carried our small old-fashioned handbags. We had been brought on board with all sorts of ceremonies and now there was no luggage. They searched the plane. They tried to telephone to locate it. Time passed. They finally did locate it, but in Tehran! There was no flight from Tehran to Bangkok for two or three days! We were traveling in an official capacity. It was the month of November, quite cold in Rome on departure. We were still in deep mourning and therefore dressed in dark gray tailored flannel suits and all black accessories. We were both Nordic tall. No ready-made clothes existed in 1961 that we could buy for the heat of Bangkok. One could have anything made in Thai silk, but they needed a little more time than overnight. Somebody managed to find a pair of low-heeled white sandals. The shoes originally had been made for a huge American girl—size 10—an enormous size by Thai standards! Then a friend of a friend lent me a white terital cotton pleated skirt. But my black silk shirt had to make do till the luggage arrived. Mother was not even that lucky. She had to wear her black high-heels and black stockings through the humid days of the monsoon. All our troubles had taken hours to resolve.

Our first evening in Bangkok, we invited Gill and Helge to dinner at our hotel, the Oriental, which is beautifully situated on the wide river. The Oriental retains its title as the best hotel in the world. I read somewhere that the manager is "a genius with his infinitely meticulous attention to detail and his ability to effortlessly keep the hotel running quietly, without glitz, and with that gentle dedication so seldom found in endeavors of this kind." After a long, strenuous day, we had an excellent dinner in air-conditioning, so we all felt better. The two long royal barges floated by on the river, part of the lovely picture. One of the reasons we felt even worse about not having the right clothes, was that since Prince and Princess Kitiakara, had been twice Thai ambassadors to the Court of St. James at the time of my parents, they had become good friends.

Princess Kitiakara was one of the most elegant ladies I have ever known. She was the mother of the Queen of Thailand. Queen Sirikit and I used to go to tea with each other in her London days. Her husband, King Bhumpol, not only held the title of King of Thailand, but also of Half Brother of the Moon and Keeper of the 24 Golden Umbrellas. The last two titles especially impressed me. The following morning, the Queen's brother, Adulkit, paid us a visit at the hotel at 11:30, and then took us sightseeing and to lunch at a Chinese restaurant. I wore my white, pleated skirt, open sandals and the black silk shirt. Mother wore her charcoal grey, woolen traveling clothes. Then Princess Kitiakara invited us for dinner Sunday evening. When thinking about what to wear, the very thought had become a nightmare. Sunday morning at seven Helge picked us up for a trip to the famous floating market. We were still wearing the same old clothes. Thank God for the "Oriental," because they could wash and iron everything over night. The market, however, was fantastic and colorful, as we floated in and out among the merchants. This was 1961. Bangkok was still a city of canals, and one could still move around.

While we were enjoying a very excellent lunch, miracles of miracles happened. The telephone rang; our luggage had arrived in Bangkok. By the time Prince Adulkit came to fetch us in the afternoon, we had been able to change into impeccable white. The nightmare was fortunately over.

Adulkit brought us to the Grand Palace. Built in 1783, it is a square mile of unrivaled royal grandeur. Its most treasured possession is the Emerald Buddha. Carved of a single piece of jade, it reposes high on a golden altar. It is not only revered as a religious icon, but also as an exquisite work of art. We were taken all around the royal compound and admired the Thai style roofs—which looked like "flapping wings straining to take flights into the heavens"—gold doors and glistening red roofs. Bald-headed monks in saffron robes walked about. Most teenage boys live for a few months in a Buddhist monastery, trying to earn karmic merit. As adults they often return for periods of retreat and reflection.

Arriving at Princess Kitiakara's pretty house on the river, Chao Phya, we found her eldest son, daughter in-law and grandchildren had joined us. Great Thai specialties were served. I have seldom enjoyed friends and surroundings more than that Sunday evening by the river—finally dressed in spotless white! In memory of my visit, Princess Kitiakara gave me a gold temple bell charm.

The last morning in Bangkok was spent alone with my camera to capture the city's dazzling sights. I wanted to be reminded forever of the color of the temple roofs, the saffron-colored robes of the monks, the life on the canals and finally the view of the River of the Kings from the Oriental Hotel. We ate our last lunch there and watched again as the royal barges floated by. Queen Sirikit was on official travel out of the country with her husband, King Bhumpol, but sent her best. I was so glad to see her family again.

The Royal Orchid Airline had SAS pilots and the most beautiful stewardesses in orchid-colored uniforms. On board the stewardesses changed into their elegant Thai dresses. The plane—a DC6—was bound for Hong Kong, and the first class cabin was paneled in yellow Thai silk. It was a very pleasant flight largely due to the smiling, helpful crew. Hong Kong's Kai Tai Airport had changed since our last visit. The runway had been extended into the bay, which made it less hazardous to land among the mountains. Hong Kong had grown too, if that was possible. SAS put us up at the Miramar Hotel on the Kowloon side. The area was more crowded than ever. There were new constructions on Nathan Road. The Star Ferry had new landing stages and boats.

The owners of the Miramar Hotel gave a superb dinner party for us. The host and hostess spoke only Chinese, but we had an interpreter. The dinner had five courses before the soup, and followed by 15 courses with several exquisite tiny tastes on each plate. It was one of the most elegant dinners I have ever attended. The owners' museum-like house brimmed with magnificent Chinese art, offering a glimpse into a world most westerners never imagine exists. I felt very fortunate indeed. It reminded us of our visit to the Kowloon Park Museum of rare photos and artifacts from Hong Kong's 5000-year history. In fact, the Portuguese came to Hong Kong in 1514 during the Ming Dynasty, but were expelled seven years later and now only remain in Macao.

My old friends, the Wallems—whom we saw on our first trip—were still residing at Sheko overlooking the golf course. At lunch with them, I overheard her speak pigeon English to the driver, "Go catch one piecy missy one piecy man, belong Gloucester Hotel." I wondered whether I belonged proper topside! Sheko was at least as beautiful as I remembered. From the Wallem's terrace we enjoyed that most fabulous view of junks, the golf course and bougainvillea. Across Repulse Bay was the rambling compound of a Chinese man, whom I was told thought he would die if he ever stopped building. As I look back now, I wonder if the same thing happened to my architect husband, Billy. In fact, right after our last renovation in Palm Beach, he suddenly died of a heart attack.

After some lovely days revisiting friends and favorite places, SAS flew us on to Tokyo. Our Norwegian ambassador fetched us at the airport. This old friend of Father's was responsible for us for three days. One day we went up Tokyo's version of the Eiffel Tower. We had a good view of the town. But what interested me most was that right below us stood the Dutch Embassy Compound where we had spent that marvelous month seven years before. Of course, our friends were no longer there, but the Japanese driver, Ivo-Hori-san, who was born at the embassy, might still be there. He had been so helpful and attentive to us, I wanted to say hello. When Ivo-Hori-san saw us, his enthusiasm was worth the trip. The return flight to Europe went over the North Pole. I was handed a certificate for crossing the pole as we watched the Aurora Borealis. We had left Tokyo Sunday night after a packed day of being wined and dined by friends. When we arrived in Anchorage, Alaska I shall never forget the airline official greeting us with a broad American accent, "Happy Sunday morning, folks—all over again!" That was my first visit to North America. Little did I know I would end up spending a large part of my life in the US. We stopped in Copenhagen before happily landing back in Rome—*with* our luggage this time. The Eternal City put on its sunny face to welcome us back. I was so happy to have been able to revisit the Far East which had forever been my "Dawn of Understanding."

Yugoslavia – Behind the Iron Curtain
CORAL PENGUIN

In 1954, we left Venice by car for a vacation on the Adriatic Coast. We passed through the US Military Zone and control before crossing the frontier between Sistiana and Rijeka. The surroundings of Trieste were arid and stony—ideal for a military training ground. But, after we traversed the Yugoslavian border, the landscape changed immediately to rolling, forest-clad mountains resembling mighty waves at sea.

We entered Croatia, and our road to Opatija took a sharp right and pitched steeply down toward the sea. The old Hotel Kvarner was enormous and stately. Outside of our hotel room was a wide balcony overlooking a tiled, circular terrace with a fantastic view of the Adriatic Sea. The large dining room held an old-fashioned elegance reminiscent of the Austro-Hungarian Empire. In the mild summer evenings, we had coffee after dinner on the terrace where golden globe lamps illuminated the open-air dance floor. Fountains were playing here and there in the park and the flowers were spectacular. A small, romantic church surrounded by palms and cypresses stood next to the hotel. From our terrace, we watched the silver moon, and listened to the ocean waves crashing against the rocky shore. In the dark night, millions of lights twinkled. The region was both Mediterranean and Alpine. Palms, roses and even banana trees flourished along the coast. Inland, the landscape was more like central Europe, where pines and vineyards mixed with wheat fields and orchards.

Even before the Romans, Istria had acted as a pawn due to its geographical setting. The Romans left roads, triumphal gates and amphitheaters. The Venetians left many campaniles (bell towers) and fortified ports. But the later Austrian imprint predicted a new future for the region. With the opening of the railroad from Vienna to Trieste in 1857, Istria became accessible to the prosperous burghers of the Austro-Hungarian society. Resorts were developed, the most fashionable being Opatija. Up to WWI, Viennese society flocked to what was then called Abbazia. You could say it was their Palm Beach. In 1954, we found the tourists to be mostly Germans, but also Austrians, French and Swiss. An occasional Swede mixed into the picture, as well as a few English and a stray American (due to the Communistic government).

Once there, I began collecting facts for my current best friend, Prince Tomislav, younger brother of King Peter. A Yugoslav prince, Tomislav was exiled and settled in England. Tommy had given me both his film and other cameras—which I was using to the best of my ability—in order to record what was happening in his homeland.

The excellent Zagreb radio orchestra played Big Band music every night from 9 to midnight on our terrace at the Kvarner Hotel. A large crowd would gather, and from our balcony, we had the best seats in the house. Most of the 18 musicians in the orchestra were students of medicine, engineering, architecture and music. The orchestra had two conductors: Miljenko Prohaska and Mikki Kerbler. One was the Glenn Miller man, the other played in the style of Stan Getz. Five of the men in the orchestra also played at the Lido from midnight until three in the morning. Yugoslavia was still under strict communist rule, so when we were out at public events like concerts, we knew we were being watched. But, because my father was an ambassador, they were more discreet about the surveillance. At first, we were not allowed any contact at all with the Yugoslavs. Then my brother, Chris, and I realized we could swim out to sea and talk with the members of the band who were very keen to befriend us. For their sake, we had to be extremely careful because the manager of the hotel was a member of the secret police.

The Hotel Kvarner—known to be the best in town—had only eleven bathrooms for 130 guests. Despite that one drawback, it looked quite spruced up due to a great deal of redecorating following the war. One of the older maids, Maria, became a part of our lives from the very first day. She was from the "old days," and like many on the Dalmatian coast, she spoke fluent Italian. Her thin gray hair was tied in a knot at the nape of the neck. She always smiled and her lively, darting eyes never missed a thing. When she brought us our morning coffee, she looked at me and said, "Fara bel tempo," (the weather will be good). No one argued with Maria. She willed it.

Since we had a car—a great luxury at the time in Yugoslavia—we took trips to several small bays towards Trieste. Palms and cypress trees grew along the coast. Here and there small, picturesque towns climbed up the hillsides with their towers, thick walls, narrow passages and small squares. Women dressed in black gossiped at the water well. We ate sun-warmed, ripe figs and enjoyed the splendid views as far as the island of Krk. The Adriatic was of a rich Prussian blue. Southwards towards Rijeka, the picture was different with mountains that were bare and wild as far as the eye could see. There were hardly any cars anywhere. People walked for miles and miles on foot. One day we drove a poor mother and her sick child to the Red Cross Hospital in Kraljenica. Had we not picked them up, they would have had to walk five kilometers in the hot sun. Kraljenica was a small town situated at the bottom of a fjord or deep bay. It had some industry, shipbuilding and a factory or two. The arid mountains round the fjord held an untamed beauty and the water was an intense deep blue. One morning, we left without breakfast, and stopped at an inn—one of many on the way—for Turkish coffee and bread. The inns were pathetically poor and small. We drove along the coast to watch tuna fishing. Men sat on top of tall ladders all day long staring into the water. Once in a while they threw down a pebble to tempt the tuna to come closer. Often they sat for days in the sunshine without seeing even one fish. But, when their luck changed, the boats went out, and the battle commenced to reel in the huge fish.

When we left Yugoslavia that first summer, I purposely left all my clothes behind. The wives of the boys in the band had very little to wear. Back in England, we sent additional clothes through various diplomatic channels.

I was eager to show my exiled friend, Tomislav, the photos and stories of the Croatian people and countryside. In return for my efforts, he gave me a coral penguin to add to my charm bracelet.

When we returned to Yugoslavia the following summer, political conditions had definitely eased up a bit. We were welcomed back by the radio orchestra members as old friends—minus the secret police. The wonderful Adriatic was ideal for expeditions and underwater fishing. One day, however, almost ended in a catastrophe. Bumbar and Kugi (members of the orchestra) drove west with Chris and me past Moscenica Draga. It was a Sunday and the pastel-colored houses in the small fishing village sat smiling in the sunshine. The landscape was peaceful, and from high points on the road we had a fantastic view of the mountains, islands and the blue-gray Adriatic. We drove 40 to 50 kilometers in search of a long, narrow fjord that reminded us of Norway. The mountains rose straight out of the water, which had changed from turquoise to steely blue. The road wound its way down a deep valley to the bottom of the fjord. An old fisherman rented us a boat, and we rowed out the fjord where the water was clearer. The sun had disappeared behind clouds by this time and a light breeze and a few raindrops gave us ideal fishing weather. Kugi and Chris grabbed their gear and dove under water. Bumbar and I followed by boat, and then found a ravine with a tiny pebbled beach. As we were pulling the boat up on land, a very forceful undercurrent got hold of the boat, waves crashed over us, and in the course of a minute everything was soaking wet. We pulled and hauled. The cameras and the clothes were placed under a rocky overhang. The boat was smashed against the rocks leaving a large hole in its bottom. Half full of water, the boat was impossible to move. We shouted after Kugi and Chris for help. They came to our aid, having already caught three fish. With combined efforts we were able to pull the boat up and somehow repair it, but it was clear it would not float. On three sides of us the mountains went straight up from the sea, unfriendly and sharp.

The only solution was to swim around the point, climb up the rocky hillside to the road—which passed a few hundred meters above us—and then walk back to the old tuna fisherman for help. The underwater swimmers tied their sneakers around their necks and a few minutes later they had disappeared from view. It was just past noon.

For the two of us remaining with our belongings, we could only hope and pray the boys would be able to reach the old fisherman. We were already soaked from the waves. On top of that we received a torrential rainstorm. There was a small cave, which kept us fairly dry, but the wind was icy cold. The hours dragged by. It was impossible to calculate how long it would take the others to reach civilization. At last, just as we had almost given up hope of seeing anyone before darkness set in, the fisherman and his two sons came rowing around the point. In addition to the rain, it had become freezing cold. The boat they brought was quite small. How we were able to float in the fjord with five people aboard was a miracle. We were on the verge of sinking at any minute. A sail remnant gave a little shelter from the rain. Eventually, we reached an old, rotten pier. The two boys went ashore and continued home on foot. Through driving rain, it took us more than an hour to row to the mouth of the fjord. At last, we were hauled ashore and brought up to the fisherman's cottage. The oven was lit and water was boiling on the stove. Not since my ski accident in Val d'Isere years before, had anything tasted as delicious as the hot tea and slivovitz (plum brandy) that the kind fisherman's wife served us in their warm and cozy kitchen. We remained a while sipping the hot tea and talking to the sweet family. Neither of them had ever been away from their little narrow valley, not even to the local cinema. The nearest telephone was at the post office, which was closed on Sundays. On the drive back to Opatija, I only had my bathing suit and a blouse—everything else was soaking wet. The long, harrowing day was finally over. We were all very relieved, not the least of whom was my father who had not heard from us all day!

Toward the end of that Croatian summer, I drove Miljenko Prohaska, one of the band leaders, and his family back to Zagreb and stayed the night with them. He lived with his parents and their adorable five-year-old daughter in a two-room apartment. We had a nice trip over the mountains and stopped to admire the new dam and other interesting sights. After lunch, the following day I returned from Zagreb to Opatija. Ozren Depolo, a medical student and saxophonist, came back with me because he was engaged to play another week on the coast. Again, the trip took about three hours. I gladly made that trip three more times, because I knew it helped my friends. On one of the trips to Zagreb, I stayed with the Depolos. Marco Polo was their ancestor and they still owned the old family house on the island of Korcula. During World War II, their washbasin in the bathroom of their Zagreb apartment had broken during a bombardment. They had been asking the Belgrade government for permission to buy a new sink since 1945. But by 1955, nothing had yet been resolved! We had to use the bathtub for everything, even brushing our teeth. There were continual similar irritations between Belgrade in Serbia and the other states, like Croatia.

We liked Zagreb so much that Father, Chris and I spent an extra few days there on our way home. One day we wandered around town to do some shopping. We went into a bookstore on Trg Republica to buy a children's book for Tommy, and then went for coffee at the café next door. Suddenly, we realized Chris had left the car papers in the bookstore. It was two minutes past two o'clock. It was a Saturday, and the shop had closed for the day. Nothing would be open in a communist country until Monday morning. Because of Father's previous commitments, we had to keep our schedule and leave Sunday morning. We telephoned the authorities because, naturally, the bookstore was not privately owned. No one seemed to be able to figure out who had the keys to the shop. After hours of searching and never taking "no" for an answer, we found the name and address of the lady with the keys. We drove out of the city limits to an old war-torn house where the lady lived. We explained our plight, and in spite of being in the middle of her dinner, she agreed to come with us. Her only request was that we would drive her home again. She was most gracious. On the way, she shyly asked if she could touch my worsted dress fabric. It had been a long time since they had had the opportunity to buy quality goods. I wanted to take my dress off and give it to her right then and there. But I'd already given away most of my clothes to friends in need. The dress was about all I had left. With a deep sigh of relief, Chris recovered our car papers, and with profound thanks, we drove the lady back home.

Beograd was 400 kilometers by "autoput" from Zagreb. Every ten kilometers there was an auto service and a restauracija. At Slavonski Brod, we crossed the bridge over the Sava River to see the minaret in Bosinski Brod, and to say we had been in Bosnia. In Belgrade, we found our way to Tolstoijeva, and were graciously received by our Minister Irgens at the Norwegian Legation. Being in a Balkan capital, the house looked very out of place, as if built for a tropical climate. Our tour of the town took us first to Kalamegdan to see where the Sava and the Donau flow together, and to admire the serene park. Then we came back over the Teracija Square, passing palaces and Parliament, and catching glimpses of the royal mansion on the hilltop, shining white among the great trees. On this trip, like the first, I was still on a mission of collecting photos for my friend Prince Tomislav. It was important to him that I bring back film and photos of places he remembered prior to his exile. To that end, we traveled from Belgrade, through Zagreb to Llubjana, the capital of Slovenia. From there we made our way up to Bled Lake. Out on an island, we could see the castle that once belonged to the royal family, where they had spent so many holidays. I believe that during my two summers there, Marshal Tito, the Yugoslavian dictator, was the one sadly enjoying it instead.

I kept in contact with Miljenko and his wife, Pavica for years. Once back in Rome, she was permitted to visit me there when Miljenko was on tour with his classical music band. As a communist ploy to ensure the parents' return, their daughter was not allowed to accompany them! Such were the conditions in 1954 and 1955. Years later, those restrictions and many other things thankfully changed when Yugoslavia broke up into the six countries of Serbia, Croatia, Bosnia Herzegovina, Republic of Macedonia, Montenegro and Slovenia.

Portugal – A One Man Legation

GOLD COIN

When, in 1946, my father became Norwegian ambassador to the Court of St. James in London, one of the first people he met was the Duke of Palmella. The Duke was the Portuguese ambassador, and had been in England throughout WWII. After serving six years, he returned to family life in Lisbon. Lady Kelly wrote in her book, *This Delicious Land, Portugal:* "One could never remember whether the Palmellas had more houses or more children. Both exceeded ten!"[1] After several of his very attractive children had visited London during the 1948 Olympic Games, I became quite keen on visiting Lisbon!

Portugal once formed part of the Roman Province Hispania Ulterior. It was in 1st-century B.C. that Julius Caesar incorporated this area into the Roman Empire. In 711, the Vizigoth King requested help from the African General, Tariq Ibn Ziyad, who became master of the peninsula. Not until 1250 did King Afonso III crush Moslem rule which held out in the region called al-Gharb, now known as Algarve. There are still many Moorish influences in the Portuguese language. At the time, this small country at the tip of Europe's edge—just four to five hundred years ago—ruled half the known world. This era was known as Portugal's Golden Age. Prince Henry the Navigator led several expeditions and developed directional devices including a huge compass dial at Sagres. He also created Europe's most powerful beacon called the Lighthouse of Sao Vicente, located at the southwest tip of the continent. Prince Henry led significant explorations to the profitable India.

In 1956, when my father decided to vacation in Portugal, society was still almost feudal, and the rule, authoritarian. Portugal's emotional preoccupation with the past was part of its charm. The people prided themselves in the past accomplishments of their Golden Age. As a country they rested on its historic laurels. No writer has surpassed the 16th century poet, Camoens, nor has any painter been greater than Nuno Goncalves of the Van Eyck Flemish School. It is said that travelers to the Iberian Peninsula in the Middle Ages arrived by the grace of God, despite stormy seas. Pilgrims survived walking across the frigid Pyrenees on foot in search of sanctuaries on the other side.

My parents and I, however, crossed the frontier between Spain and Portugal by car at Guarda. The border station house was decorated with wonderful azulejos, the famous Portuguese tiles. Azulejos may be a blend of two Arabic words, azraq (azure) and zalayja (polished stone), introduced by Moors. The blue decorated tiles were adopted by the Portuguese to such an extent that today they are a vital part of the country's heritage. On our way south we stopped in Coimbra, the seat of the ancient university, where Dr. Antonio Oliveira Salazar taught before he became a dedicated Presidente do Conselho. When we arrived in Lisbon we found our way out to Estoril and the *Hotel Albatroz*. It was built on a rocky point in Cascais Bay, just north of Estoril by order of the Duke of Loule. Every window held a dazzling view across the deep blue Bay of Cascais. Small, brightly painted fishing boats bobbed on the waves. The only noise was that of the sea lapping against the rocks below. An orchestra played by the pool below us. My wonderful friend, Manuel Palmella, had left me an enchanting welcome gift of a gold portafortuna, a good luck piece in my room.

It was the summer of 1956, and no sooner had we settled in, but Father was called back to London by the British government because of Middle East trouble. Fortunately, the interference did not last long and he rejoined us after a week. "When has there not been trouble in the Middle East?" my father asked philosophically.

In spite of so many tourists, Cascais was—as it has always been—a charming fishing village. Since 1870, when the Portuguese Royal family first moved to Cascais, the aristocratic great families followed in their wake, and many still reside there. From the bridge on the Estrada de Boca do Inferno, one sees the spectacular villa of a grand clan. The family house resembled a boat, decorated with blue and white azulejos. It was understatedly elegant; casual and intimate at the same time. I loved being there for lunch. The pastel pink *Villa Italia*, also near Boca do Inferno, was where King Umberto II spent his years in exile. Though he left Italy after it was declared a republic in 1946, he never abdicated nor abandoned his hopes for a restoration of the Monarchy. King Umberto was not allowed to visit Italy, and after nearly 40 years of waiting, he died in 1983, and was sadly buried—outside of his country—in a rural valley in French Savoie. After I returned to Lisbon in 1957, I saw him at parties, and he was always interested in any gossip from Roma— in Italian, of course! Both Don Juan of Spain and King Carol of Rumania lived in nearby Estoril.

The Palmellas spent part of their summers in their Bay of Cascais home. The grey stone house looked as if it belonged on the coast of Scotland, rather than in Portugal. Regardless of which house they were in, it was their practice to gather their family for Sunday dinner. We were happy to be included before Father left for London. The "Padre Familia," Domingos Palmella— one of my favorite human beings—was married to the most charming lady I ever knew. She had such a deep melodious voice. I always called her "My Favorite Fairy" because she was always so special. Domingos Palmella's sister, Marquesa do Tancos, had a grander house in the Scottish style right next door in Cascais. Colorful fishing boats crowded the port and white sails speckled the blue Atlantic. We joined a wonderful family get-together.

While my father was in London, we went sightseeing with the Duchess of Palmella and her son, Manuel, my dear friend. We drove via the royal city, Sintra, as mist clung to its peak. The Portuguese kings prized the chilly summer weather of this ancient Arab stronghold. Dom Luis, the poet king, built the first palace, which Lord Byron described in his epic poem, "Childe Harold." Sitting high above Lisbon, the town was surrounded by lush forests. Atlantic rain clouds intercepted by the mountains created the damp climate.

Fern and moss grew on ancient oaks, and the luxuriant scent of jasmine filled the air. A winding road led up to the enthralling *Palacio da Pena*, where flowers and specimen trees from throughout the Portuguese Empire bloomed in profusion. Property walls in Sintra stood tall, but we could still catch glimpses of towers, shrines and fountains, arches, benches, and bridges bending over sparkling streams. The road down from Sintra ran passed the *Palacio de Seteais*, and it was suggested we stop there for a cup of tea. As we approached the palace we saw the two neo-Palladian pavilions across the wide stretch of lawn. In 1800 when Marquis de Marialva bought the *Seteais Estate*, he erected a Triumphal Arch between the two identical pavilions in honor of King Joao VI. The house became a hotel in the early 20th century, and was beautifully remodeled and redecorated. It was a real treat to sip tea and admire the panoramic view extending to the Atlantic coastline. The drive continued past the *Palacio de Queluz*—without a doubt, one of the eighteenth century's finest gifts of Rococo architecture. Comparisons with Versailles are unavoidable, even though *Queluz* is not much bigger than a large country house. From there we went on to Lisbon.

The Palmellas lived in a palace on the Rua Escola Politecnica at the corner of the Rato. Lady Kelly again, mentioned in her book: "The palace in Lisbon and the country house at *Calhariz*, both seigneurial on the 18th century scale, but thanks to the taste of the Duchess, both are homes, as she lives in each just as busy, but as homey a life, as she did when she transformed the Portuguese Embassy in London, when her husband was Ambassador to the Court of St. James during the 40s."[2]

An Italian architect built the Palmella Palace with debris from the Estrela following a historical earthquake. The front entrance was from the Rua Escola Politecnica, but since the street ran up a hill, most of the living rooms were on the second floor. At the top of the stairs was a great man-high Sevres vase, which had been given to the first duke by Talleyrand after the congress of Vienna. I remember it was of the deepest blue with white medallions. Nearly all the ceilings were decorated by Italian and French artists in the best Pompeian style. One of the bedrooms had a painting of the Holy

Family, classified in Italy as a Raphael. The palace was also rich in Romneys and Gainsboroughs. The ballroom was left intact, full of late 18th-century furniture covered by splendid Aubusson tapestries. Large chandeliers lit the rectangular dining room. "As family or guests always drop in for meals, I think we are never less than about twelve, and on Sunday night we are at least the double of that. Domingos and I never have a *tete-a-tete* dinner, Monsignor and Nanny will at least be there," Maria do Carmo said to my mother with a smile. In one of the special rooms, the duchess had hung hand embroidered muslin curtains found in an old 18th-century trunk. In the same room hung a portrait of the first Duke of Palmella, by Lawrence. The crowning glory of the house, which I shall never forget, was the private chapel on the top floor of the palace. It was brought from Italy and had a rich combination of vert-antique marbles, elaborately carved woodwork of the late Renaissance with green gold leaf and embossed leatherwork. In the small entrance hall to the chapel was a St. Jerome by Guido Reni.

I later learned to my horror, that this palace was seized during the 1974 revolution and turned into Palais de Justice. I was even more revolted to hear that communists had set fire to the splendid chapel on the third floor. I thought to myself, "What a waste, and what did it prove?" In 1957, during my employment in Lisbon, I continued to appreciate this fabulous chapel at family mass on Sundays, as well as the wonderful family and their generous hospitality. Joao, the doorman, would greet one at the palace front door. I would mount the stairs and often look in at Domingo Palmella's study, where I was invited to sit down on a stool and listen to his many enchanting tales. I remember how he used to play with a small silver barometer on his desk. After he died, my favorite friend among the daughters, Bebinha, gave it to me in memory of her father and it's been with me ever since. She knew how much I appreciated him. Even after 37 years, Nanny hadn't learned Portuguese and Monsignor did not know a word of English, although they'd spent dinner together every night. On Sundays, the large family usually appeared at the family mass at noon in the green embossed leather Italian chapel, and they returned again for supper at a long table in the gracious dining room. The younger members in the family used to gather after dinner in a cozy living room on the bottom floor. In front of the fireplace was a leather-covered fender which had heard many an intimate conversation!

In 1961, a bridge was built across the Tagus. But when we first went to *Calhariz* in 1957, we had to take a ferry. The Arrabida Peninsula "on the other shore," was a 21-mile stretch of Atlantic coastline, paralleled by a low green spine of rolling mountains, rich vineyards, fruit orchards and cork trees. From the ferry we drove, according to Lord Carnarvon, through "hills fragrant with lavender and rosemary, and finely clothed with olive, pine and cork." I loved the color of the cork trees on the road that led to *Calhariz*. Dom Francisco de Sousa, an ancestor of the present owner, who married Helena of Portugal in 1684, built *Calhariz* as a hunting lodge. It was always a great sight to see everyone dressed for a shoot with feathers in their hats. The men assembled in front of the palace's front entrance portal with its broken impediment emblazed with the family coat of arms. The first Duke of Palmella remodeled *Calhariz* in the early 19th century. He, too, was ambassador in London for many years and was a compadre of both the prince regent and the writer, William Beckford. The palace opened into a large baroque-style hall. The opposite wall held a huge stone fireplace with a painting of Diana the Huntress surrounded by spears, arrows, hunting horns and other emblems of the chase hanging above. I was later told that when the communists tried to take over *Calhariz* during the 1974 revolution, the Duchess of Palmella—with only old Nanny at her side—was able to chase them out of that hall in her wheelchair. The communists had already jailed her son Luis, expropriated his house opposite the *Palace of Queluz*, and overrun her Lisbon home, the *Palace at Rato*. *Calhariz* was a "Grand Ducal seat" in every way. The large courtyard had a cluster of outbuildings, and opposite the house was a large fountain pool for watering the horses. *Casa do Calhariz* had all the main rooms on the ground floor with French windows enabling the whole floor of the house to be thrown open at an instant. All the doors facing the garden were aligned, which provided a vista that penetrated to the end of the house and beyond to the chapel. When the Palmellas were in residence, the family assembled for Sunday mass, and sometimes returned for supper. The 18th-century chapel had an impressive inlaid marble altar, which filled the entire end of the chapel. It was one of the major works of its type to survive from the Joanine period. The memory of the chapel's warm atmosphere lingers with me, and will continue to throughout my life. The simple exterior of the house was white-washed stucco with plain grey pilaster strips at the corners. The lower part of the immense façade of the house was clad in blue and white azulejos. Terraces towered over the formal gardens, with steps that led down to the lower terrace. A double staircase led down to the box parterre with its classical rotunda. The surrounding large trees softened the solidity of the distant limestone mountains. Garden designs drew from English, French, Italian and Moorish styles. Portuguese gardens were unlike any other in Europe. They included elements of fantasy, humor, and caprice as well as vast reflecting pools added to the parterres. It was the iconic azulejos, however—the white, blue and yellow tile extravaganzas—that set the gardens apart.

Among the Duke of Palmella's treasures was also the *Convento do Arrabida,* a group of small irregular white-washed buildings precariously perched above the blue Atlantic coast. The spot is sacred to birds and occasional pilgrims. The year I was there, the duke was restoring the second convent. It had been erected by one of his ancestors, Dom John de Lancastre, the first Duke of Aveiro, who was a great-grandson of John I. Early in 1539, the Duke of Aveiro had asked the Carthusians to bring a new order. The monks were friends of Saint Teresa. But it was the Franciscans who came instead of the Carthusians. There were forty minute cells on seven different levels and seven chapels in the convent. A microscopic terrace full of orange trees and water gurgled down the hill. Domingos Palmella was attempting to restore it to its original 1830 state, but the order was suppressed. The whole place appeared ageless with its thick white walls, outside staircases, steps and fountains. It was such a romantic place, and I thoroughly loved it.

CONVENTO DO
ARRABIDA

After our wonderful first vacation in 1956, a couple of the Palmella boys came to London during the following winter. One evening, Manuel Palmella and I went to an event at the Dorchester Hotel. By the time we returned home, dense smog had descended over London. Driving the car was out of the question, so we walked home following the wall on the south side of Hyde Park and Kensington Garden. At one point we ran into a man with a thick scarf covering most of his face. He asked us, "Could you tell me the way to London?" The smog was so thick he did not even notice he was already in London. The smog ceased to exist after open nutty coal-burning fireplaces were finally banned.

I definitely wanted to spend some time in Portugal. Of course, I could not go for any length of time without having something specific to do. My good friend, Pedro Theotonio Pereira, the Portuguese Ambassador, came up with a great idea. In those days young girls of good families did not work in Lisbon, but Pedro spoke to the Pakistani High Commissioner in London, and found that he needed a secretary. Seeking to escape England's gray skies, the High Commissioner had requested a position in Portugal, as well. It seemed perfect, except for the requirement that the secretary must speak Portuguese. Pedro insisted I could easily learn the language, so off I went. During the first ten days in Portugal, I stayed with the eldest Palmella daughter, Maria. To help me learn Portugese, I was locked in a roomful of children and heard nothing but their language for days. After this intense schooling, I left to stay with Tareca and Luis Fayal. Luis was the eldest of the Palmella sons, and Tareca was Pedro's niece. Luis ran the 25,000 acre estate for his father. He was an agronomist devoted to modern farming methods, and was the first to establish an eight-hour workday. Moreover, the Fayals gave each of the 250 families residing on the estate two and a half acres of land, free medical care, housing, electricity, water, milk, and olive oil. Their bread was baked for them and their children went to primary school on the property. "Few of our people ever leave, they are like part of the family," Luis Fayal told me.

One Saturday night, Tareca and Luis brought me to a party. I was seated next to Carlos Champalimaud, a happily married man with six children. We talked about airplanes, and I mentioned that I'd taken some aeronautic lessons in France. He invited me to go flying sometime. It sounded fun. Not wanting to worry anyone about my safety, I kept it under my hat. At three o'clock on Sunday afternoon, Carlos picked me up on the Rato. By seven o'clock I was back. Joao, the doorman looked horrified when he opened the door and exclaimed, "Oh Menina!" I mounted the staircase to the second floor and met one of the footmen. He also exclaimed, "Oh, Menina!" I continued up to the bedroom floor where I saw Manuel and asked, "What is the matter with everybody?" Manuel told me that Bernardo, one of the older brothers had seen me get into Carlos's car. I said, "But I only went flying for an hour and, besides, it was so much fun." I was over 27 years old, but apparently, had provoked a big scandal. At Sunday supper nobody spoke to me except for Monsignor who couldn't hear and one of the sons-in-law, Zecas, who was married to my beloved friend Bebinha. Zecas also was very deaf! I certainly learned my lesson! My *faux pax* seemed soon forgotten when the Champalimauds gave an enormous luncheon party in *Marinha*. The 150 guests included King Umberto, the Countess of Barcelona, diplomats and friends from every age group. *Marinha* was a most lovely property. The low, enchanting house was placed among wonderful pines, overgrown with my favorite flowering plant—bougainvillea.

Queen Elizabeth paid a state visit to Portugal early in the year, which put my secretarial skills to the test. My boss, the High Commissioner and the Begum Ikramullah arrived for the visit. Ikramullah asked me to arrange several official visits for him at the Ministry of Foreign Affairs. This put my Portuguese to the test and, trembling, used my best accent and kept talking. I must admit that as soon as Ikram had left the room, I called back to see whether I had made any sense. The answer was—fortunately—positive, and I kept my job. Queen Elizabeth arrived in Lisbon on February 18th. After one stormy day, the sun was shining over the Portuguese Royal Barge, rowed by 80 men, the Praca do Commercio and a parade of uniforms and flags. It was a marvelously colorful scene. The Duke and Duchess of Palmella were part of the festivities. We admired my Favorite Fairy in grand gala and magnificent jewelry. Then the Palmellas gave a big luncheon at *Calhariz*, where the queen went to stay for the weekend. Jose van Zeller Pereira Palha, Tareca's father, also gave an outdoor lunch in the queen's honor at his *Quinta do Cabo* at Vila Franca de Xira. Luis Fayal and Jose Palha were on horseback with several other men of the Portuguese nobility. The men looked arrestingly elegant dressed in black with their wide brimmed black hats. Jose Palha—who was an amateur horticulturist and gentleman cork and bull farmer—looked like Don Quixote as El Greco might have painted him. There were 200 campinhos on horseback, a magnificent and beautifully staged scene. It was obvious that Queen Elizabeth was delighted. These members of the Portuguese aristocracy were as cultivated as they were charming. They all spoke English and French fluently. They thought nothing of flying off to Paris, Madrid or London for clothes, fun or business, and yet they seemed to live in a world of their own.

Vila Franca was up the Tagus, off the road to Santarem. I had driven out with Pedro Theotonio, Paolo da Cunha, the foreign secretary and his wife Dona Maria Amelia. The traffic was heavy so we felt privileged to be in an official car. That night the queen gave a dinner on board the Royal Yacht

Brittania. We were late returning to town, so I went with Pedro to his quaint old pink house in Dafundo to help him put on his decorations. As his car was nowhere to be seen, I hailed a taxi—albeit—a small one. It was quite a sight to see the very tall Pedro with his long legs in the tiny taxi in white tie and tails and decorations! I couldn't help but giggle!

Pedro Teotonio was tall and calm and handsome. I'd never heard him raise his voice and he had a strikingly decisive air. Behind his benign smile was a man who knew what he wanted, and was determined to get it. At 29, he had already become Under-secretary for Labor and Social security. He had been trained in Switzerland and at the University of Lisbon as an economist and mathematician. The legislation—prepared by Pedro as Under-secretary and later, as Minister of Commerce—was an essential factor in the rehabilitation of national finances. This feat revealed his brilliant talent for negotiation, eventually leading him into diplomacy. He was ambassador to Spain before WWII, and in 1945 he was sent to Brazil. He always had great contacts with England and became Ambassador to the Court of St. James in 1953. He ended up serving as ambassador in Washington for three years. Back home again, he became Deputy Prime Minister. He was a devoted father to two daughters and a son, and my very loyal friend. He had given most of his life to public service, but like Dr. Salazar, didn't seek power for its own sake. He loved his yacht *Bellatrix* and ocean racing. The fine points of seamanship fired up his imagination more effectively than personal ambition. It is said that "his strength lay in a detachment unusual among Latin Statesmen. The yachting was only incidental. It reflected a philosophic temperament and a steady nerve. His one public aim was to keep Portugal on the move."

That evening, I went to dinner with Pedro's daughter, Clarinha. We joined other friends to watch the spectacular fireworks from a beautifully situated house on the river. From then on I was considered part of Lisbon's social life. Queen Elizabeth left Lisbon on her *Brittania*. Both my powerful friends, Ikram and Pedro returned to London the same day. Ikram then said to Pedro, "I have left my 'one-man legation' in Lisbon!" It was I, Evelyn Prebensen, the secretary who was left in charge with an office in the Tivoli Hotel!

The Portuguese people are passionately nostalgic. A favorite saluta-
tion is "saudades" which means nostalgia or melancholic longing. Portugal's
emotional preoccupation with the past is part of its charm and a sign of the
people's deep attachment to their land and folklore. This showed in their
devotion to the small, yet striking woman, Amalia Rodrigues—the greatest
of the Fado singers at the time. Accompanied by two guitars, she mourned
the past sadly because it is the past. She sang of a man lost at sea or a gypsy's
unrequited love. She was equally popular with the man in the street as she was
with Lisbon's chic socialites and the titled exiles who had settled near Estoril.
A favorite activity after a dinner party was to go listen to the fados! Life in
Lisbon returned to normal—or *pianissimo*. However, in the Palmella Family,
there was always something going on.

One night *Carnide* (the home of Bebinha and Zecas), suffered a bad
fire. Bebinha was pregnant and had had several miscarriages already. She
escaped out a window, but when she was taken to the hospital, her family
feared the worst. But happily, her pregnancy was not affected and afterward
she stayed with her parents at the Palace in Lisbon. I spent a lot of time with
her. She was exactly my age. When Easter arrived, the doctor decided to
induce the baby, because of prior history. Domingos Palmella and I had gone
to midnight mass at the Irish church as Favorite Fairy was in bed with sciat-
ica. The mass was being said for Bebinha. One could feel the whole church
praying for her. Two minutes before midnight, two of her brothers came into
the church to tell their father that Bebinha had a son and that all was well
with both mother and child! The happy news spread like wildfire. She had so
many friends. I have never heard a more jubilant 'hallelujah' since then. It was
the happiest Easter Sunday I can remember.

Since they had such a large family, the Palmellas gave only a couple
of formal dinner parties during that winter. The first one was in honor of
the British Ambassador, the Stirlings. And a second one was for the Spanish
Ambassador, Nicholas Franco, the Generalissimo Franco's brother who was
smaller. He had a fine beard and was most "simpatico." I was fortunate to
be included in both dinners. The palace glittered from top to bottom. The

four footmen wore knee-breeches and coats. It was all so lovely. Other guests included Antonio Eze de Queroz, The Magalhaes (Bebinha's professor), a Monsieur Salvan from the Gulbenkian foundation, Maria do Tancos, Maria Pinto Cunha. My white wool short evening dress by Balmain and red and gold shawl from India had great success. It gave me confidence and contacts for the events I had to organize for the Pakistanis, both in the summer and the autumn. As always I looked forward to weekends at the Palmellas. One lovely Saturday, Domingos and Maria do Carmo, as well as Bebinha joined me in the garden where I was sketching. Later, Manuel returned around seven. I stayed for dinner, and afterward I was taken out for a movie and a drive under a full moon. We first went to a lovely spot above Lisbon's lights and then to the coast where it was even more beautiful with the waves gently breaking.

When I was first invited to Sintra, I luckily chose a dreamy, clear spring day. I took the train where I was greeted by Caroline di Robilant's husband at the station. He was very tall and elegant and had been one of Italy's most famous pilots. His sister Olga had married the Marquez do Cadaval, and lived on a lovely property outside of Sintra. The wide landscape unfolded below creating a fantastic view. The setting was so beautiful that Bertie Lansberg, who owned the Villa di Malcontenta near Venice, redecorated Olga's neighboring house and made it his permanent residence. (The Cadaval heirs were to receive it—with all the improvements—at the time of Bertie's death). The second time I went to Sintra, Caroline met me at the station. We had lunch with Olga Cadaval before going to the Lansbergs—arriving just in time for a fabulous tour of house and gardens. I have seldom met anyone with such imagination and taste as Bertie Lansberg. The house had a view of both Castelo di Pena and the Atlantic Ocean. There I first met Lady Barkley whose name was Molly. I liked her immediately. She owned a castle in Assisi and a tower in San Gimignano in Italy. Her adopted son played the boy in the film *Never Take No for An Answer* created after the book by Paul Gallico.

At a party for young friends, one of Manuel's friends happened to fall while he was dancing with me. It was not a graceful fall. I went down too and hurt my back. From the time I started working in Portugal, I was supposed to be a paying guest at the home of Regi Hassel, who was an old friend of my parents. The problem was that Regi lived in Estoril and I worked downtown Lisbon, so Tareca came up with the idea I should be a paying guest with her old spinster aunt. None of us had realized that her house had no heating of any kind. It was constantly freezing as she never let in one ray of sunshine for fear of damaging her furniture. On top of that, the aunt lived with a companion who was a witch, and hated me before she'd even met me. Here I was laid up from the fall in terrible surroundings. Noticing my back pain, Manuel, along with two of his siblings were driven to the famous Fatima on May 13th to pray for me and bring back holy water and a blessed medallion. I had already sent a letter of apology to the Norwegian Ambassador for not attending their 17th of May celebration. This holiday is marked with many flags and parades to commemorate the Norwegian constitution of 1814. The day also honors the release of the Union with Sweden in 1905, when the Norwegian people elected Prince Carl of Denmark as their King. He took the name of Haakon VII. In Oslo, grade school children parade through the streets and end up in front of the Royal Palace to greet their King. National costumes are seen all over the country. It is a colorful and happy day of celebration. As soon as the Ambassador had received my note and learned of my living conditions, Consul Stadheim came into town and packed my suitcases. He refused to take no for an answer and immediately brought me to their sunny abode outside town. I was carried from Ingrid Stadheim's home (she was my friend, Lillemor Soveral's sister) and placed on the embassy terrace for the National Day festivities.

What followed, however, was more important. My friend Salvador Soveral—with whom I'd taken drawings lessons at Andor Hubay's studio— turned to me at the reception and said, "Be ready in the morning, we are flying you up to Oporto. I know a fabulous doctor there who will see you." Tell me it was only coincidence, but I believe there is more between heaven and earth than can be explained! The back injury paved the way for more care for my chronic circulatory issue. Our plane thundered towards the north. The landscape below was an intricate pattern of well tilled fields, wide rivers and islets. We were met with the dense, humid fog of the ocean, the grey, dark houses of the turn of the century, and a large bourgeois town that had an English accent. I flew up in the morning and Doctor Frias Fereira insisted I stay for the next three weeks. Lillemor arranged for me to stay with her aunt, Mrs. Wiese's sister out at *Figueria da Foz*—an inviting seaside resort on the coast just outside Oporto.

"The Tripeiros" are very proud of their city and claim that its origin goes back to the creation of the world. It's a town poor in palaces, but rich in churches. Foz de Douro had an immense promenade bordering the sea. On Sundays the population of Oporto came out in droves, by car or otherwise hanging in layers on the outside of the old whining trams. A few black-shawled old women passed along to and from church. Calm elderly gentlemen sat on the pier trying their luck with fishing gear where the water of the river Douro met the Atlantic. It was a God send to stay with the da Silvas at Foz. They all knew Dr. Frias Fereira's treatments. I met with him for six hours a day. It was hard, but I had the weekends off. Alexandre, the youngest of the Palmella boys, was stationed in the army in Oporto and often took me out to dinner. We went to small, cozy French restaurants and had the best time. He had the legendary Palmella charisma, too.

Some three centuries ago during one of the frequent disagreements between England and France, shipments from the port of Bordeaux were blocked, cutting off supplies of Bordeaux wines, for which the English had developed a special taste. Wine merchants searching for solutions had discovered the red wines along the upper regions of the river Douro in Portugal, and began shipping it to England. The merchants found that the wine traveled better and was more popular in England. When mixed with a little brandy, the beverage 'Port' was born. The descendants of these shippers still hold interest in the port trade and though many of these families have lived in Portugal for generations, they remain quintessentially British. They play or watch cricket every Saturday at the Oporto Cricket and Lawn Tennis Club and send their children to English schools. "My family started in the business in 1780," Johnny Graham said over a glass of his own vintage port named

"Churchill." His family's old business was eventually sold to the Symingtons. Apart from carefully culled vintage port, there are three basic types: Tawny, Ruby and White. The white port is a great aperitif wine. Among Portugal's many other wines is "Vinho Verde," inexpensive and refreshing with a simple fish dish and a hunk of fresh bread. In the fields, you can see the peasants reclining in the shade of a cork tree eating handfuls of olives and bread as they drink their local wine. It was among these families that I spent part of my time in Oporto. Since my father was Ambassador in London, I was made to feel very welcome by the English contingent. There was a single track railroad that followed the course of the Douro River. At the Pinhau railway station, detailed tile panels told the story of the area's wine cultivation. Not far away from Foz was the—strongly smelling—fishing village of Matezinhos, as well as the port of Leixoes. Climbing and cascading roses bordered the roads.

Such was my impression of entering the Minho, the most historic area of Portugal. The Moors never went north of Braga. The Minho was colorful and varied, surprisingly rich in original beautifully wrought details. There were green fields and orange groves. And everywhere, like "guirlandes," the climbing vines passed from tree to tree. Vines decorated houses as well. Many delightful, small houses were typically overgrown with vines, and surrounded by magnificent hydrangeas. We caught the last rays of the sun, arriving in late afternoon. A friend of Dick and Lia's joined us for dinner. He was a delightful gentleman of around seventy-five and extremely amusing and entertaining. Friends even came up from Lisbon to distract me and we drove to the handsome city of Guimaraes. Three miles south of it sat the *Casa do Sezim*—seen from a distance—perched half-way up a hill. A long broad verandah with slender columns ran the length of the house, giving it a colonial look. The verandah overlooked a formal garden. The roof had retained its ancient tiles—now rich with patina. It was the home of our friends Ambassador Pinto de Mesquita and his family.

When I returned to Oporto a friend brought me to Nunes Pinto—a very talented dress designer who had worked for several of the big Houses in Paris. I needed something for the upcoming Pakistani festivities. I decided on a raw silk suit and a dress—which had the same print as Princess Grace's dress—and a beige redingote I couldn't resist that would be ideal in London.

That Sunday I received the terrible news that Domingos Palmella had had a stroke. He was taken straight to the hospital when he returned by plane from Paris. Manuel called me every day although the connection was at times atrocious. He told me his father had been unconscious for the first two days, but was somewhat better. However, he had to stay in the hospital for a couple of months.

As for my medical problems, the only thing Dr. Frias Fereira could guarantee was to ease my intense pain. But again, I said to myself, "Never take no for an answer." What Enocksson in Sweden had started, Dr. Frias Fereira more than continued. I had not apprised my parents of my health status in order to shield them from both worry and false hope. But when I realized I was so much a rag that I couldn't even pack my suitcases, I called London for help. "Please mother, could you come and pack my bags, I need you to bring me back to Lisbon." As soon as the words left my mouth I realized I sounded like a spoilt brat, since they did not even know I had gone to Oporto! I explained the situation, and my mother flew down at once. She spoke with Dr. Frias Fereira, and packed my suitcases. Then she thanked the Da Silva family profusely for all they had done for me. After that she took me to the Palace Hotel in Estoril for two weeks. And that did the trick—beach and rest!

After my mother returned to London, I moved to Bebinha and Zecas' at Villa Maria, between Cascais and Estoril for a month. They were the nicest family. And I shall never forget what a wonderful friend Bebinha was. As I have mentioned she was just my age and totally absorbed in her 'Easter' child. She had a superb dressmaker, and we did girlish things together, like having clothes made. She had such great taste.

When I went back to work, my first duty was to arrange an official naval visit. The Pakistanis had acquired their first destroyer, the *Babur*. They were fetching it in England and bringing it by Lisbon. Pakistan and Portugal had a common bond in their political difficulties with India—Pakistan over Kashmir and Portugal over Goa. The official naval visit lasted several days.

The day the *Babur* arrived in Lisbon, I put on my new raw silk suit. As an official representative I was piped on board. And since I was the daughter of a naval officer, I almost died with emotion. I sent my father a telegram to tell him the great news. I was extremely impressed with the *Babur* and its crew—not to mention its captain. He was both very nice and outstandingly handsome. The Ikramullahs came from London for a couple of the engagements. But I was left alone to see the destroyer leave. The night before they left I was invited on board for a drink. The American Naval Attaché and his wife accompanied me as chaperones. I don't think I would have bothered with a chaperone had it been the present day!

I had a few days off after *Babur* departed. I was staying with Lillemor and Salvador Soveral at the time. Lillemor, Gerd, her niece, and I took a trip south. Our first stop was the ancient town of Evora, where the best-preserved Roman temple in Portugal, crowned a hill. I had always wanted to see the Alentejo, since one of my good friends was born there. *Quinta de Nossa Senhora do Carmo* was set in the rolling hills of the eastern Alentejo. Its simplicity of style was typical of the Alentejo's domestic architecture, though its interiors were very luxurious. King Joao IV had built it for one of the ladies of his court. We drove south via Beja and arrived at Faro, the capital of the Algarve, from where we turned west. This southernmost province of Portugal was wildly beautiful, but also very poor due to its infertile soil. Picturesque century-old fishing villages harbored brightly colored wooden fishing boats that brought in their catch. I had brought my sketching pads to capture the beauty. I was so impressed by dramatic rocks surrounding the beach at Praia da Roixa. I wanted to buy some land there. Father thought I was crazy and it came to nothing. The year was 1957. In the early sixties land values had already doubled in the South. Modern hotels were built along the beaches of the Algarve, air service from Lisbon started in the mid sixties and the property owners began to dream of another Riviera in the making. My father was a marvelous man, but never a financial genius!

Back in Lisbon, Mrs. Herbert Scoville, a lovely American lady invited me for tea. She lived at the *Quinta da Bacalhoa* situated on the Arrabida peninsula. It was one of Portugal's old surviving palaces—set in a rural area—known not only for its grapes and olive oil. Narrow roads twist through a patchwork of pine and eucalyptus forests and ancient groves of shimmering grey-green olive and cork oak trees. Built at the end of the 15th century, it was a mixture of Italian renaissance with touches of Moorish influences. King Manuel I commissioned it for his mother. It fell into ruin. Albuquerque created this estate, but died without children in 1581. After years of various owners and tribulations, on a 1935 trip to search for azulejos, Mrs. Scoville came across an innumerable collection of tiles at this palace. "Every room of the palace and every corner of the garden had azulejos with designs of seemingly inexhaustible variety," she wrote. She fell in love with Bacalhoa, bought it and lovingly restored what she called her "Museum of faience, softened by flowers and trees." Passing through the gate, one entered a large square courtyard. The house itself sat across the courtyard to the left where an imposing staircase led up to the "piano nobile." From the columned loggia was a lovely view of the verdant and enchanting garden. In one part of the garden, a pool was flanked on one side by an elegant pavilion with walls that were tiled in a Moorish pattern of green and yellow. Mrs. Scoville saved the garden. Bougainvillea and roses scaled the walls. Amazing flowers crowded the raised beds. The famous garden designer, Russell Page, wrote in an article: "For sheer boldness and simplicity of plan, the garden is one of the most striking in all of European art." We had our tea in the columned loggia!

As the summer turned to fall, we started on the work for the upcoming State visit of the President of Pakistan, General Iskander Mirza. Ikramullah, 'my' High Commissioner had asked me to stay for it. I begged for a diplomat to come to my aid. We also needed a cypher specialist, but when he finally arrived, he had forgotten to bring his books! A very pleasant and intelligent Pakistani diplomat, Aslam Malik, did arrive with a beautiful wife, but he came so late that I had had to make rather important decisions before his arrival. Fortunately for me he was in full agreement, in spite of my being a woman. I had been given special help at the Portuguese Department of Foreign Affairs, not to mention the NATO office. The British Embassy was also of immense help. I could not complain. But certain specific problems turned up. We had asked for the music to the Pakistani National anthem. The notes for the music only arrived in Lisbon a couple of days before the visit, and it was for a hundred man brass band! I had arranged for an Italian dance band to play at the banquet. I had even rented tuxedos for them. Ikram did not approve, but it was too late. Fortunately for me the Italians came through on the National Anthem. The Pakistan Presidential party consisted of The President and The Begum, The minister of Interior, Mir Ghulam Talpur, the Commander-in-Chief of the Air Force, Air Vice Marshall Ashgar Khan, Mr. And Mrs. Hajid Ali, Mrs. Abdul Quadir, Chef de Protocole, Brigadier Mirza Hamid Hussain, Chief of the Military Household, Colonel Nawazich Khan, Aide de Camp, S.A. Ahmed and Mrs. Ahmed, Mr. Quereshi and Mr. Pir Mahfuz Ilahi. It took me some time to learn the names of the party. They were all being put up at the Queluz Palace. The Portuguese found various difficulties in their arrangements and in the end begged for me to stay at Queluz too. The first evening we had a pleasant dinner at Queluz. Even though I did not understand a word of Urdu, the atmosphere was great. Then we were off to San Carlo, the opera house. I was seated in a box with the Pakistani Chief of Protocol and Pir Mahfuz Ilahi, which really made the performance even more colorful. Back at the Queluz over soft drinks, I had a talk with Jorge. The colonel waited up, and various things were organized before bedtime at 2 a.m. The next morning started at 6 a.m. What a life! Every night I had to move furniture in front of my door to block unwelcome entry, as there was a slight misunderstanding about my duties! Jorge Braga de Oliveira, my friend from the NATO office, was staying in the next room. I would knock a signal on his wall and he would immediately call me on the phone to interrupt any secret nocturnal visits.

That morning the rain poured down, and the program for the day had to be changed. No air display could take place. We ended up sightseeing in Alcobaca and Batalha in the morning, and then took in the military parade. The ladies instead had lunch at Quinta da Torres, and went touring across the river at Arrabida. When the invitations went out from the Portuguese

President, for his State visit Dinner, I learned they used lists of family names that went back to before the times of titles. The response was that so-and-so died several hundred years ago. So, for the Pakistani President's party I borrowed friends' wedding lists and added every title I could find, and everyone turned up. Since we had no residence in Lisbon, the Portuguese Government kindly allowed us to give the official dinner at the Queluz Palace. We had one hundred people seated for the party, with the responsibility of seating arrangements falling on me. Terrified, I borrowed an ingenious "table-placer" from the Portuguese protocol office—and it worked.

Queluz was a royal summer palace in the hills outside Lisbon. The transformation of an old manor house, which existed on the site, into a palace had begun in 1747, but in the end it was developed along the lines of Marly, Louis XIV's woodland retreat. The palace reception rooms opened directly onto a terrace surrounding a sunken box parterre with two rococo fountains. William Beckford stopped at the Queluz gardens one evening after a visit to the Alcobaca monastery. He met the Infanta, daughter of the king, and later wrote, "Cascades and fountains were in full play; a thousand sportive *jets d'eau* were sprinkling the rich masses of bay and citron drawing forth all their odors, as well-taught water is certain to do on all such occasions. Among the thickets, some of which received a tender light from tapers placed low on the ground under frosted glasses, the Infanta's nymph-like attendants, all thinly clad after the example of her royal and nimble self, were glancing to and fro, visible one instant and invisible the next." We had "son et lumiere," and that was how I would want to remember *my* remarkable evening. When the day arrived for the Pakistani president's party, as I mentioned, the band had been able to manage the anthem. I thought all was in order until I discovered that the cigars and case of brandy had been left behind at the office. Queluz was 20 kilometers from Lisbon. With some quick thinking, I asked head of the secret police—whom I knew—to send some officers to fetch the forgotten items. The dense crowds outside the palace made it impossible for our cars to pass. He agreed. All the guests were entering through the side door by the Cozinha Velha, except for the Portuguese President, the Cardinal and Dr

Salazar who were arriving via the front entrance. We were already lined up inside the hall to receive Dr Salazar at ten minutes to nine, the Cardinal at five to nine and the Portuguese President on the hour. Dr. Salazar arrived and we were all introduced, after which he passed into another room. Then—to my horror—just then, the case of brandy was being pushed through the front door. There was no time to remove it, so I quickly had it stuffed under the train of my evening dress. The Cardinal arrived. But I forgot I had to genuflect and smacked my foot hard on the brandy case. Stifling my pain, as soon as the Cardinal was out of sight, I shuffled backwards, scooting the case till I reached another exit. With two seconds remaining—despite two sore heels—I found my place to welcome the President of Portugal. Phew!

The Duke and Duchess of Palmella joined the official guests at the Banquet. Their presence renewed my courage, as I was extremely nervous about the seating and the playing of the National Anthem during the meal. The music sounded all right, thank God, even though Ikram had requested a military band. I wondered if he would mention it later. The rest of the Palmella family arrived elegantly dressed and wearing lovely jewelry, ready for the special reception to follow. The main guests left shortly after the banquet, but not until Dr. Salazar complimented me on the success of the party (while in the company of the Palmellas)! I was greatly encouraged and gratified. When the President of Pakistan, the Cardinal and Salazar had left, President Iskander Mirza sent for me and asked, "Do you think the band could play 'Happy Birthday?'" It happened to be his birthday. President Mirza, the Begum and the younger guests danced well into the early hours. The guests included: the Carnides, the Campilhos, the Bellos, the Faials, the Mendias, the Vilas Boas, the Soverals, the Stadheims, (Ingrid Stadheim was responsible for the Emerald Green gala-dress with the train that had hid the Brandy case earlier in the evening), the de Murcas, the Soares Francos, the Schonborn-Wiesentheids, Jose Pulida Garcia, Madalena and Leonor de Lancastre, Manuel de Braganca, the Pinto Bastos' and many more. Of course, it meant so much to have Pedro, Manuel, Zinha and Alexandre Palmella there with me. It was a colorful and beautiful sight—an evening I will never forget. There was no mention of any 'mistake' regarding the musicians.

We gave an official luncheon for thirty-five people at *Seteais*, the lovely palace outside Sintra. Before we left *Queluz* I brought the Begum to the small salon of Dona Maria Francisca Benedita, Princess of Brazil (1746-1829). The salon was decorated in a light Neo-classical style including mirrored doors and *trompe-l'oeil* on the domed ceiling. It was such a gracious room. I loved the week I spent at the palace. While there I accompanied the presidential party—this time dressed in gala blue—to an event given by the Portuguese President. I also attended every sightseeing trip as well as the Military Parades, which I loved.

As exciting as these events were, they were equally exhausting, and I soon found myself back in Oporto at Dr. Frias Fereira's office. While residing at the Aviz Hotel, I suddenly contracted the worst triple ear infection which developed into mild meningitis. My hotel-room maid, named Aida, took phenomenal care of me. There were a few days where I was not even conscious, and just lay there with a silk chiffon scarf around my head. Dr. Frias Fereira sent the specialist, Dr. Jose de Sousa Campos. I shall never forget how he sat up with me for two nights. Somehow, I survived and I shall never forget any of them. They finally got me up on my feet.

I packed and was set off on a plane for London. Father and his Ambassadorial car drove right in on the tarmac and picked me up. Those were the days! What a wonderful thing to have friends and family.

The following year, before we moved to Italy, I stopped for a check-up with Dr. Frias Fereira. Both Manuel and Alexandre Palmella were at the Lisbon Airport to ensure my safety as I changed planes to Oporto. Sadly, this happened to be the last time I would see the great doctor before he died, as it was several years before I could return. But in the early sixties, I got another opportunity to go to Lisbon. A friend in Rome got wind of my trip and asked me to bring a wedding gift to Prince Juan Carlos with the promise to personally deliver it into the hands of his sister, Dona Pilar. I agreed, but wanted to know why such a fuss. He explained that when he—the great

Principe Lancelotti—had sent a telegram to Athens, Greece for the official engagement, he had received a 'thank you' note addressed to Mr. Maccelaio (Butcher) and was mortally offended. Then he asked, "How come you are so sure you can see Dona Pilar?" "I told you I would do it; I am not telling you how. It is rude even to doubt me," I said. I knew that Dona Pilar daily lunched with the Palmellas at their palace in Lisbon while she was taking a course in nursing! And I was staying at the palace for some days. Giovanni's wedding gift for the Royal wedding—which I brought on the plane with me from Rome—was a book that weighed twenty pounds. At least he had given me the courtesy of a lift to the Rome airport!

The Castle S. Jorge has the most superb view of the river. The Tejo Tagus offers life and beauty to Lisboa and sailors from far off lands. It gives the daily bread to a great part of the city's population, through commerce, shipping and fisheries. The Tagus River is the Princess' lover—an ever-present and jealous one. He shows himself violent when he throws temper tantrums, but also loving as he caresses the quays. As a generous lover, he has given Lisboa a great fortune: one of the most valuable ports in Europe. For more than four centuries the Tower of Belem has watched this great love story. The renowned Castel S. Jorge Back, Lisboa's tiara, was where the Moors resisted the violent attacks of Afonso Henriques for four long months. One can still see the gate where Martin Moniz died, and baptized Lisboa a Christian with his blood. "Lisboa Moderna, Lisboa Antiga…"[5] The city with its flowers, pastel colors and beautiful iron works serves as Europe's balcony towards the open seas, the neighboring continents, and perhaps the future. One of the most beautifully situated capitals is reigning on seven hills. "One must either have an Alpine stick or a full purse," an old Irishman once said to me. And how right he was! The streets are covered in cobblestones, a punishment for high heels. In the mornings the *varinhas*—barefoot women with flat baskets of fish on their heads, and their clogs on top of the fish—walk the streets and shout in a shrill voices to advertise their wares. They are joined by small donkeys tripping along, pulling their yellow carts. The Spanish knife grinders walk the streets as well. The trams whine down the streets and the oldest taxis cough their way up the steep and narrow ruas. My favorite square is Terreiro do Paco. It was especially lovely the day Queen Elizabeth arrived on an official visit riding a barge rowed by 80 men. In addition to the colors, the banners and flags, 6000 men of the armed forces had been assembled on the square to greet her, while a band of the Royal cavalry trotted slowly past the royal party.

The River Tagus passes one of the most beautiful churches I know called the *Madre de Deus*. Founded by the pious Queen Leonor—wife of D. Joao II, and sister of the brilliant King Manuel—it has the loveliest cloister and most superb azuleijos. The chapel is richly decorated with wood carvings, gold and marble as well as Portuguese primitives and relics. A little further out the river meets the ocean. The temperamental and grandiose Atlantic rages and throws enormous waves with incredible force against the rocky coastline…Saudades!

In 1984, my husband Billy gave my daughter, Alexandra a graduation present. She chose a trip to Europe as her gift. We stopped in Italy and France first, and then crossed the border to Spain, hugging the Mediterranean coastline. Scenic and white, Cadaques had retained its old flavor with small boats dotting the sea. Slowly, we continued along the Costa Brava's rugged coast, etched by cliffs and inlets. Barcelona, Spain's second largest city, and capital of Catelonia, was counted as an architectural jewel—with its Barri Gotic and modernista turn-of-the-century style. From Barcelona we turned inland to Lleida, then to Zaragoza, the capital of Aragon, from where we continued toward Madrid. About 80 kilometers before Madrid, near Seguenza, we turned off on a smaller road to the west. It ran on the mesa for a while and then dipped down into a valley. I called it the "Valley of Shangrila." My old childhood friend, Turid and her husband Javier had remodeled an old mill in the valley. They had collected antique doors and window frames from all over Spain and turned the mill into an utterly enchanting weekend cottage. My architect husband loved it and was very impressed. We had a divine time.

We met up with our dear old friend Adele Emery in Madrid. She insisted on renting a car from there on. She knew Billy thought her a dangerous driver, but she did not want him to drive either. The responsibility fell on my shoulders to drive—much to Alexandra and Elizabeth's great amusement, especially in a Latin country where men usually do the driving. Going south we went by Cordoba and hurried on to Seville. We passed a few lovely days before crossing the border to Portugal. Ever since an earthquake reduced the Castel San Jorge to a golden shell, it became inhabited by black ravens, white swans and peacocks and two old tortoises. At its feet lay the part of town called Alfama. This enclave has kept its atmosphere of former days with steep, narrow slippery streets filled with children, stray cats, guitar players and street vendors. Alfama was a mixture of sailors and workmen. But sprinkled in were blacks, pirates, and travel-weary seamen. But if Alfama's streets were poor, its churches were very ornate. Alfama has retained its Arab name since the Seigneurs of Alcova took their summer residences there, enjoying the air of the sea and the Tagus. I showed my family and Adele Emery what I had come to love, from the beaches beyond Cascais, to the Alfama and everything in between. Best of all, we had been invited to lunch at Calhariz on the other side of the Tagus. The duchess, my Favorite Fairy was holding court and both Adele and Billy were enchanted. Not to mention, my two daughters who were so happy to meet the younger generation. Billy immediately adored the duchess and never forgot her.

More than half a century has passed since I first went to Portugal, but I remember every detail as if it were yesterday.

Morocco – A Thousand and One Nights
MALACHITE EGG

Between the 8th and 13th centuries, Moroccan sovereignty extended from the Atlantic to the Gulf of Sirte and from the southern reaches of the Western Sahara to the Ebro Valley in Al-Andalus land, now known as Andalusia. The 40-year long French Protectorate in Morocco had divided Morocco into two parts: French Morocco and Spanish Morocco. The French Protectorate ended in 1956 and Morocco returned to being one country.

Prince Moulay Ben El Mehdi Alaoui, the Viceroy of Tetouan, Spanish Morocco, was sent as Moroccan ambassador to the Court of St. James in London. His wife, Princess Lalla Fatimah Zohra, was the daughter of Sultan Abd-el-Aziz. The sultan had refused to accept the French proposal in 1916. He, therefore, was exiled first to France and later to the Freeport of Tangiers on the African mainland. Prince Moulay Abd-El-Aziz lived in gentlemanly retirement in Tangiers surrounded by the remnants of his extensive harem until he died in 1943. Lalla Fatimah Zohra, his only daughter, had been given a modern education; first, at the Italian school and then at the French college. Her father supervised her education and instilled in her the idea that she would one day serve her country.

He also found a husband for his daughter—Prince Moulay Ben El Mehdi Alaoui—who was the previously mentioned Viceroy of Spanish Morocco, and also happened to be Lalla Fatimah Zohra's cousin. After their wedding, they lived in the Mexuar Palace in Tetuan and had one daughter named Lalla Keltum. During her stay in London, Princess Lalla Fatima Zohra and I had become close friends—partly due to our many common interests. She loved the theater, ballet and art as much I did. She loved shopping for elegant European clothes, and enjoying the freedom that life offered in London. In 1958, Lalla Fatima Zohra planned her very first trip to the former French Morocco to visit her cousins in the Imperial Cities. She invited me to come with her on this most adventurous trip. It was an invitation I could not refuse and, while initially hesitant to consent, my parents fortunately agreed to it. I had to go to Portugal anyway to see the doctor for my chronic circulatory problems. Here, again my lifetime ailments led me on a trip that many say is truly unbelievable. To have spent more than three months with princes and princesses in palaces of such grandeur was an unrepeatable experience—especially by today's standards.

To me, North Africa always had a "Maghreb," or African feel, even though it had been deeply influenced by the Islamic east and Europe. Before the time of Christ, the Romans arrived in Morocco followed by the Spanish and the French who remained in power for more than 40 years. The Imperial Cities were Fez, Marrakech, Meknes and Rabat. The latter housed the royal palace and various compounds accommodating the sultan and his entourage.

The first city, Fez, was founded in the early 9th century by Idriss Ibn Abdallah and his son Moulay Idriss. It was modeled after the main centers of the Islamic civilization, i.e., Baghdad in the reign of the Abassid Dynasty and Damascus under the Umayyad Dynasty. The second Imperial City, Marrakech, was built of dried mud. It was a Saharan creation of 11th-century Sultan Yusuf ibn Tashufin, who hailed from the outskirts of the desert and planted a palm grove of more than 80,000 trees. Meknes, the third city, was built amidst olive and fruit trees. Moulay Ismail, brother of the founder of the Alawite Dynasty, Moulay Rashid, made it into his fortress and capital in the 17th century. Rabat was the fourth of the Imperial Cities and the capitol of Morocco. It was a Carthaginian trading post that became a Roman colony known as Sala Colonia. It stood on the site of present day Shella at the junction of three entities: the city of Sala, the Rabat headland and the Andalusia city. The Imperial cities were among the places I was invited to visit, and about which I was very excited.

At the end of the summer of 1958, I flew from London to Gibraltar. The 16-seat propeller-driven airplane left Gibraltar for its twelve-minute crossing of the Strait. The brief flight was the proud boast of British Airways because it operated the world's shortest intercontinental flight. We touched down in Tangiers between the gate of Hercules on the European shore, and Djebel Moussa on the African shore.

Father had sent a telegram to the princess with my arrival time, but there was no one to meet me at the airport. I was surrounded with Arabic-speaking people. I finally found an interpreter and asked him to telephone the royal residence where also only Arabic was spoken. However, the interpreter understood that I was to proceed to the great mansion on the *Vieille Montagne* or Old Mountain. I found a taxi, whose driver did not believe I was really going to the *House on the Mountain*, as the locals called it. He drove around the area for some time, before I finally convinced him to actually climb the driveway. The villa was situated at the very top of the mountain above Tangiers with a superb city view, including the bay and the strait. We stopped in front of the villa's large front door. The driver insisted I pay him before he let me out. Then he proceeded to throw out the suitcases and sped off. I didn't know what to do because I had not yet seen a living soul. In fact, I wasn't even sure if I was at the right place.

After the taxi disappeared down the hill, however, the imposing front door opened, and several women dressed in pastel-colored robes appeared. The women greeted me in Arabic as my luggage disappeared into the house. I was then invited into a lovely garden where they served me mint tea. I was later told this was the ceremony of hospitality. A tray was brought in carrying three boxes, one with sugar, one with mint leaves and the third with tea. A second tray contained glasses and a metal teapot. The tea was always made in front of the guests. They all chatted with me but, unfortunately, I didn't understand a word. Nor did I have the foggiest idea where my friend was or whether it actually was her house! After a while, they realized I might be tired from traveling, and they brought me upstairs to a grand European bedroom with a large bathroom. There was also a small salon with large windows facing the sea. It had the best view of the strait and the lights of Gibraltar beyond.

The Rock of Gibraltar has flown the British flag since 1704 when it was first hoisted on the tower of an ancient, Moorish castle. The Phoenicians named the Rock one of the Pillars of Hercules. Despite its barren aspect, Gibraltar grows a great range of flora and fauna. There are palms, jacaranda, lavender, clematis and honeysuckle, not to mention native orchids. Thousands of migrating birds use the rock as a stopping point on their flights between Europe and Africa. The area's famous monkeys without tails are the only primates living wild on the continent of Europe. Legend has it that if the apes leave the Rock, the British will lose Gibraltar!

A wonderful older woman, whom I later found out was Turkish, had already unpacked my bags for me. But I did not speak Turkish either, so I knew not a thing more about my surroundings. However, it did appear that I was expected, so I calmed down a bit, cleaned up and changed my clothes. As darkness descended and lights popped up here and there, some women brought me a delightful dinner and a basin and a jug of hot water with which to wash. They also brought forks and knives, which they typically don't use, and dropped them on the table. I felt like I was in a goldfish bowl as they stayed to watch me eat.

After dinner, a woman finally arrived from the former Vice-Royal Palace in Tetouan. She spoke Spanish. At last I understood that Lalla Fatima Zohra's mother had received my father's telegram, though she could not read it and just left it with the incoming mail. The sultan, King Mohammed V, had called Lalla Fatima Zohra to come to Rabat to help in an advisory capacity. She would be back in a couple of days!

This was how my North African fairytale began on a dark southern night. That night the moon was almost full and the wind was blowing hard outside, but inside all was silent and peaceful. Unlike during the day you could hear the wail of the muezzin—the men calling the faithful to prayer five times a day from the countless minarets.

The next morning, I woke up to brilliant sunshine and a cool breeze whistling through the trees. The bougainvillea and the greenery looked splendid against the shiny white walls. The elderly Turkish woman turned out to be my personal maid. While I was still in bed, she served me a breakfast of sweet coffee, a rich variety of breads and sweet cookies. My clothes were laid out for me, freshly cleaned and pressed. I took a long leisurely time dressing. Arabian music sounded beneath my windows, and dogs barked in the distance.

A book about Morocco on my nightstand inspired me to learn about the fascinating country. I read that along Morocco's eastern border, the vast deserts are crisscrossed by oeds and oases, and along Morocco's western seaboard, the Atlantic coast stretched as far as the eye could see from Cape Spartel in the south to the custom posts of Nouadhibou, with its age-old Portuguese and Spanish fortified towns. To the north, seafaring folk came up against the dense and shady Rif mountain ranges, the citadel of resistance soaring above the Mediterranean, from Tetouan to the Spanish enclave, Melilla. Scythe-like slashes were created by the Berber mountains, the plateaus of the Middle Atlas, with their harsh, rugged solemnity above Fez. The snow-capped peaks of the High Atlas, visible from Marrakech, arose sheer out of the Haouz plains; and the arid ridges of the Anti-Atlas stood tall as though to guard the first approaches to the Sahara. Tangier is the tip of Morocco that reaches out and almost touches Europe.

On my second day, I visited the ruins at Volubilis, and was most impressed with their central heating system and running water baths. It had been ravaged by vandals in 429 AD, and little was left of the Roman town save a few Corinthian columns.

Lalla Fatima Zohra was still away that second afternoon, so the Spanish-speaking driver took me sightseeing. We went to the Casbah and the Medina—the Muslim quarter of Tangier. The houses boasted beautifully carved ceilings and doorways. Pillars and walls were covered with attractive multi-colored tiles. He also showed El Minsah, the most luxurious hotel in town, which featured a spacious patio, and beautiful tiles and mosaics on the walls and staircases. Marvelously situated in the middle of town, the hotel—previously a private residence—had a splendid view of the sea. Our driver passed homes of present and former luminaries, including Tennessee Williams, Aaron Copeland, Henri Matisse and Barbara Hutton. My friend, Lord David Herbert, a charming English aristocrat who had lived in Tangier since the thirties, chronicled their lives and scandals from the Duchess of Windsor to Malcolm Forbes.

Later that afternoon, I was introduced to the princess' mother, who suggested they take me to the souk—the Moroccan market. The rush of spicy aromas, raucous cries of the people and colorful fabrics made the souk magical. My shopping companions were all dressed in drab, grey djellabas and dense, white silk veils, as were many other Moroccan women in the marketplace. They looked like big grey birds. I had great difficulty identifying which group was mine and it was also easy to get lost in the maze of lanes. The sweet-scented spirit of the souk proved a mesmerizing experience as much for the ladies as for me, because they rarely left the villa.

Monetary exchange consisted of not only Moroccan francs, but Spanish pesetas as well. It has been said that the souk is an institution and should not be reduced to some historical memory. It is like a magnet that pulls the people of the "bled" together and serves as a forum for city merchants. The weekly festivals are essential to Morocco's rural life.

Colorful tiles adorned both interior and exterior walls of the houses in the Casbah, part of the Arab Tangier. Decorative stone work embellished roofs and arches, and framed carved wooden doors. Street signs were written in Arabic, Spanish and French.

In spite of the language challenge, my lovely group of women took great care of me. We all had a wonderful time. When we returned to the villa, however, the women vanished without a word. I was left behind in the car with the driver who, fortunately, spoke Spanish. When I asked what had happened, he explained that Lalla Fatima's stepson had arrived for tea with some friends, and that Moroccan women could not be seen by men. So, I entered the drawing room alone pondering how much I had to learn!

Since the visiting prince and his friends had been educated in Spain at the Military Academy of Saragossa, they spoke Spanish. This was a welcomed break for me after these first few strange and somewhat solitary days. The boys told me how Tangier's schools and mosques were built as early as 707 AD, making the city an ideal check-point for Muslim Spain and the Kingdom of Morocco. They said the Portuguese made it their home for over a hundred years until the Spanish ousted them after the "Battle of the Three Kings." The English then occupied it before they were driven out by Moulay Ismail in 1684. This pleasant interlude of tea and conversation settled my state of mind.

Until the beginning of the 20th century, Tangier was the diplomatic gateway to Morocco. This was where the sultan had assembled the various consulates of the coast from as far away as Mogador. It became an international zone for years and still is a free port. The foreign population has grown to include not only the accepted diplomatic group, but also a mini-society of journalists and writers, like Mark Twain and Alexandre Dumas. Famous painters, composers and celebrities such as Barbara Hutton and my rather eccentric friend, Lord David Herbert, and a host of others spiced up the mixture. A French writer once described Tangiers and wrote about a metropolis of more than a million people where illegal immigrants rub shoulders with lovers of all that is not quite "above board." Someone also wrote, "Tangier is an essentially anachronistic city, it is always a survival of something, precisely when that something no longer exists, or one no longer manages to put a name to it." It is nostalgic for the dream city of yesterday." This was the city in which I found myself when Princess Lalla Fatima returned from Rabat, and life returned to normal.

On her first day back, we lunched with the princess' husband, the ambassador and his family at his house in the part of Tangier called Shakespeare. There I met two of his previous wives and two more of his sons. Lalla Fatima Zohra, being a royal princess was the official wife. As I mentioned, she and the former viceroy had a daughter, Lalla Keltum. The ambassador's handsome house stood inside tall walls, and the interior was furnished in Moroccan style with comfortable sofas along the inside walls, and large cushions strewn about. On top of the house was a room with a stupendous view of the strait towards Spain, the Atlantic Ocean toward the west, and the Mediterranean Sea toward the east.

When we returned to the *Villa on the Mountain,* we received a visit from the Jalifat of Marrakech who was touring Tangier. The Jalifat was Lalla Fatima's uncle. He was so strict that his 50 year-old daughter did not dare have tea with us without his permission. This is so hard to imagine nowadays! Another day we drove about 60 kilometers over a desolate mountain road until we passed the customs house between the territory of the free ports of Tangiers and Morocco. A short time later we arrived in Tetouan, a city unlike any other in Morocco. In the late 15th century, Moorish and Jewish refugees from Spain built the city on the rocky slope of a mountain. They drew upon the finest traditions of Andalusian architecture. As a result, the medina, or old quarter, was filled with beautifully designed homes that featured tile roofs and elaborate wrought iron balconies reminiscent of the old Moorish towns in southern Spain.

We left the car in Plaza Espana and walked through a maze of narrow passages until we arrived at an ornate, heavily carved wooden door. Here we left the bustle of the world behind. We were led through a dark passage into a sunlit atrium. A fountain played in the middle of the patio—the hub of home life. On the opposite wall was a wide alcove, slightly raised from the patio level. The perimeter, as usual, held low, comfortable sofas with oriental rugs and pillows. Doors and shutters were painted in bright colors and a staircase led to an upper floor gallery. Upstairs, several handsome salons, beautifully furnished, opened up one after another. Large mirrors with multi-colored frames, precious brocades and Oriental wall-hangings adorned the walls. Venetian chandeliers of great value hung in every room.

We were at the home of one of Lalla Fatimah's greatest friends. A low table was brought in and placed in a corner of a small salon. Once we were seated on comfortable cushions around the table, lunch was served. We enjoyed an exquisite meal while I was given my first lesson in Moroccan eating customs. I sat on my left hand to remind myself that I could only eat with three fingers on my right hand. It took me quite a while to get used to eating this way. But, eventually I became quite proficient. The other guests spoke Spanish, which was very helpful. Homemade bread came in a basket with a pyramid-shaped lid. Course after course of heavenly smelling food covered with the same kind of lid was served and placed in the middle of the table. Everyone partook from the same plate. The first course was a delicious fish in an onion sauce served with eggplant in vinaigrette. The second course was chicken in saffron. Each person tore a piece of their bird, which was complicated with only three fingers. The third course was apples cooked with cinnamon served over meat. For the last course they served melon, grapes, pineapple and finally, Turkish coffee. Afterward, we lay on sofas and gossiped away the afternoon. This magnificent, tasteful, Moroccan house breathed an atmosphere of peace and tranquility.

Eugene Delacroix was the French painter who had been deeply impressed by the great beauty of Morocco. As a primary leader of French Romanticism, he visited the country for six months in 1832. While there, he filled seven notebooks with sketches and notes. He transformed the sketches into oils during the rest of his life. John Singer Sargent, the famous American also was inspired by his travels to Morocco. After lunch, I, too, sketched my surroundings before I was brought to see the vice-royal palace, where Lalla Fatimah had lived with her husband, the viceroy, and their daughter.

The Moorish part of Tetuan was behind the palace. Some streets offered only shoemakers, while others had a variety of craftsmen. Women from the mountains sat in the market square selling their goods. They were dressed in white with red woolen scarves around their waists and enormous straw hats on their heads, the brims kept up by colored woolen cords. Workers sat cross-legged in the doorways of their tiny shops as darkness fell. Lamps were lit in the evenings, and the town teemed with activity. Behind the palace, the souks—the Bab El Rouah gate and the Place de l'Oussa with its lovely fountain and vine-covered trellises—were popular tourist spots.

Once, during our stay in Tangier, we had an eleven-hour long lunch with the Caid of Alcazar-el-Quivir. He lived with four wives—some of which were ten years apart. The wives seemed quite congenial toward each other. They never stopped chattering with Lalla Fatima Zohra in Arabic, so I took the opportunity to bring out my sketchbook and had a field day sketching everything and everyone in the palace. They all loved my sketching, but when I tried to bring out my camera, it was different story as I was met with some hostility. A large fountain was placed in the middle of the garden and palm trees stood guard in the corners. The palm trees were referred to as

Mohammed, the prophet's "blessed tree." The Swedish botanist, Linnaeus, considered the palm to be the "prince of the plant world," and it has thrived in that part of the world for thousands of years.

When Lalla Fatima Zohra returned from Rabat, she brought an invitation to go and stay with Princess Lalla Aicha. Lalla Aicha was King Mohammed V's eldest daughter. The visit with her began our great journey through Morocco. We left Tangier one afternoon in a Volkswagen Beetle. Lalla Fatimah—in her blue linen djellaba and a pink silk veil—drove and her bodyguard, in his djellaba and fez, sat in the back seat. I had managed to get a couple of comfortable A-line cotton dresses to wear to enable me to sink gracefully to the floor. The route ran along the sea and some orange groves. It was evening by the time we reached Rabat, where a cluster of white buildings lay like seashells along the magnificent beaches of the Atlantic Ocean. That was when Lalla Fatima Zohra realized she had forgotten to bring the daily password necessary to enter the royal residences. We had to drive over to the youngest princess' house (she was five) where security was less strict.

Finally, we returned to Lalla Aicha's villa with the correct password and were warmly welcomed. It was almost midnight, but Lalla Aicha had postponed supper till we arrived. In her garden, there was a long pool with a loggia at the other end, which looked like a mini Taj Mahal. A full moon lit the fairytale scene. We were seated around a huge engraved, polished brass tray set on legs to make a circular table. Servants carried our supper on their heads in tajines. A tajine is a glazed earthenware dish, consisting of a shallow platter and a pointed, hat-shaped lid. We ate Chicken Tajine, made with almonds, lemons, prunes and a long list of spices such as coriander, cumin and saffron. Couscous was served and we drank grape juice and finished off the meal with luscious fruit.

This area of the city, called Sala Colonia, was built on the right bank of the Bou Regre. It was a vast medina from the 11th century encircled by ochre walls. Bab-el-Mrisa, "the gate of the little harbor," was designed to let boats and vessels through. Pirates set up their lair in New Sala, which is present-day Rabat built on the outer bank. Rabat was named for the rock of the

Oudaias. The Moors, fleeing from Extremadura in 1608, found refuge in the old casbah, which was now a hive of tourism. Rabat, being the Capital and seat of the King, was also a busy center. The Sultan of Morocco is the symbol of national unity, and is responsible for the administration of his subjects, as well as military Commander-in-Chief. But, he is also "Caliph," the successor of the prophet Mohammed, and the defender of the faith.

One day, we went to a lunch in Lalla Fatima's honor at the Minister of Communications' magnificent villa, about 20 kilometers outside of Rabat. We ate while lying on mattresses around a luxurious swimming pool. The minister was dressed in an odd, striped pajama jacket, an off-white robe, Moroccan wide trousers and slippers. Then, on the Sunday, Lalla Aicha gave a huge luncheon. Her younger brother, Prince Moulay Abdallah came with his friends. The party also included some of the younger diplomats and lasted until late afternoon. This put us off schedule because we had planned to go to Casablanca that day. Luckily, Moulay Abdallah offered us not only his house in Casablanca, but also insisted he drive us there in his fast, white Cadillac. Like all good Muslims he did not drink any form of alcohol so I did not realize what we were in for. The drive only took the prince 35 minutes, in spite of the fact that it was a 100 kilometers between the two cities! At one point I wondered aloud speeding so and encountering traffic. Moulay Abdullah quietly commented, "Don't worry, I told the police to clear the road." "What about the black pigs?" I asked innocently. "Do you have them under police control too?" We all shard a good laugh and somehow, arrived safely in Casablanca at 1:30 in the morning. Moulay Abdullah left us at his very nice bachelor house just outside town, and then drove the long distance back to Rabat in the dark with his friend, Farim Rachid.

In the morning, we awoke to delicious coffee before Moulay Abdallah told us about a whole day of sightseeing he'd planned. He had arranged for the police to come and collect us later that morning. Who better to show us around Rabat than the police? Their presence granted us admittance to any place of interest. They escorted us through neighborhoods where flaming bougainvilleas covered modern villas. We took in magnificent vistas and drove along palm-lined boulevards and the waterfronts. We visited the port and town center and even the "Prefecture," or police headquarters. From the Prefecture's tall tower, we had a marvelous view of the "quatres coins," or four corners of Casablanca. We admired the magnificent arches and mosaics of the Tribunal (courthouse), as well as many other wonders of the exciting port city. I imagined the *Casablanca*-esque atmosphere during WWII—full of spies from both sides in the casbahs and bars. France's Marechal Lyautey called this city the "New York" of Morocco.

After a delightful lunch at the restaurant, Sacha on the water's edge and then coffee at the Lido, overlooking the Atlantic, we were again picked up by the police who continued sending radio messages to Moulay Abdallah: *"La princesse laisse la place un telle pour se rendre a la residence du prince,"* which means "the princess is leaving this and that place to return to the residence of the prince." For a while I felt very important. At this point, we thanked our official guides, collected the Volkswagen and our bodyguard at Moulay Abdullah's house and proceeded towards Marrakech. Halfway between Casablanca and Marrakech where we crossed a river, the color of the soil changed dramatically from black to red. If the dirt was black, the houses were whitewashed—but if the ground was red, the houses were also brick red. During the years of the Protectorate, the French Marechal Lyautey made sure that new constructions outside the old town walls were the same color as the ancient houses inside the city. His legacy also included a first-rate network of roads.

Marrakech, the gateway to southern Morocco, may be no match for Fez, but, to me, it had a mysterious charm of its own. It was an oasis of fruit and flowers on the edge of the great Sahara. The old military encampment of Yusuf ibn Tashufin became an imperial capital. It did lose its status to Fez, but eventually gained it back. The mosque and minaret of the Koutubia served as model for the Giralda in Seville, Spain and the Hassan Tower in Rabat. The reigning sultans during the 19th century built the Bahia Palace and restored the great gardens. On special occasions, the royal family still uses the dazzling reception rooms.

As soon as we arrived at Marrakech in the afternoon, we drove straight to the Bahia Palace. We entered an enormous gate where we were royally received by the guards. They led us through white archways, a patio full of exotic trees and lovely flowers. We passed mosaic-decorated niches and climbed up narrow staircases. Prince Moulay Abdallah had paid me a special honor and lent me his apartment. It was upstairs with a fabulous view out to the Sahara. My apartment consisted of a row of rooms, chicly furnished with Moroccan leather and attractive white and camel-colored wools. Adjoining the bedroom was a modern bathroom—quite unusual. The refrigerator was filled with everything one could desire in the realm of drink and food. The only thing I had to promise Moulay Abdallah was to watch the sunrise over the desert at the earliest hour of the morning! What an easy promise to keep because it was an unforgettable sight. Below me lay the enchanted gardens and courtyards. Night and day I heard the guards' footsteps echo through the courtyards as they performed their duties.

Since my 1958 visit, I was told the Bahia Palace "riyad es-ghir" was completed in 1989. It is known as the "blessed garden," because of the riyads. All it takes to create a riyad is a few orange trees, a cypress strung with bougainvillea and wisteria, four palm trees and a courtyard. In the land of Islam the garden is first and foremost intended to create a feeling of intimacy. Of course, the sultans also created gardens of monumental proportions as in the Al-Badi Palace in Marrakech. I read that Brice Matthieussent spoke of Marrakech as a city of light and open air where the movement and joy sweeps you along. The whole city exudes the warm character of the straightforward and friendly people of the south.

For a while, the Bahia was referred to as the Glaoui Palace. It had been renowned for its banquets, dancing girls and young boys—or slender "Chleuhs"—whose effeminate gestures and perverse eyes were very appreciated by the feudal pashas. Homosexuality in Morocco, as someone described it, was nearly a "national institution." El Thami Glaoui, the Pasha of Marrakech was known as the Lord of the Atlas and the uncrowned King of Southern Morocco. His reign lasted for nearly 40 years until the return of the then Sultan Mohammed V. El Thami Glaoui could be very cruel, but had intensely refined taste. I was told he had a falcon face and long, artistic fingers. He held western sympathies and tangled roots in the past. He entertained distinguished foreign visitors and kept a magician at his side. At the end of his life—as a tired, old man of eighty—he humbly asked forgiveness of his sovereign for his past disloyalties. The sultan gave his royal pardon and El Glaoui died in Marrakech.

After I was settled in the Bahia, we drove over to the palace of King Mohammed's 100- year-old aunt. The aunt's palace was situated next to the Koutubia Tower and the Mamounia Hotel with its beautiful gardens. We drove through a tumbledown gate, up an overgrown drive and stopped dead at an old wall. Around the corner was a small door, which led into bare corridors and finally into a magnificent patio at the center of a superbly beautiful palace. The doors were extremely tall and made of the most exquisitely sculpted wood. The wall was embellished with lacy stonework reliefs and mosaics tiles, as were the majestic pillars. In the middle of the patio, a lovely fountain played round the clock. The floors were shiny marble. Four sides of the patio led into magnificent rooms with fabulous ceilings of carved wood. We were surrounded and heartily welcomed by several women in gaily-colored Moroccan costumes—some of whom were Lalla Fatimah Zohra's cousins. I regretted having to use an interpreter at times, but it didn't seem to affect the conversation. On arrival we were served hard-boiled eggs and coffee—the custom after a long trip. Dinner started with soup, followed by chicken, pigeons with almonds, meat with tomatoes and Moroccan vegetables, four salads, and finished with pears, watermelons and grapes. We drank almond juice scented with orange blossom.

We lunched and dined superbly every day in this lovely palace. I felt extremely honored as the first European the aunt had admitted into her palace since the Protectorate had been established more than 40 years earlier! When we left, we were led through other mosaic-decorated rooms and through an overgrown orange and lemon grove. We walked along the outer walls of the palace which give away none of the beauty and charm of the interior. This was the fascinating mystique of the Moorish houses. I found the Moroccan cuisine was the best and I could understand why the cousins were a bit rotund. The trouble was they hardly ever left the palace. Once we went sightseeing with Princess Lalla Moulrit, who was married to Moulay Idris, a brother of Mohammed V. She nearly collapsed from overexertion and required cool footbaths when we returned to the palace!

One day, we all had a *hammam*, which is a Moroccan bath ceremony. In a sauna-like room, a hefty woman beat us with birch branches, after which gallons of perfumed water were poured over us. Our skin soon turned baby-soft. In the hammam, we sipped a special drink called a zuri'a that was made of crushed melon seeds, whole milk, rose water and cinnamon. Despite the lavish culinary fare and luxurious surroundings, the toilet accommodations were sub-standard, consisting of an ancient bathtub and rusty water closet. Running water was also in short supply.

At night, as Lalla Fatima stayed with her aunt, I was alone in the Bahia except for the guards. There was a war on in neighboring Algeria, but it seemed so far away. When I walked in the gardens, I felt totally safe. I read once that the Thousand and One Nights' garden was not a dream, but a faithful mirror of the divine world. Everything delighted my eyes about the Moroccan gardens: the symmetry, the cleanliness, the layout of the trees, the abundance and unusual species of the fruit, as well as their freshness and beauty.

As I promised Prince Moulay Abdallah, I kept my curtains open at night and woke up to see the legendary sunrise over the Sahara. A glorious red and gold light colored the horizon and played over the rooftops, palms and cypresses. I was totally lost in the beauty.

Days were spent sightseeing. Marrakech was a window into an incandescent world. Beyond the miles and miles of ramparts, the nomad's plains stretched to the foothills of the Atlas Mountains. Dawn and sunset were the two most striking times of day in Regal, Marrakech. The sunset cast a golden light illuminating the palm trees against the ramparts, the folds of every burnoose, as well as the heavily laden donkeys.

The Palace of Dar-es-Said once belonged to the brother of the Grand Vizir in the Bahia. Today, the Dar-es-Said museum featured Moroccan utensils, rugs, carpets, dresses, arms, pottery and art. From the Dar-es-Said we had mint tea and almond cakes at the Dar-es-Salam, a Moroccan tea house, which had once been the residence of one of the former Caids. When the current owner realized our party included the royal family, he felt so honored that he refused payment.

In the Djemna-el-Fna, the market square, we listened to local musicians with iron castanets and observed various other attractions. The bustling crowd represented all the different faces of North Africa. People of every color and creed were dressed in their fezzes, turbans, burnoose and djellaba. We sauntered through one of the two most famous souks in the world. The second one is in Fez. We wandered aimlessly, yet managed to leave with wonderful treasures, from fabric to spices and everything in between. (To this day, these items remind me of wonderful times spent in that world.) Evening descended as if a curtain was suddenly drawn. The golden light of sunset blanketed the red buildings, and the Koutubia Mosque and stately palms and cypresses created black silhouettes.

Leo Africanus wrote: "Marrakech had 24 gates and very beautiful and strong walls, built of chalk adobe and coarse sand mixed with gravel."[1] The number of gates here pointed to the greatness of the city. It was with great sorrow that I left my apartment in the Bahia, taking in for the last time the magnificent view. We walked down the steep staircase, passed lovely patios and white-washed archways to reach our car. We had planned to leave that morning, but Lalla Fatimah Zohra was asked to stay through lunch. The last lazy day was spent day with cousins in the familiar atmosphere of "dolce far niente!" I drew a few more sketches at their request, then, for the last time, sat cross-legged around the low table with this kind and hospitable family. The princesses and ten of their beautifully dressed women saw us off, praying that God would bless us and keep us safe always! "Salama, salama!" It was a touching goodbye as the princesses sent their best wishes to my parents and family. The marvelous stay in Marrakech ended on a lovely afternoon just as siesta rested over the city.

Halfway to Casablanca we crossed the river, leaving the terracotta soil behind. Casablanca's gleaming white houses sat under a rosy haze. The medina teemed with people and a million deadly cyclists. By evening, we were back in Rabat and drove straight to Moulay Hassan's house. Moulay was Lalla Fatimah Zohra's older brother, and Sultan Abd-el-Aziz's only son. Moulay Hassan avoided politics and had been allowed to live quietly in Rabat even after his father's exile. He was never permitted, however, to see his father again. Not even on his father's death bed did the French give their concession for a hospital visit, or even to attend the sultan's funeral. Moulay Hassan received us warmly, dressed in the wide Moroccan trousers, white shirt, yellow slippers and a white and yellow cap on his head. We stayed with him for dinner.

Friday was the Muslim Holy Day, 'jour de priere.' At one o'clock we were brought to the royal palace to see His Majesty ride in a procession to the Mosque. It was one of the most magnificent sights I could possibly imagine The royal lifeguards were dressed in white uniforms with finely pleated trousers, turquoise, red and black caps and red belts. The cavalry led the procession, followed by the military band and the infantry. After that, came His Majesty's gold and purple carriage followed by Crown Prince Hassan and several dignitaries on foot. Finally, the royal guard brought up the rear. By the time the procession returned half an hour later, I had gotten a superb position to use my camera, and caught it all on color film. His Majesty returned to the palace riding on a striking white horse—a grand red parasol held above his head. It was an unforgettable sight with the White Mosque on one side and the expansive royal palace on the other. Masses of multi-colored flowers amidst an equally colorful human throng completed the scene.

Moulay Hassan entertained us for lunch before we started our chain of visits. Our first visit was to Lalla Aicha where the four princesses were resting in the drawing room. Lalla Aicha, Lalla Malika, Lalla Naissa and Lalla Fatima were waiting there for their daily film show. Having promised to return with Lalla Aicha by dinnertime, we left to pay our respects to the Crown Prince Moulay Hassan. Our last visit was to the Directeur de Securite National. A very charming man who spoke excellent French, he asked us for dinner and persuaded Lalla Aicha to join us rather than dining at her house. Outside her own domain, she was even more open and charming and exhibited incredible intelligence. Having tracked us down, Moulay Abdallah suddenly turned up, as well. I was able to repeatedly thank him for his generous hospitality. He was quite delighted that I was so pleased.

The modern town of Tamara was the design brainchild of the French Marechal Lyautey. On our way back to Tangiers that evening, we stopped for dinner with the former Caid of Alcasar el Quivir and his family. One of his guests was a famous poetess and member of a prominent Saharan family. She was dressed in black. I was totally fascinated by her personality and dazzling intellect.

One of the royal lunches had taken 36 hours to prepare! From pastella to tea, it took eleven hours to eat—something very new to me! As we sat motionless, a thick, opaque, mist rolled in from the sea. It had been a very long day!

The next evening, we drove out to Faro da Malabata to see the fantastic view of Tangiers' nightlights. The town climbed up the surrounding hillsides. The lights reflected in the water's edge of the lighthouse. The white *Stella Polaris*, a former Norwegian grand yacht, was in the harbor that night, at that time under Swedish flag. The wharf offered another magnificent vista on that still African night.

We were again invited to Rabat. All four princesses joined Moulay Ali, the fiancé of one of the sultan's daughters, for a late-night supper that started at eleven thirty. Among the guests were Jaqueline and Jean Macel and Farim Rachid's sister Chedela. Farim Rachid had been with us on Moulay Abdallah's wild ride to Casablanca. An excellent Moroccan orchestra with a great lead singer entertained us until the early hours of the morning. While Lalla Fatima Zohra and the boys were with His Majesty that afternoon, I seized the opportunity to walk around the area. By chance on one of the main streets, I met Jean Macel who offered to take me to the souk through the busy narrow streets. In some of the craft stalls, we came upon magnificent Andalusian-inspired doors of heavy, carved wood. Pink lights shone on white walls of the densely populated passages and beautiful minarets. As we passed through the former street of the consuls, Jean reminded me of Rabat's origins and how in 1600, when the Muslims were all exiled from Spain, they settled in this area. We ended our tour in the Casbah where the Macels were living in an old pirate's house. Here, we admired the last light of the sunset on the river. Before we left Rabat to go to Meknes, Lalla Aicha insisted we take one of her new, large American cars. The idea of riding in a Volkswagen Beetle was incomprehensible to her. So, our little guard in his djellaba and red fez followed behind in the Beetle with our luggage. As usual, it was quite late when we arrived in Meknes that evening. I learned that Moulay Ismail was instrumental in the history of the city. He turned it into a stronghold with 25 miles of bastioned triple walls of dizzying heights. His magnificent larger-than-life palaces, gardens, stables and ornate gateways were built to dwarf normal human proportions.

Morocco may be the land of gates, but nowhere was that more evident than in Meknes. It is the sheer number and scale of its sculpted stone gates that other Islamic cities are measured against. Above the grandest Bab Mansour Gate was the inscription, "To the glory of Moulay Ismail and his son, through whom Islam appeared holding firm the standard of the crown." The colossal gate is unforgettable. We drove straight to the Pasha of Meknes' palace. The Pasha Moulay Hassan was married to the youngest and favorite sister of King Mohammed V, the charming Lalla Mina. We stayed with them for a long, enjoyable week. The opulent palace featured rows of rooms, charming courtyards, and a beautiful patio, where we dined, with another singing fountain in the middle. Usually men and women dine in separate areas. But here, occasionally a remark was exchanged between the two tables. Here comes the part where I felt I let my friend, Lalla Fatima down. As a foreigner and the guest of honor, I was given the honor to gouge out the eyeballs of a lamb's head and eat them. The whole lamb's head was put in the front of me. I apparently went absolutely green. Lalla Fatima Zohra had to save me. I felt ashamed, but I don't think I could have managed it even if I'd known of it in advance!

I was given a European-style room—one of two in the palace. I awoke at 5 AM to roosters crowing and water playing in the fountains.

Another evening, Moulay Abdallah and a couple of his sisters joined their aunt and uncle in Meknes for dinner. The sultan had sent Moulay Abdallah up to Ifrane in the Atlas Mountains to study for his exams. Before they left that night, Moulay Abdallah insisted that he give a lunch for me the next day at Ifrane. We drove up in separate cars to the royal palace which sat atop a hill in a vast park with magnificent old cedar trees. Under these giants by pools of water three low tables, masses of cushions and Oriental rugs had been placed on the grass for lunch in the Moroccan style. The latest music wafted through. Lunch was served at three tables. At the first table Moulay Abdallah sat with all the men. Lalla Fatima and I sat at Lalla Aicha's table with Lalla Mina and Jaqueline Macel. Sometimes Moulay Abdallah came over to exchange news and jokes. As before, men carried tajines on their heads filled with every delicacy that Morocco could possibly provide. The grand mountains surrounded us in the bright fall sunshine.

When we had arrived at the palace, the military guards paraded for us. After lunch, the men went shooting and returned with an enormous monkey as their kill. While the princesses and I were discussing l'amour, we were presented this horrible monkey. Ugh! A hideous sight!

While Lalla Mina and Lalla Fatima Zohra were away visiting the sultan for a few days, I walked the beautiful palace park. I enjoyed the huge trees and woodsy perfume against a blazing sunset. A caravan of guests from Ifrane, led by Moulay Abdallah were escorted by police racing down the mountain. The pasha had arranged a fantastic dinner party in the vast Moorish salon upstairs. Prince Moulay Abdallah hosted and placed Lalla Malika, a French doctor and his wife, Jaqueline Macel, his French teacher, Moulay Ali and me at his table. I sat next to Prince Moulay Abdallah. It was a great evening full of many interesting discussions. When Moulay Abdallah had to leave and go back to Ifrane, Lalla Aicha took his place and we continued to converse in French, to my delight. A seven-man orchestra played after dinner until five in the morning when some of the guests left for Rabat.

Another day, before we left Meknes, Princess Lalla Mina and Princess Lalla Fatimah were again called to go and see the sultan and his harem in Ifrane. The day dragged on because I heard nothing but indecipherable Arabic. So, in the afternoon, Moulay Ismail and I decided visit the Holy City Moulay Idris and Volubilis. We found large Roman ruins, of beautiful columns and fragments of magnificent mosaic floors. The water system was almost intact to this day and was a reminder of an amazing culture and their technical knowledge. The Pasha of Moulay Idris received us for tea in his white villa. The pasha was one of those men who just oozes charm. Moulay Idris was built on the top of the hills and had an amazing view. While we were having tea we also enjoyed a fiery sunset behind. When the princesses had not returned the following day, the pasha very kindly planned a visit to Fez for me, accompanied by one of the princes. For me, going to Fez, was a dream come true. Fez was founded in 808 AD and is one of the best

preserved medieval cities in the world. To begin with, the city ruled over
the fragile "Kingdom of Fez," fighting wars on all sides. When Yussuf ibn
Tashufin—founder of the Almoravid dynasty—made Marrakech his capital
in the 11th century, he constructed a military base at Fez. Two centuries later
Fez entered its golden age and became western Islam's greatest trade city, as
well as Morocco's intellectual and religious hub. It was then the firmly established capital of Morocco.

I was taken to the famous souk and to the "intelligent disorder of its
unique Medina," its maze of ever branching lanes confronting life of "some
unfixed past." Weavers, woodworkers competed with sales of doves and car-
rier pigeons in cages. Wonderful smells came from a bakery where there was
an oven for the public to bring their cakes or loaves to be baked and then
picked up later. Fez is the present gastronomic capital of Morocco and best
known for its "pastille," a miraculous pigeon pie. In this labyrinthine city, I
enjoyed our visit to the ancient university in the center of the city—one of the
great centers of learning, culture and wealth, like a North African Florence.
We returned to Meknes very late that night, having first driven up on a hillside above Fez to admire the lights below us with the minarets appearing
like black arrows against the sky. For once, I had dinner with the men under
the stars. The evening air was delightfully fresh and relaxing. Moulay Ismail
ended the evening reciting Spanish poetry to me.

After two days the princesses had still not returned from Rabat.
Consequently, the two princes and I went sightseeing in Meknes. As a special
courtesy to me, the pasha opened the royal palace. It had not been kept up
and certain parts were literally falling down. Inside, however, immense gold
treasures decorated the ceilings, walls, doors. The enormous proportions of
the rooms and patios were particularly amazing, built by Moulay Ismail, who
needed a great deal of space because, apart from having 400 wives, he also had
140 sons and over 200 daughters!

The evenings brought sights of camel caravans trailing through the
main square. Rosey sunsets blurred the signs of decay and reflected visions of
past grandeur. Since the princesses did not arrive back until evening, I was

given the rare honor of spending the day just with the men, including eating with them, which was unheard of. When they did return, before I went to bed that last evening, the princesses came to my room and presented me with a gold bracelet as a memento and "thank you" for having been their guest! Unfortunately, this bracelet was one of the things the robbers stole in Rome.

The next morning there were grateful goodbyes to our most hospitable royal hosts before once again traveling through Meknes' grand gate, Bab-el-Mandour.

Arriving back in Tangier where the Atlantic meets the Mediterranean felt like coming home. We had been on the road for a long time. I realized how Tangier's mixture of Berber, British, French and Arab cultures created a true international free-port. Tangier was beautiful and there I was mesmerized by the "smell of Africa." Luxurious villas dotted the *Mountain*. But, in the middle of the Medina, any old door may have lead into a sumptuous house. As ever, Muslims believe in keeping their wealth, as well as their beautiful young women, a guarded secret. "What is not known cannot be stolen!"

Lalla Fatimah Zohra and I both returned to London. However, my father was soon transferred to Rome, Italy. Before I saw Lalla Fatimah again, I had been married. It had been several years when Lalla Fatimah Zohra and her husband had a tour of duty as ambassador to Italy. In fact they were in Rome when my second daughter, Elizabeth, was born. I don't think my husband, Billy, ever forgot when Lalla Fatima came to visit me in the clinic. When he walked the princess to her car, he found it surrounded by a group of colorfully clad women, and he subsequently invited them all for ice cream at the Gelateria in Parioli! Of course, Lalla Fatima came to dinner in our gorgeous penthouse apartment on my Roman rooftop. She also visited us— before moving back to Morocco—at *Shenandoah*, our beloved Tuscan home. She was one of the most marvelous friends I ever had. Unfortunately, I saw her less after we moved to the States. She served her country admirably, was known as "The Princess of the Poor," and founded the Moroccan Women's Union. After our first foray into the beautiful land of French Morocco in 1958, she continued to travel throughout Morocco to help the cause of women.

Sultan Mohammed V was on the throne when we started our adventure in 1958. Years later, when Lalla Fatima Zohra returned from her ambassadorial duties, King Hassan II, the new sultan encouraged her ideas and work. Her husband, Prince Moulay Ben El Mehdi, died in 1984 and Lalla Fatima then lived permanently at her beloved Mansion on Vieille Montagne. After her untimely death, it was written in one of the London papers that "Princess Lalla Fatimah Zohra was always held in enormous affection and esteem by Moroccans and by the large expatriate community." And also, "The princess was a remarkable bridge between old Morocco and new, and between Moors and Europeans." She had been appointed commander of the Legion d'Honneur of France. She was only four years my senior. Lalla Fatimah was remarkably kind and compassionate and I never stopped loving this fabulous friend. Lalla Fatima Zohra always had, from early on, a terrific presence and a wonderful old-fashioned aura, yet she had no airs about her. This Moroccan fairytale could not have been written had I not had the privilege of such a rich friendship.

New York City – First Trip to the USA
COQUETTE

It was 1961 when Alitalia Flight 602 left Rome at 1:30 in the afternoon. The New York bound flight left Milan around 4 p.m. and proved to be a smooth flight. The majestic Alps shone white with snow and the wide Atlantic Ocean lay calm beneath us. Later, clouds veiled Nova Scotia and Halifax. Over Boston, clearing skies revealed a heavenly red sunset as we headed south along the United States eastern seaboard.

My old friend, Albert Rothschild had arranged an art show in New York. All my paintings were with me by special permission from the Belle Arte in Roma. We landed around 7 p.m. at New York's Idlewild Airport. My brother, Nicken, and his wife, Else met me in their red Rambler. From the windows I saw the fabulous Manhattan skyline for the first time. We crossed the George Washington Bridge in the brilliantly lit New York night. Once across the bridge, we turned north, and drove up the Palisade Interstate Highway to Alpine, New Jersey.

When the Palisades Interstate Highway was constructed, it went through the Rionda 300-acre estate and actually—I believe—through old Mrs. Ellen Goin Rionda's living room! As a result, Mrs. Rionda decided to collect New England stone houses and rebuild them on her property. After WWII, she left them to be used by servicemen. The homes were perfect for young families and dogs to live in pleasant surroundings. My brother, his family and their dog, Coffee, were among the lucky ones to live there, and had stayed for ten years. It was a very cozy and charming cottage. The children's newly built school was so close they could walk through the Glen Goin woods with only one road to cross. A policeman was stationed there to help the children cross safely.

My first unusual experience in New York happened when Nena and Dick Downar invited us for lunch in Manhattan. Else and I drove across the George Washington Bridge down the Westside Highway to 56th Street where we turned east, and crossed the famous avenues. After we all had a delightful lunch, Nena and I sauntered up Fifth Avenue. Near the public library, Nena noticed a well-dressed woman sidle up and try to give me an injection in the arm! Nena yanked me away and we jumped on the first bus. The incident left me so rattled we went straight for a stiff drink at a very good jazz bar to soothe our jagged nerves. I then returned to Glen Goin.

The following Saturday, Nicken suggested we drive up the Hudson to visit West Point and to admire the blazing fall color upstate. As an artist I have especially enjoyed the autumn leaves. We decided to have lunch at Bear Mountain Inn. In the middle of our meal, I suddenly had a strange feeling and apparently turned pale green. Certain something awful had happened, it seemed urgent to return immediately to Glen Goin. Appearing as if I'd seen a ghost, Nicken and I ended lunch abruptly, paid the bill and sped toward New York City. As we turned into the family driveway, Else was on the stoop and shouted that Mother was on the phone from Rome. I burst out, "Father has died!"

My father had been hospitalized before I left for New York, but the doctors advised me to go anyway, so as not to worry him. They assured me that he would be all right—at least until I returned. I asked Mother what time he had died, and she confirmed that it was the moment we were at lunch! My beloved father had died of a heart attack. I felt very strongly that his spirit had come to say "goodbye" and perhaps to give me special strength—as he had done all my life. If Nicken had not been there with me, I would not have had the courage to relate this incident.

Father had suffered a fall in Moscow the year I was born. As a result, he battled a measure of lameness all his life. In spite of his illnesses, including what some doctors thought was a form of Multiple Sclerosis, he bravely persevered—a characteristic passed on to me. He was ever a pillar of stability and wisdom and held many positions of great responsibility. In 1944, he had been a member of the eight-man civil service council for the WWII Resistance. After the war, he became head of the Ministry of Foreign Affairs. Father helped to reorganize the Norwegian Foreign Service. At the young age of 50, he was appointed the Norwegian Ambassador to the Court of Saint James. I was, am, and always will be extremely proud of him. He will forever be my inspiration. When he died at age 65, he left a cavernous void—not only in the lives of his family—but of everyone who had known him. I don't believe I've ever loved anyone as much as I loved my father.

Nicken and I flew back to Rome the following morning. I sold a few paintings in New York, but the art show was cancelled.

Since Father was an accredited ambassador in Rome at the time of his untimely death, the Italians and the Diplomatic Corps gave him a fantastic send-off. The day began with a beautiful service at the English Church on Via del Babuino. The British Ambassador hosted the memorial service honoring Father for all the years he served as Ambassador to London.

After the service, Mother and I were busy thanking and greeting people. We hadn't noticed the Italian-led motorcade had departed for the Ciampino Airport. I could almost hear Father laughing—wherever he was—having been accustomed to twelve years of British punctuality. Fortunately, I knew the route. So we raced across Rome and joined the stately motorcade on the Lungotevere. Deftly, we filed in ahead of the British Ambassador, Sir Ashley Clarke, who was one of the pall-bearers. The other pall-bearers included Gaston Palewski who was the French ambassador, the Finnish, Danish and Swedish ambassadors, as well as Conte GianVico Borromeo, my godmother's husband, who was representing the Italian government. The Italian military band played Chopin's Funeral March as we slowly walked behind the coffin. Not an eye remained dry.

The Norwegian Royal Air Force dispatched a military plane to bring their ambassador home. Nicken and our good friend, Consul Einar Riis, accompanied the coffin. Chris and I flew Mother home on a commercial flight and tried to boost her spirits knowing that difficult times lay ahead.

A telegram from Queen Elizabeth honoring Father and expressing her "sincere sympathy" to Mother deeply touched us all.

In Oslo, we held a perfectly beautiful church service. An enormous flower arrangement from His Majesty King Olav brightened up the stage. Numerous officials, family, and close friends were there to pay their respects. Father was a unique human being and had led a life of outstanding service to people all over the world—first and foremost—to his country! When the coffin disappeared for cremation, a hollow spot formed in the pit of my stomach!

The following morning we brought the urn down to Risoer, the White Pearl of the south coast. The urn had passed the night on the dresser in my brother's room. Citing the excuse to help avoid car sickness, we sat mother in the front seat of the limousine. The real reason was, of course, to separate her from the urn. It seemed disrespectful to stow it with the luggage, so the three of us rode with it in the back seat. Our late October drive down to the south coast was spectacular. The flaming fall leaves shimmered in the sun as we arrived in Risoer, Father's home town. Only a small chain of islands and rocks protected this charming town from the open sea. The town's people always cared for their cemetery as if it were a park full of well-kept flowers. We held a final graveside service and left Father's ashes in the fenced-in family plot. The grounds were a gift due to our generations-long relationship with the town. Since then, whenever I returned to Risoer, I visited the garden-like cemetery to pay my respects. There was, however, one humorous story. One year, the gate in the cemetery fence had been removed. Mother worried that people might walk on Father's head! He must have enjoyed a good giggle.

When we left Oslo after the ceremonies, we knew life would change dramatically. Brother Nicken returned to life in New York and my brother, Chris went back to the university in Oslo. Mother came to live with me in Italy. Arriving at the Via Appia Antica in Rome where our family had been so happy, the decision of our next direction lay before us. It was all so very sudden and unexpected.

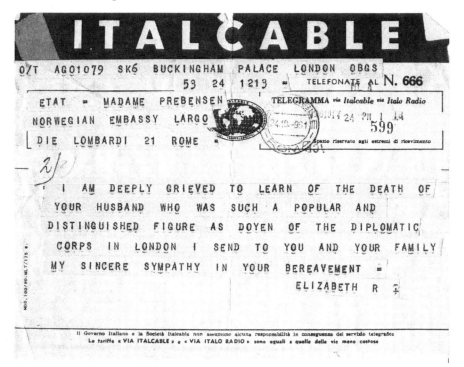

Telegram sent by Her Majesty Queen Elizabeth on the occasion of my father's death

Rome – Life in Trastevere
VIKING SHIP

After Father died, I remained in search of sunshine, which meant Rome for the time being. Mother spent six months with my brother, Nicken, in the States. It had been with heavy hearts that we packed up the embassy on the Appia Antica. We had enjoyed so much happiness there. Some things were put in storage until I found a newly remodeled townhouse in Trastevere, a charming area across the Tiber. I rented the top floor and penthouse. When mother returned from New York she took the apartment below me.

The fashion industry had always fascinated me. Knowing that I could not make a living off of my painting, I turned to designing women's wear and set up a studio and fashion atelier on the bottom floor of our "narrow-minded," four-story townhouse. The building was situated on one of the squares near the Isola Tiberina. My tailor, Lidia and her seven seamstresses worked on another square. Lidia had worked for large clothing houses, but her bad temper kept her looking for other work. Although she was difficult, she was a great tailor. At the time shoppers patronized dressmakers rather than large department stores. Customers would come for fittings in my atelier on the lower floor. We produced high fashion women's wear including dresses, belts and knitwear (coordinating sweaters and skirts). I had great fun with it. Leather was of a marvelous quality in Rome. We used it to trim many of my creations.

I often gave dinner parties on the penthouse roof terrace. Two of my friends were great chefs. Dom Radziwill was a meat griller and Giovanni di Borbone was an all round specialty chef! He even wrote a cookbook with "Simonetta"—of fashion fame—called the *Snob in Cucina* (*The Snob in the Kitchen*). Other friends often asked the musicians at the trattoria below us on the square to come up and play for us on the rooftop.

Life in Rome was very pleasant, even though Father's death had changed a great deal. I would take early morning horseback rides with friends before work, and go sailing with other friends on the weekends. It was during this time in Rome that I met William Henry Harrison III (Billy), my soon-to-be husband.

Our lovely stay in Trastevere ended abruptly one Sunday night when robbers entered the rooftop and broke into the penthouse. I was out to dinner with my mother and Billy. He and I had just become engaged when the robbery occurred. It must have been an inside job because the previous Friday I had temporarily taken my jewelry out of the bank box to show Billy, intending to return it on Monday morning. When we got home that

Saturday evening, I immediately noticed the lights were on full blast. "How silly of you to leave the lights on," Billy chided.

"Of course, I did not!" I snapped. "Somebody has broken into the apartment,"

The thieves were still there and had bolted the front door from the inside. They escaped over the rooftops with all the loot before the police arrived. Unfortunately, they stole my favorite camera that I used for travel articles, heirloom jewelry that had been passed down through generations, as well as my mother's antique Russian silver. Fortunately, I was wearing my father's gold bracelet, so that was saved. It had belonged to him when he was in the Norwegian Navy. I was also wearing a necklace of the Empress Catarina 1767 gold ruble, a childhood gift from my parents in Russia.

The Italian Foreign Office and the Department of the Interior offered their assistance in apprehending the burglars. The Roman police, however, acted complacent until I received a ransom letter from the thieves. Then the Italian Foreign Office gave the police a plan. The criminals wanted me to leave money in an urn by a mausoleum in the protestant cemetery. All the gardeners were replaced with policemen to guard me. Off I went with a bag of fake money provided by the police. At one point, I noticed a man standing on a corner reading a newspaper. This seemed strange. I asked the police afterwards who that man was and they said, "What man, why didn't you tell us?" "Excuse me," I thought, "the police had 20 or 30 men on the spot and none of them noticed him?"

The police scheme was so obvious that the robbers wrote me another letter saying, "This time, no police, or else..." So, the next time the officers provided me with a phony fiancé dressed up in a new suit. I trotted off again to the cemetery, arm in arm with my policeman. It was like a scene out of a bad movie. The thieves were again brighter than the police and, unfortunately, my valuables were never recovered.

After that disturbing incident, we left our brilliant life in Trastevere. Mother was so fearful that she moved to Campo dei Fiori to live in an apartment above its well-known trattoria. She felt safer there, and enjoyed the delicious meals sent up from the restaurant.

Billy had previously married an Italian named Eloise during WWII. Her mother was an American from Cincinnati. Eloise had not yet obtained an annulment from the Vatican after she divorced Billy, and we knew that could take some time. So we decided to get married in London, my old stomping grounds. In order to marry in London, you had to be a resident for three weeks prior to the event. So we settled in at the Savoy Hotel. Arriving in an Alfa Romeo, we were received at the hotel with ovations by the innumerable Italian waiters. Billy happily divided his time between his tailors ("Huntsman" on Savile Row), and hunting in Leicestershire with the Belvoir, the Quorn, and the Cottesmore, out of Melton Mowbray. I remained in London with friends and prepared for the wedding. When English acquaintances asked me how I could possibly marry an American (and by the way, where was he?), I told them he was foxhunting in Melton Mowbray. Their reply was always, "Then, he can't be all bad!"

One day, Billy called me from Melton Mowbray and said, "You've got to come up here and buy a table." I thought he had lost his mind, but I went anyway. I arrived by train and found Billy was out hunting, but had sent his groom, Bill, to take care of me. The groom drove up to the top of a hill with me to watch the hunt. I saw the pink coats far below and heard the yelping of the hounds. Suddenly, I saw the fox quite near us, and I swear he winked at me as he went on his way. Obviously, the hounds had lost his scent. I did buy the gorgeous rent table and own it to this day.

Our marriage service was performed at Caxton Hall. Durru Shehvar, the Princess of Berar, was my matron of honor. The Molesworths, head of the Tate Gallery, gave us a lovely reception and my mother gave the wedding lunch at Claridge's. It was her favorite hotel in London. We drank Chateau Ausone, Billy's prize wine from the sommelier at Le Grand Vefour in Paris! That night we went to the theater and saw Diahann Carrol in *No Strings*. To this day, that lovely actress seems never to have aged. Our dinner was at the Dorchester, a place that holds so many memories for me. Then we said goodbye to the Savoy, our home away from home for three weeks, and the Alfa Romeo took us across the channel to France where our adventure continued.

Back in Rome, Billy and I began married life in his bachelor pad, which was a penthouse near the Via Condotti and our favorite bar—before taking a five-month honeymoon in the States. His "mistress," a specially built green Bentley, came with us to the States. I always said it had a fancier Rome address than we did. It was kept in a garage under the Spanish Steps after Billy's divorce. The garage space cost more than our apartment. Any time we took it out for a drive, we had to ask the police to help us move half the parked cars in the square. It was like taking Queen Mary out of port. We did have a second car—a sporty Alfa Romeo—but it lived its life on the street.

USA – American Honeymoon
GOLD MOOSE

Three years after my first US visit, I was back in New York. I had married "another continent." He was an architect named William (Billy) Henry Harrison III. We were married in London on the condition that we take a real American honeymoon across his wide and wonderful country. We came over on the beautiful French ship, the *France*. It was later acquired by my old classmate, Knut Kloster, and converted to the cruise ship, the *Norge*. We joined the *France* in Le Havre where we spent a couple of days with my good friends, Nicole and Pierre Rufenacht and their enchanting daughters. They lived in the large white Rufenacht family house on the hill above Le Havre harbor. They saw us off on our voyage to New York. Nicole was part of my beloved Fraissinet family. Once again, they were present for an important event in my life.

The Atlantic crossing was wonderful. I enjoyed special treatment from our French steward. He loved my clothes so much that he asked if he might iron them every day—at no cost to me. We gorged on caviar, drank the best wines and danced our feet off. As we approached the Big Apple, I climbed on deck to watch our cruise into the harbor. An inspiring bridge sent me down to ask Billy its name. "What are you talking about? There is no bridge there," Billy said. Obviously, it had been a while since he last sailed into New York's port. The bridge was called the Verrazano. The Italian who christened it turned out to be one of our future neighbors in Italy.

Once again, Nicken met us and greeted me with a hearty, "Hello, Dolly!" After all, it was 1964, the year that show opened. We had brought Billy's wonderful magnolia leaf green 1961 Mulliner Bentley. She carried us for our honeymoon around the United States when I had insisted I wanted to know his country from the view of a car, not just from the 30,000 foot level. On arrival at the St. Regis Hotel in the Bentley, the doorman begged us to park right in front of the entrance. How wonderful. She was such a beauty.

Billy had arranged for theater tickets, knowing how much I loved shows. He asked me to dress up because we were going to the famous night-club, "El Morocco" after the theater. I wore my diagonally pleated red chiffon gown, an evening coat and my handmade Chanel evening shoes. Before we went to the theater, Billy took me to a drug store for a hamburger. I felt very strange, sitting on a bar stool eating a hamburger in my finery, but he said Americans did it all the time! When we arrived at "El Morocco," Billy sent me upstairs to check my coat so I would have to descend the imposing curved staircase. The maitre received me at the bottom of the stairs and brought us to the very best table. Billy turned to me and said, "I guess you passed the test!" I had no idea what he meant, but was glad he seemed so pleased. Many of the passengers we had seen on the ship were also there, but I was told that they had all been seated in "Siberia" far from the choice tables.

On our first day in New York, Uncle Bill Bolton came to lunch with us at the St. Regis. He was Billy's stepfather, and he and I adored each other on sight. We became the best of friends, and kept close contact till the day he died. He helped me understand many, new and strange things about the United States and its people.

One evening we were invited to dine with Bill and Molly Rockefeller in Rye. Bill and Billy had been roommates at Yale. I was immediately wel-comed and enjoyed a lovely time over dinner. When we returned to New York City that night, however, Billy took a wrong turn and we ended up on 125th Street in Harlem! It was eerie that not a soul was on the street. We cautiously made our way south in the Bentley. "Imagine if we'd suddenly had car trouble in that part of town!" Billy exclaimed. "You've always bragged that

Bentleys and Rolls Royces never break down, and don't you remember when you once asked how much horsepower the Bentley had and your answer was 'sufficient!'" We opened the newspaper the next morning and discovered we had been driving around same area where the 1964 Harlem Riots had ignited just hours after we left! That was my initial experience in our action-packed five-month stay in the States. Billy would later give me a lovely gold charm in memory of our good fortune.

Our special friends, Linda and George Post brought us out to Syosset to have lunch with Alexandra MacKay, Linda's mother. Her divine house was a copy of one she'd seen on the Yangtze River while honeymooning in China. I admired her moon gate so much that I later copied it in both Tuscany and Palm Beach.

The night before we left New York, we dined with my brother, Nicken and Else in Glen Goin. We had brought their two small children, Karen and Preben, up to the country the day before to see Harvey Fite's sculptural masterpiece. As a new uncle, Billy offered them any size ice cream cone they wanted. I think Preben ordered a double-double something. Karen was overjoyed when he was unable to finish it!

We reluctantly left the great St. Regis, the theaters, family and friends in New York because it was time to go west. In 1964, there were no turnpikes to Cincinnati, Ohio. So, we took Route 50 and maintained a steady speed to make 6 o'clock cocktails with Billy's step-mother! The house on Brill Road in Indian Hill had belonged to Billy's father, who was related to the Virginia Harrisons. One of the family members had moved to Cincinnati when President William Henry Harrison was stationed at North Bend, Indiana. We intended to stay in Cincinnati for some days. Billy's adorable (and recently widowed) Aunt Peggy, who had visited us in Rome, was hosting a large family dinner in our honor. Other friends and family also treated us to many wonderful parties.

Aunt Peggy's dinner party—which was a wonderful occasion—turned out to be the last time we enjoyed the Wulsin family home. *The Hermitage*, a gracious southern mansion, had always been filled with musicians and music.

The Wulsin family owned the Baldwin Piano Company. Billy, being an only child, had often been included in family events, and had seen many famous artists entertained in that marvelous house. Soon after we left Cincinnati, the property was sold and the wonderful *Hermitage* was no more. In its place was erected an apartment building, which today is the address of quite a few friends.

One sunny summer day, we drove to see Billy's cousins, John and Roz Wulsin in their large white-frame house. Two flags—the American and the Norwegian—flew over the front porch, making me feel welcomed. In later years, when we moved to Cincinnati, Roz and John continued that flag tradition, both in Cincinnati and on their boat house in Canada. Each year we were gifted a three-week vacation at their Captain's house on the channel between Sault St. Marie and Georgian Bay. From then on they included us in every family Christmas celebration. We drove up yearly from Cincinnati through Ohio and Michigan, always stopping just before the Mackinack Bridge to buy fresh lake trout and white fish. At night we often took the canoes for a quiet paddle among the islands, and shared supper with friends along the channel. The scenery reminded me of the film, *On Golden Pond* with Henry Fonda and Katherine Hepburn. Early mornings saw us roaming through the trees to various piers to enjoy the sunrise.

After a few weeks of being wined and dined in Cincinnati, we packed the Bentley and commenced our America tour. We stopped at a restaurant in Indianapolis for our first less-than-satisfactory dinner. Since it was a Sunday, wine was not served. So, Billy went out to the car and took a swig from his flask—just on principle. I asked for a salad and was served a tired lettuce leaf with half a canned peach topped with marshmallows. I tried to say I had not asked for dessert, but this was 1964 and green salads had not yet seen the light around the country. We, however, happily joined "Route 66" and passed one night at Mickey Mantle's hotel in Joplin, Missouri.

The next day we picnicked in the serene Missouri countryside. When we arrived in Amarillo, Texas, we impulsively joined a club for a night just to enjoy the wonderful wine. Then, from Albuquerque, New Mexico, our tour took us to Santa Fe, which sits at 7,000 feet. The air was like champagne. Billy went into the nearest shop and bought a large cuff bracelet that had five rows of turquoises. It forever reminded me of the great Indian chiefs. Years later the bracelet paid the cost of some needed medicine!

Having passed Flagstaff, Arizona, we left Route 66 and headed to Las Vegas, Nevada. Billy had intended to stay one night, but we had such a good time, one night grew into five. We stayed at the Desert Inn, where at five in the morning, Jimmy Durante came into the nightclub with several beautiful girls, joined our table, and joked the way only he could. That year, the nightly shows included Maurice Chevalier and the Follies Bergere. Sunning and swimming were still on, and the weather was blissful. After an exciting five days in Vegas, we drove through San Bernardino to Los Angeles. We had heard that Beverly Hills Hotel was the most elegant on the west coast. The plan was to hear Lena Horne sing, whom we had sailed with on the *France*. Her performance at the Cocoanut Grove was unforgettable.

For a few days, I felt part of Hollywood's celebrity life and saw several movie stars along the way. Over a drink at the Beverly Wiltshire bar, Van Johnson sat down on a stool next to me. As we drove our green Bentley down one street, Fred Astaire sped up beside us at a traffic light in his black Rolls Royce to see who in Los Angeles dared to have a smarter car than his! And once, at the San Ysidro Ranch near Santa Barbara, a car parked next to us and out stepped Bing Crosby! He smiled at me, whistling a happy tune!

In Santa Barbara one evening, we decided to eat at the restaurant on the pier. I was dressed in elegant slacks and a blazer. To my surprise, I was denied entrance into the restaurant, and had to go back to the hotel and change into a skirt. These days I might not have even owned a skirt. It actually reminded me of a similar occasion in Italy during the era of the miniskirt. I had gone to a well-known restaurant in Rome wearing a black velvet Valentino pant-suit. Again, the maître would not admit me. So I took off my black velvet trousers and gracefully handed them to him, as if checking my coat. My velvet tunic was longer than most miniskirts. The maître was speechless and we had a great dinner anyway!

We drove north on Highway 1 along the Pacific Ocean, stopped at San Simeon's Hearst Castle, and arrived in Carmel for the night. That Seventeen Mile Drive with its pristine golf course of every shade of green, and the fabulous Pacific vista, was a beautiful experience. We had telephoned the Fairmont Hotel in San Francisco from Santa Barbara, but found that the Republican Convention was taking place, and every big hotel in town had been reserved. I sounded so disappointed that the dear young man at the Fairmont felt sorry for me and told me he knew they still had a room at the Huntington—also on Nob Hill. The situation could not have turned out better. Although it was much smaller, the hotel was delightful with a most elegant clientele. Billy felt quite at home. We had actually reached San Francisco, a city I had dreamt about since, as a little girl, I first saw the film *San Francisco* with Clark Gable and Jeanette MacDonald. I was so excited.

Friends in San Francisco took us out for dinner at the Ondine, a delightful restaurant across the Golden Gate Bridge with a magnificent view of the bridge and the bay. Hugh Johnson, the interesting old politician, joined us. The next day, the head of the Wells Fargo company—also a good friend—brought us up on the bank's rooftop after a wonderful lunch. There, again, we experienced a gorgeous, sweeping view of the city. On our last day in San Francisco, we gave a luncheon in the Captain's Room at Trader Vic's. Having had too good a time the night before, Billy had to take off his shoes to make it down the steep hill! I ordered seafood, cheese soufflés and strawberries served on an ice sculpture. An old friend from Father's London days, Peruvian Ambassador Berkemeyer greeted me from a corner table. Even 6,000 miles away from London, I felt the world was still quite small. When I suggested to Billy we might settle in San Francisco, the old "east coaster" said, "Do you ever want to see your family in Europe again? Don't you realize how much further Europe is from here?" My reaction to that argument was, "Well, then let us send a telegram to Tuscany that we are ready to buy the old ruin!" And that's exactly what we did.

We had gone as far west as we could go. The time had come to turn around. First stop was Reno, Nevada. Billy got quite nervous because his last visit, two years before, was on the occasion of his divorce. To our dismay, Reno was overcrowded, and we ended up in Carson City, the state capital, for the night. The only motel room we could find was cheap and utterly dreadful. "I will make up for it with a real treat for dinner," Billy promised. "They have a marvelous restaurant here set up for all the divorces." The restaurant was overcrowded, so we had a drink at the bar while we waited for a table. I sneaked a look at the barman's name card, Halvor Smedsrud. One could not find a more Norwegian name. So I asked him, of course, whether he was Norwegian and told him I was. When he heard my maiden name he said, "Do you by any chance know a man named Per Prebensen? I knew him on a delegation in Paris in 1939." "He happens to have been my father," I said. Well, Halvor went into superlatives about Father, and we became fast friends in five minutes. We invited Halvor and his wife, who was the lady cook from Boston, for a cognac after hours. They invited us for dinner in the mountains on their night off. Not only that, but Halvor arranged lodging at the best motel in Reno for the rest of our stay. I was only allowed to play the nickel slot machine in Las Vegas, and the same rule prevailed in Reno. When once I played the dime machine and won the jackpot, Billy disowned me and went to the bar. He was too embarrassed to see me scooping up the mass of coins that, in those days, would roll all over the floor. Then we went to Bill Harrah's car museum. Since we still had the Bentley, they waived our parking fee, insisting it was such an honor to have the Bentley in front of the door. Billy's mood improved instantly! Harrah's had a fantastic collection of cars that had little to do with today's productions.

Next stop was Denver, Colorado with dinner at Brown's and lodging on the 22nd floor of the Denver Hilton. Lazing about in the morning, as honeymoon couples do, window cleaners suddenly appeared on scaffolding outside our glass plate windows. Stark naked, Billy walked with great dignity across the room and pulled the curtain. I laughed so hard I hardly survived it.

It was in Denver where Billy gave me the gold moose charm in memory of the fabulous Wild West. We also bought gear for a visit to a dude ranch in Wyoming. It was the only time Billy bought me blue jeans. He hated them and made me solemnly swear to never put on another pair as long as I lived. I got around it by wearing jeans in other colors! The ranch was situated near Dubois on the Wind River in Wyoming. Billy had been there the year before, and we received a wonderful welcome. Not only that, but as a wedding present, they gave us four days alone with a cook and a wrangler at their cabin on Simpson Lake up on the Continental Divide. It was a virgin lake and the trout fishing was indescribably rich. Wildflowers grew everywhere. Billy went dipping in ice cold ponds and we fished while he rowed and I angled. Once ashore, he insisted that since I had caught all the fish, it was my duty to clean them. He went into the cabin and left me outside to fight not only the messy fish, but also vicious clouds of mosquitoes. I could have murdered him at that moment. My efforts did not go unrewarded, though. Billy gave me another charm—a gold fish crewel! The best time we had on Simpson Lake was when the four of us rode horses together. David, the wrangler, showed us all the area's treasures, including wild goats on the mountain ledges. When we stopped to picnic, chipmunks sat down next to us to share our bananas.

After four days of utter freedom, we returned to the ranch. Henry Alexander—the head of Morgan Guaranty in New York—and his fifteen-year-old daughter, had arrived in the cabin next to ours. We recognized him from a recent cover of Time Magazine. I suggested we invite him over for drinks. He seemed lonely to me. "But you can't do that," Billy said. "He is too important." "Not out in Wyoming," I retorted. "Anyway, my father always used to say the more important you are, the easier it is to come up with an excuse without offending anyone." Of course, he accepted the invitation and came over with a drink he had already poured himself, but was ready for a divvy. We had a great time and promised to visit him in New York before we returned to Europe in the fall. The morning of our departure we took a final horse ride.

Then we drove off for Cody, ten-gallon hats and all. At the Irma Hotel during lunch, Billy—to his chagrin—heard a voice he recognized. It was the busybody wife of his late godfather. Right in front of me, she asked, "Who is this woman you are traveling with?" Billy drew himself up to his full height and looked down on this snobbish, elderly lady and said with great aplomb, "Aunt Helen, this is my wife, Evelyn." It did not appease her much since he had not communicated it to her formally. Billy, however, was not rude in return. He didn't tell her he had intentionally avoided her. She made us promise to see her in New York, and she did come to stay at Shenandoah a few years later. Sometimes the world is too small. I could not wait to get away from Aunt Helen, so I escaped to the marvelous museum of Gertrude Vanderbilt Whitney. Among the museum's treasures was a wonderful collection of paintings by Remington and Russell.

From Wyoming, we went straight to Chicago to see Billy's best friend, Eddie Hurd from his St. George's school days. Eddie and his wife lived in Lake Forest. Their dinner party, which was to celebrate our marriage, had all the trimmings including speeches, champagne, best friends and good wishes. We were to meet them at their club for lunch the next day. Billy called their house in the morning to thank them and confirm our lunch. But, to our shock and complete surprise, Eddie informed Billy that the couple had gotten divorced that night! We felt so badly until their best friend called us up to ask whether they had said something wrong. Eddie asked us to please stay on a few days to cheer him up. Of course, we stayed a week. I never did find out why they split up. Having just come from Europe, the suddenness of this event was very strange to me. Eddie came to stay with us in Italy several times and remained our devoted friend.

We returned to Cincinnati, packed our things and said goodbye to friends. It was time to head to the East Coast. There were three older gentlemen who had taken me under their wing when I first arrived in the "Queen City." They were: Jack Emery of Seven Hundred Acre Island, Maine; Bill Chatfield of Camden, Maine; and John Mitchell of Vermont. All three had debated, in their words, about "whose jurisdiction I was in"—or rather, who would host us first in their summer houses. It was fun to have them fight over me. Our route took us via Buffalo on to the New York Throughway. The first night, which was my birthday, was spent in Batavia. As a present, Billy let me telephone my mother in Rome. The following morning when Billy went to pay the bill, the cashier looked at him with great sympathy and said, "Your wife must be the biggest chatterbox in the world. Thirty dollars for a telephone call to Rome, and it is only thirty miles up the road!" Obviously, she had confused Rome, New York with Rome, Italy.

Once through Burlington, Vermont, we zipped over the Canadian border to see Joris and Sonja Arnold-Foster in Montreal. Her parents, the Refords, were old friends of my delightful Ludens. George and Evelyn Luden had spent the war as Dutch Consul General in Montreal. Both Sonja's brothers, Boris and Alexis also lived there. Joris and Billy became best friends at once. In fact, we all got on like a house on fire.

We gave a superb lunch at the Montreal Ritz—one of the finest of the Ritz Hotels. I remember when we left Montreal we passed by the Reford family compound on Lake Magog. It brought back such pleasant memories of many long telephone conversations throughout the years. Of all the Refords, I knew and loved Boris and Sonja the best. Later, it was with immense sadness that I received the news that all three siblings had died of cancer within three months of each other. Joris had "fallen off the perch" (in his own imitable words), even before Billy did. To my great joy I still keep in contact with Boris' son, James, dining with him in Palm Beach whenever life allows.

We then headed for Camden, Maine and stayed with the Chatfields. Their large, white-frame house had a charming veranda where we would have drinks and look out to sea as their black-belted cattle grazed nearby. We had such fun, especially the afternoon spent with Bill Chatfield's daughter, Helen. She made my Billy transport a snapping turtle from the harbor up to their lake in his precious Bentley. The turtle ate through a brown paper bag and part of the rug in the trunk. Finally, we saw the turtle disappear into the lake. Billy's face was unforgettable. Imagine anyone or anything harming his beloved Bentley, even if it was a Chatfield! Since we were so close, we took several boat excursions to see Jack and Babs Emery on Seven Hundred Acre Island. Their privately-owned island hosted the entire Emery family in summer. It was absolutely delightful!

After we moved to Cincinnati in 1975, we would often find our way back to Maine on our annual driving adventures during the children's summer vacations. We would visit friends in various places like Northeast Harbor and Frenchman's Bay. But Camden and the Chatfields—especially Bill's son, Freddie, and family—would always hold a special place in our heart.

In New York, we again saw Nicken and Else in Glen Goin between serious shopping at Bloomingdale's in Patterson, New Jersey. We knew we wouldn't get the chance to shop like that anytime soon.

And so the summer honeymoon came to an end with a last visit to see Henry Alexander at Morgan's in New York City. The great departure day arrived. Since we wanted to be on American soil as long as possible, we had booked passage on the *United States*, the fastest Blue Ribbon-winning liner on the Atlantic run. Linda and George Post saw us well onboard with a bottle of Dom Perignon to help me through my post-trip unpacking! We traveled in splendid style with our 21 pieces of luggage. I guess we almost emptied Bloomingdale's to furnish our grand new home in Italy. On board daily feed was my favorite caviar. We also had our last bottle of Billy's favorite ice-cold Chateau Yquem before we landed in Cherbourg—with a glass left for the wonderful German sommelier, of course. It is too sad that the magnificent *United States* ship was put in mothballs soon after because Americans could not afford to keep it in operation. I never understood how this could happen in the great country of the United States of America!

Shenandoah, Tuscany 1975

Elizabeth in the garden, 1972   Alexandra in the gazebo, 1972

Shenandoah guests: Mattis, my godchild, his parents, Karin and Goffe Greve with Billy, Pallazone 1966

Mattis, my godson, and Janeke Greve, 43rd anniversary, 2018

Adrian Chanler, 1968

Lela Emery Steele, 2006

Happy newlyweds, Billy and Evelyn, Rome 1964

Anna Ferri in another moon gate, Shenandoah 1978

Giulio and Marcella Falini wedding, Cortona 1973

Billy, the girls and me at one of the three moon gates, Shenandoah, 1974

Don Giuseppe, beloved parish priest, Pergo di Cortona, 1987

My godson, Enrico Falini on his wedding day, Cortona 2004

Beautiful bride, Adele, Billy's daughter,   **Billy and grandson, Giacomo, 1972**
Rome, 1969

Grandson, Giacomo and granddaughter, Giulia, Tuscany, 2016

Princess Berar, Alexandra, Billy, me and Elizabeth, QE2 bound for the US, 1975

Billy Harrison, wife Evelyn, daughters Elizabeth and Alexandra and dog Polly

The Harrisons, Cincinnati Post, 1975

Rogers' Regatta, Cincinnati 1978

Paulie Ilyinsky, Winthrop Wulsin, the girls, Cincinnati 1979

Harrison and Payne Tyler, Alexandra and me, Sherwood Forest Plantation, Virginia 1990

Natalie and Russell Walden and children, John and Susannah, Santa Fe 2003

Daughters, Alexandra and Elizabeth, and granddaughters, Katt and Dee Dee, Kravis Center, West Palm Beach 2000s

Great grandson Salem with parents Charlie and Katt, 2020

Great grandson Dresden, St. Augustine 2019

Louise Hitchcock
Stephaich and her
granddaughter, Andrea

Louise Stephaich and me, Jason Tuttle's anniversary
party, Palm Beach 2018

Palm Beach Reading Group: Miriam Rosengarten, Evelyn Harrison, Edith Eglin,
Carol CollinsCindy van Husan, Anne Cox, Mary Bolton, Cinders Tilney, Didi
Ballinger, 1990s

Alexandra and me, Trianon view, Palm Beach, early 2000s

Granddaughters, Katt and Dee Dee, Tampa 2001

The Duke of Norfolk and Carolina Herrera, Hospice Ball, Palm Beach 1994

My best friend and brother, Chris, Brussels, 1989

Brother, Nicken and wife, Else, Newlyweds, England 1955

Nicken and Else, 50th anniversary, France 2005

Chris with children Cecilie, Per Christopher, Christian, Anne-Sophie, Alexander, and Carl Martin, Norway, mid 80s

Chris and wife, Anne with daughter Anne-Sophie, doctor and tri-athlete Christian and rising star, Carl Martin on Norwegian National Day, 2016

Nephew, Preben with wife, Annie and lovely children, Charlotte, Nicolai, Harry and Tom

The above Prebensens all grown up, 2019

God-daughter, Karen Bunting and son,
Oliver, 1986

Oliver, his wife, Kath and daughter,
Isla, 2018

Per Christopher, and wife Barbro,
Augusta and Benjamin, 2018

Anne-Sophie, Stian with Matthias, 2018

Cecilie, my beautiful goddaughter

Chris, my inspiration and knight in shining armor

Alexandra, daughter, friend and fellow survivor

Italy – Our Shenandoah

PRINCESS BERAR'S HYDERABAD COIN

After Billy and I were married in London, my great friend, Alain Vidal-Naquet, suggested we come up to Cortona—an Etruscan hill town in Tuscany—to find a weekend cottage. Alain had bought a house in the hills just behind Conte Umberto Morra di Lavriano's beautiful villa. Umberto was another old friend of mine who had served as head of the British-Italian Alliance in London.

The *Autostrada del Sole* between Orvieto and Florence had not yet been completed. So it took us six long hours to drive the narrow, winding roads from Rome to Cortona. The town is famous for its Etruscan Museum and the Diocesano Museum. The Diocesano is filled with works by Fra Angelico, Luca Signorelli and other Tuscan artists. The Santuario di Santa Margherita was named after the 13th century patroness of Ascension Day. When the *autostrada* was finally completed, my friend Umberto described the road as only he could, "Cars maneuver like epileptic eels on perfectly paved highways lined with blossoming plants; if one were a voyeur and not a participant in the stream of traffic, one would enjoy the spectacle of Italians attempting—by means of outracing and outwitting one another—to demonstrate that life is short and manhood long and enduring; as it is, one sweats and sometimes squeals!"

We spent the weekend with Frantz and Giuliana Passerini at their handsome Villa on the hillside overlooking the open valley of Val di Chiana.

The Passerini family had belonged to the valley for centuries. We could see across to the proud hill town of Montepulciano. I remember waking up in the mornings to the sound of the Pergo church bells and throwing open the shuttered windows to the same views that inspired famous painters. In the evenings we dined *al fresco* on the vine-covered terraces overlooking acres of olive trees. Tuscany instantly appealed to me with its tranquil rural regions. Medieval villages capped the rolling hills. Stately cypresses and vineyards surrounded old farmhouses. The area's history was as fascinating as the vistas.

Although Italy's early Etruscan civilization was short, their legacy lasted long in the area. Their origin was a mystery, their language unknown—yet had these talented people united, Italy might well be called Etruria today. In fact, in 1965 all across central Italy, dozens of towns and cities with romantic names like Florence, Siena, Volterra, Cortona, Orbetello, Arezzo, Populania, and Chiusi celebrated "The Year of the Etruscans." Perhaps it was the element of romance that captured us as our host, Alain, took us around to look at properties. We had been leaning toward a farm house, but instead we came across an ancient, large villa next door to the Passerinis. The owners had fallen on hard times, and had rented it out to six families.

The property was set high on a hillside overlooking the tranquil Tuscan plain with its many fields and vineyards. We learned this nearly 30-room structure had once been a convent, and had also been inhabited by the famous painter, Pietro da Cortona. The foundation dated back to 1200 A.D., and an inscription above the main door stated it had been remodeled in 1665. Those were good enough reasons for us to move forward on the house! Everybody, however, thought we were crazy to even consider the place as a viable dwelling. So, we left for our American honeymoon without making any decisions. Traveling from the East Coast to the West, our trip took us across the continent, arriving in San Francisco on a July day. I fell in love with the City by the Bay and wanted to live there. That is, until Billy reminded me we would be 6000 miles from our family in Europe! The Tuscany property had played on our minds throughout the entire honeymoon. The day our reflection ended, we sent a telegram to Cortona to secure the house. It was also during this trip that Billy and I chose an American Indian name for our future home. To make it easy for Italians to pronounce, we picked the melodic sounding *Shenandoah*.

We crossed the Atlantic on the fast and beautiful ship, the *United States,* and drove straight to Cortona to begin our acquisition. Initially, the renters that were living in Shenandoah had to be moved out—which took the next six months. The day came to sign the final papers, but the lawyer advised us to wait until the last family, the Falinis, moved out. I completely trusted Vittorio Falini's honest, chiseled face and signed anyway, despite Frantz, Billy, and the lawyer's disapproval. The Falinis were the first people to help renovate the house and turned out to be dear and lasting friends. So, it was with great anticipation that we took on Shenandoah's major renovation. During the first cold winter, we spent weekends in the Passerini's guest wing above the fragrant, but icy cold Limonaia.

When we began to rebuild *Shenandoah,* we acquired a penthouse apartment in Rome. It was in the vicinity of Palazzo Farnese, the French Embassy. It had been a boarding house so it needed a great deal of work. We had a "field-day," because it was just the kind of work that intrigued us both. One of the problems with the place was the unruly mass of TV antennas on the roof where we wanted to create a livable terrace. It took great tact and effort to make the other people in the building understand that we did not expect them to pay anything. We just wanted to create order. When I got pregnant, we tried to install an elevator because we lived on the 5th and 6th floors. It was voted down because the other tenants didn't believe it would stop on any floor but ours. That was how suspicious they were in that part of Rome. After our second daughter was born, we had to give in and sell the apartment to an actress who liked taking the stairs to keep her figure. I did not mind the stairs either, until I had to carry heavy babies. But while it lasted, we had more fun on that splendid rooftop. Our views of Saint Peter, the Giannicolo and Tosca's church were unsurpassed.

In Rome, we had a crook-of-a-contractor, which caused extra headaches, but the end result was spectacular. First, we doubled the front door to insulate against the noise in the building. When we sold the apartment, we brought this five-hundred-year old door to *Shenandoah*. Billy insisted on even taking it to America. We did and the door ended its life at the Harrison Tyler's Pocahontas Museum on the James River in Virginia.

The apartment library and dining room were combined to make a large space measuring thirteen meters in length. The dining room was defined by a polished copper wall. The library boasted ceiling-high bookcases trimmed in copper and leather-covered doors. We built a fireplace in the library flanked by two "dog houses," which we had copied from *Amalienborg Castle* outside Munich. To assist in the perfect library fireplace, we sought out an expert. He arrived wearing a bowler hat, and carried a suitcase. He made some calculations for the fireplace upstairs in the drawing room and started to leave. I asked for his telephone number, in case his plan was defective. The man in the bowler said it wasn't necessary because he had never failed. He was right. His plan was perfect, which we employed in all our future renovations.

The walls of that old apartment were two feet thick. The rooms were fairly small, so we installed built-in furniture in the master bedroom, the dressing room and the guest room. The drawing room one floor up had vaulted ceilings and a large terrace. In spring, summer and fall we ate most of our meals outside. Two of the arched windows in the drawing room framed the Gianiccolo and the Tiber River. From the terrace door we had a superb view of Saint Peter's Church dome.

We were away from the Roman apartment much of the time working on *Shenandoah*. When we would return to Rome from the country, I used to telephone my fabulous Maria. She and her husband, who was a roving butler, would arrange everything for a perfect dinner by the time we arrived. Aside from being the best chef I've ever had, Maria also kept the apartment spotless. Well, those were the days!

Back in *Shenandoah*, our first job was to fence in the 13 acres surrounding the house and chapel. No longer could trespassers make short cuts through our property, and—more importantly—our animals were kept in and other animals kept out. Then we constructed a three-car garage with an apartment above it featuring a good-sized living room, a bedroom, kitchen and bathroom. We still kept the apartment in Rome, but spent every moment we could above the garage while we remodeled the big house. Next, we removed every outside appendix. To create a front door to the hillside, we dug down to the foundation where we found colossal stones dating back to the 13th century. We removed a three-story interior stone wall. How these huge rocks were moved back in those days is unfathomable. We ended up with a pyramid of small boulders on the lawn and later used the stones to build a raised pool. Removing an interior wall resulted in a large dining room on the ground floor, a generous drawing room above it and a wonderful playroom on the top floor. The spacious dining room had a grand fireplace at one end and a small greenhouse at the other end, which was especially charming in winter. The ground floor also included an unusual "Arms Room" leading into Billy's study. We built a big country kitchen which led into an equally large pantry/laundry room. We also added a special room with freezers and a wine cellar.

Old stone stairs led up to the second floor. In the middle was my adored library with its view over the valley and Monte Sepoltaglia. At one end we left an old stone fireplace and then built floor-to-ceiling bookcases on the two other walls. Our beautiful Georgian desk was placed with my back to the view of the garden. The lovely rent table, which Billy had insisted I buy in Melton Mowbray reigned in the middle of the apple-green carpet. The second floor held the master bedroom and the large salon bathroom, the walk-in closet, two children's bedrooms and the emerald green bathroom were located. Apple-green taffeta curtains were hung on the four windows of the inviting drawing room. The room also held our best antiques and a one-of-a-kind 1904 Baldwin grand piano. Leading off the drawing room was what we called the American Room. It featured a copper sheeting wall—which Billy was always excusing himself to polish—and a long leather-covered bar with brass trim made by our expert Roman carpenters. One cork-covered wall hid the refrigerator and other appliances. The American Room was the entertainment center. Backgammon and cards were played, TV was watched, the drinks flowed, but more importantly, it was the musical soul of the house.

From Classical to Broadway and from Cole Porter to the Beatles, music was played every night, which often lead to singing and dancing. Alexandra and Elizabeth were frequently asked to dance for the guests either in ballet tutus or Charleston gear. What fun we all had!

The house came with no running water or heating system, just some open fireplaces. We decided to install radiators along the spine of the house because drilling through the two to three-foot thick walls was impossible.

All the guestrooms were found on the third floor. The main guestroom held my mother's majestic four-poster bed that had come from the London Embassy. Enormous in size, it featured large lion feet and golden eagles in flight. I never understood how the men hauled that bed up the stone stairs. The Pink Room faced our formal rose garden. The Blue Room had a preferred view to the courtyard. Then, there was a single bedroom furnished with my father's mahogany bed. My studio at the southeast end had a view of the rose garden. One of the guest bathrooms had formerly been a kitchen. We left its big fireplace in the corner. If special guests came we'd set a fire before their pre-dinner bath. Billy usually sent up their favorite drink to keep them company.

That second winter when we worked on the house, we passed a weekend with Marchesa Mary in the Abbruzzi. The house was unbearably cold. We found ice on the water jug in the morning because Mary was too stingy to buy wood. She pretended to be so grand that the mayor owed her the wood for free. All she had left were wood shingles from the 1915 earthquake. During meals, she would only burn four of the shingles at a time in the fireplace. My hand froze to the silver soup spoon. I have never been so cold before or since. Billy had fortunately brought his two woolen hunting undershirts, which we never took off. We were snowed in by a ferocious blizzard for five days and nights. Not surprisingly, nine months later Alexandra was born!

Throughout my entire pregnancy, I told the workmen they had better finish on time because I did not want to see them once I came back from the clinic with the baby. As I grew bigger, more men joined the workforce. Italians knew not to joke with nature. The contractor was a very pleasant man who joined his father's firm after he returned from being an Air Force pilot. Billy was an architect and I had studied architecture as well. So we both had lots of design ideas. The contractor thought we were totally mad, but was very amused. He gave up making suggestions. He just said, "Signora, you just do what you like!"

Many years later, when we were back on a visit, I recognized our contractor looking rather downcast on a street in Cortona. I greeted him, "Signor Carresi, how nice to see you." When he recognized me, he said with a wistful smile, "Signora Harrison, I haven't had any fun working since you left!"

Since we had very few shade trees, we built a loggia with a huge open fireplace. In the summer we served breakfast and lunch there. The brick paths were laid just wide enough for my "Rolls Royce" to pass. I had it made by the local artists. It was a large cart constructed of lightweight aluminum with bicycle wheels and spaces for bottles and glasses on top. The kitchen was at the opposite end of the house, so this cart was quite useful. The arched loggia was on one side of the rose garden, and the chapel—which was covered with Blaze Rose (a spectacular sight when in bloom)—was on the other side. My dolphin fountain played happily in the middle of the roses, which were bordered with white candytuft and blue ageratum. Lined with Juniper horisontalis, my dreamy cloister led to the French doors of the chapel. Along the cloister eaves were twelve begonias in steel mesh hanging baskets made by my beloved gardener, Gino. In front of the chapel doors I planted rhododendrons and camellias. A three-tiered fountain played gaily in the cloister garden.

I loved my chapel where I placed three, antique pries-dieux. The quiet times I spent there every day were priceless. A very ugly painting above the altar was removed. We broke through the wall and created a window with a cross, which extended the view to the great Tuscan hills. It was an idea we had gotten from a small church in Jackson Hole, Wyoming. One of the French doors faced the cloister, another opened to the rose garden. The quiet beauty of the rose garden inspired me to pray even more intensely. In fact, I was further inspired to build a spiral staircase descending from my bedroom to the rose garden. That way I could escape the constant flow of guests—often with my beloved Labrador, Polly—to steal some peace and quiet.

Next, we constructed a driveway to make privacy for the chapel and to add protection from the oldest hilly road that went from Umbria to Tuscany. We planted Japanese craetagus with their white flowers and bright red berries along the driveway, all the way from the gate to the dog kennel—which we covered with the world's most beautiful pale pink Clair Matin floribunda roses. Along the old road, the fences dripped with masses of wild, pink roses. Pink roses also climbed up every pole and pillar of the open hay barn, woodshed and porte-cochere.

To create vistas, we planted a long cypress alley to the east. We bulldozed through the olive groves in front of the house to the south, creating a wide view of the valley and Mount Sepoltaglia. Westward, we enjoyed a superb sunset beyond the Alamo, our adobe style playhouse. Confederate jasmine framed the French doors to the garden of the main house welcoming guests. Their lovely fragrance wafted downstairs to every room. A flagstone terrace ran the whole length of the façade. The raised stone pool was erected at the bottom of the rose garden. A laurel hedge divided the pool and the roses.

We spent many happy times at the pool, with the exception of one morning when I was having breakfast with guests in the loggia. I got a funny feeling in the pit of my stomach. Something was wrong. I jumped up, ran to the pool by leaping over the rather high hedge and the pool wall. There I found my two-year-old daughter, Elizabeth, face down in the middle of the pool. I dragged her out, turned her upside-down, and forced some hot tea down her throat to make her vomit—which, thankfully, saved her. A mother's instincts and reactions are so strong!

From the pool, a hundred yards of espalier led down to the tennis court. We also added a skeet shoot, a one-hole golf range, a maze and a small lake. We planted umbrella pines and kept a lot of the original olive trees. Our neighbors, the Falinis, always helped harvest olives. I shall never forget Anna Falini's beautiful smiling face shining through the silver-colored leaves of the old, gnarled olive trees. We also kept the old grapevines, which were, strangely, empty of grapes up to the same height of our beloved Polly's reach.

A serpentine wall, modeled after one at the University of Virginia, separated the front lawn from the vegetable and cutting gardens. Magnolia grande flores faced the garden while cherry blossoms nodded their graceful heads above the wall. A wide herbaceous border sported several hues of blue delphiniums, rich pink peonies, summer phlox and pink hollyhocks. In the cutting garden we grew lupines, snapdragons, zinnias, sweet peas and dahlias, as well as enchanting, pastel-colored columbines—all ideal for arrangements in the house. My vegetable garden also had a special pattern: one bed of flowers—like marigolds, verbenas, snapdragons and asters—separated two or three beds of spinach, lettuce, carrots, parsley, radishes, onions and green beans. Fields of melons, watermelons, eggplants and cucumbers grew further out. Lastly, I threw seeds of wild flowers underneath some old apple trees. An ancient rosemary bush seemed to enjoy the sight as much as we did.

The old rose-covered well in the middle of the front lawn was topped with an iron grill for the children's safety. It became necessary to dig more artesian wells to service the large household and the rather extensive gardens. Fortunately, my beloved gardener, Gino, had a special divining talent and could find water underground with only the help of a twig. He divined three wells, including the one for the swimming pool which was of the clearest mineral water. We surrounded one of the wells with white and pink oleander. Only later did I realize they were lethal to horses. To the west of the front lawn, we kept the tall row of old lilac bushes because of their wonderful scent. On the other side of the lilacs we planted apricot, cherry, and almond trees as well as gooseberries and currants.

Guarding the front lawn was my boxwood elephant sculpture, which Billy affectionately called "My Taft Republican." From the day that we decided to leave Shenandoah, strangely, the boxwood elephant would lose its appendages one by one. By the time we departed, only a stump was left. It didn't want us to leave.

We knew a French decorator who found a very handsome gazebo for us in France. We bought it from a photograph. Early one morning, I got an unexpected call from our local railway station. The gazebo arrived and it turned out to be 40 tons of stone and a wrought iron dome in a French railroad car. At seven o'clock in the morning I had to produce manpower to unload it, or else it would be returned to France! It took seven strong brick-layers to transport it to the house and assemble the puzzle. Fortunately, the pieces were numbered. It was installed on axis with the house and we planted Queen Elizabeth roses around the base and framed it with azaleas and yellow forsythia, which was very pretty in spring.

By this time we dreamed up the idea to create a trail all around the property so we could inspect our work. We planted almost 7000 trees and seedlings along the "Mile Garden" including beech, birch, linden trees, weeping willows, maples, oaks, chestnuts, pines, and elm trees. Every day we brought the children, as long as they were small, on a tour around the property that was almost a mile long. We started down cypress alley, skirted the pond, continued down the canyon where we joined the arbor and continued through the pins parasols forest up to the playhouse and the yarb garden. The garden path started down the cypress alley with glimpses of the vegetable beds and the peach tree blossoms. It then passed by the largest well to the small lake we had created by damming the creek. Billy kept a rubber dinghy there to take the children for boat rides around the little island in the middle of the lake, where a lone weeping willow admired its own reflection. The path continued past the lake, down through the valley of lovely shrubs of hibiscus and weigelia, viburnum and japonica. It then dropped down below the dam through clumps of trees to the "Grand Canyon." I found the Canyon one day when the gardeners and I were cleaning up a horrendous mess of thorns and vines in the creek. I never walked around the garden without my pruners. The children used to say they would have to bury me with pruners in my hand. The trail went past the tennis court and continued to the Grand Stairs of Versailles, which were made from railroad ties and adorned with varieties of sempervirum, subulata, primroses and wild forget-me-nots. Walking down the path one would see my favorite grove of umbrella pines, the wild flower garden and finally, Billy's last creation—the Chicken Palace. It was a lovely round tower with a roof terrace where Billy could have a quiet drink, while addressing his "Senate," which consisted of Japanese Bantams, guinea hens, ducks and various species of ordinary chickens. Billy enjoyed it there, emphasizing that they never talked back! It was tragic when one day I found that, overnight, a fox had killed Nanette, one of the pair of bantams. Her husband, Peter the Great, died of a broken heart two days later.

Then we would pass by the ancient fig trees—both the green and plump purple variety. On to the western border there was a heaven of sunflowers, the herb garden and the flagpole. The herb garden was laid out as a wagon wheel with brick footpaths as divisions. I was told by a New Englander that I should call it a "yarb" garden. The trail then looped back and ended at the playhouse.

Some of my favorite architectural details on the property had been discovered while honeymooning in New York. We had lunched at Jack Emery's sister's (Mrs. McKay) beautiful house on Long Island. *Chelsea* was modeled after a house on the Yangtsee River banks in China that Alexandra McKay had seen on her honeymoon. Among the many fantastic details in her garden was a Chinese Moon gate, which we adored and copied several times, both in Italy and in America. In fact, we ended up with three Moon Gates in Tuscany, all on axis—two on each end of the rose garden and one to cut off the courtyard from the garden terrace. It wasn't just the architecture and the gardens of Shenandoah that captured our hearts, it was the people, the animals, the neighbors and the Italian way of life.

When we were at *Shenandoah,* Giulio and Marcella Falini and Anna and Guido Ferri ran the property with us. Elsa Pareti also joined the crew. Her daughter, Vilma married Anna's son, Ivo! Giulio and Marcella had two children, Enrico and Elisabetta, who are both now married with children of their own. Enrico is my godson, and even though we left for the States many years ago, we still stay in constant contact. His son, Tommaso, had his first communion in recent years and is now a great tennis player.

I always treated the animals in my life as members of the family. When we first moved to *Shenandoah*, we had the most wonderful black poodle named Coquette. She had been my loyal companion in Rome after Father died. She would go to most restaurants with me. Owners would insist that I brought Coquette and hardly allow me in if I had come alone. In fact, I may have married Billy simply because Coquette approved of him. I was destroyed when she turned blind and could no longer get around without hurting herself. Billy gave me a charm in memory of this faithful friend.

After Elizabeth was born, we acquired Polly—our beloved yellow Labrador—from Peabody, Massachusetts. The dog was to be flown to Italy when she was three months old. So, we drove three-and-a-half hours to Rome's Fiumicino Airport to pick her up, but she was not there. When I called the kennel in Massachusetts, the American owner said, "I couldn't send her before I had a check in my hand." I replied, "How can I pay for something I haven't seen?" His next remark was something else. "Well," he said, "You are a dishonest Italian." Horrified, I told him, "You may think what you want about the Italians, being a New Englander, but I am an honest Norwegian." Of course, he won, and I sent the check. Once more, we drove all the way back to the airport. At first, we still could not find her, but then realized that the Italian pilots had taken turns walking her and giving her water. She jumped into my arms and my heart, and stayed there forever. Polly intuitively understood everything, in good and in bad times. She was my best friend for 14 long years.

We also had cats. The first was called Uncle Lucien. Once while away for the weekend, there was a chimney fire and he died of smoke inhalation. I was given his sister, Emi. She had various children living with us: Happy, who always walked in the garden with me, and Kitten and Fernandino, who belonged to Alexandra and Elizabeth. When we had to leave for the States, Emi went to stay with Marcella's mother next door. A year later, I returned to *Shenandoah* for a month in the summer. I sat having breakfast the first morning on the terrace when Emi turned up. I greeted her with enthusiasm; she just gave me a terrible look, put her tail straight in the air, turned on her heels and walked off, never to set foot on the property again. She was going to show me who was leaving who! Though I was shocked and brought to tears, I understood.

One of the many fond memories of *Shenandoah* was of the big, white Chiannini oxen. They were still in use for agricultural work when we arrived. I loved it when the large, docile animals faithfully arrived at olive-picking time to transport the crop to the mill. The oxen had an aura of majesty and peace that was reminiscent of 18th-century life. In fact, I still have the metal flag that combines the Medici balls and the oxen of the Val di Chiana—the Passerini coat of arms—which was given to me by Frantz Passerini when we left Tuscany for the States.

Lorenzo Passerini, Frantz's older brother, owned the biggest residence in town. Pope Leo X, originally known as Cardinal Giovanni di Medici, came on a visit to Cortona in November 1515. Lorenzo di Medici told his student, Cardinal Passerini, to build a spectacular palace to honor this visit. The construction began in 1521 and took six years. The building—simply called *Il Pallazone*—has proportions that are vast and impressive. As a one-year-old toddler, Alexandra would slide in her play device along the vast expanse of the palace's living rooms, while we were offered Vin Santo (anno 1849 and 1863) from his cellar, Renzo was a great friend. He still lived at *Pallazone* during our early years. He later gave the palace to be used by the University of Pisa, keeping only a tower apartment for his use. Renzo and his wife, Lyndel, celebrated many a Christmas with us.

However, my favorite neighbor was Umberto Morra di Lavriano who became a most loyal and great friend. He lived only a mile away as the crow flies. He had been in London as Director of the Italian Institute during my father's time as ambassador. After Umberto returned to Italy, he worked in Rome at the *Palazzetto Venezia*. He was an active anti-fascist, an outstanding writer and a great anglophile. During the Resistance, Morra played a large part in anti-fascist activities, acting as a link between the Central Committee for National Liberation in Rome and its branches in Tuscany. Later, he became the private secretary for the Parri government. He came from an old Piemontese family, and his father, General Morra, had been the Italian Ambassador to Russia. Umberto spent part of his childhood in St. Petersburg. When he returned to Italy, he brought with him his Russian toys including a large brown mechanical bear and a gilt model of a troika, which thoroughly intrigued my children. In his villa at Metelliano, his study and its many frescoed walls were modeled after Napoleon's tent at Malmaison. Umberto received and concealed many anti-fascist friends, including Salvemini. He always received many foreign friends and guests from all over the world, among them, for instance, the French President Francois Mitterand and T.S. Eliot. Whenever he had interesting guests, during my Tuscan years, he would include us, and we did the same for him. He also spent all his holidays like Christmas and Easter with us. Lord Ashley Clarke wrote of him that he was a friend who's sweet character, intelligence and absolute sincerity was a great joy. Umberto published a book about another good friend of his named Bernhard Berenson. *Conversations with Berenson* presents a vivid picture of the famous connoisseur.

Iris Origo, also a good friend of Umberto, lived at *La Foce*, which was situated between Chianciano Terme and Montepulciano. She was a well-known author whose childhood had been divided between three different worlds: her American grandparents (the Bayard Cuttings of Long Island); her Anglo-Irish grandparents of County Kilkenny; and her mother's years lived at the Villa Medici (Fiesole) in Florence, Italy. In 1924, Iris married the Italian Marchese Antonio Origo and they bought and renovated the property, *La Foce*. She was a legendary figure during the Second World War and lived right on "the gothic" line. *La Foce* became a wartime refuge for children, peasant families and Allied Airmen. The couple was warned that they would be in the line of fire. Marchesa Origo kept a diary in 1943-44 that she published entitled *War in Val d'Orcia.* One very dangerous evening she escaped with the children and crawled with them through the fields and ditches towards Montepulciano. They had to dodge the low-flying planes. Finally, when they reached the church of San Biagio (one of my very favorite churches), the inhabitants of Montepulciano saw them and came down and helped them on the last climb. We loved the church of San Biagio so much that we often went across the valley from Cortona to visit it. Billy dreamed that our daughters would one day be married there. Life turned out differently.

Marchesa Origo also wrote an autobiography called *Shadows and Images*. In it she wrote: "During the Second World War Umberto Morra worked in the prisoner of war section of the Italian Red Cross and in times of crisis, such as the great advance of the [Nazi] 'Desert Rats,' he was much in demand to decipher the often garbled information that was telegraphed from North Africa. He became the Italian representative of the International Red Cross Commission which inspected the Allied POW camps all over Italy, in particular at the castle of Vincigliata where the English generals were kept. Here, Morra's tact and humor were as useful as his thorough knowledge of the English language and character."[1]

The happiest part of Umberto's last years, I was told, was spent in his Tuscan villa in Cortona. He was always surrounded by friends and admirers of every age, class and range of political opinion. My daughter, Alexandra—as one of his youngest friends—started her social life at his dinner table at the age of eleven months, nodding intently as if following the conversation! And it is in the hearts of his many friends that he will forever be remembered. Umberto Morra di Lavriano died the seventh of November, 1981. It was a very sad day when I received the telephone call from his friend Mario.

Being an artist all my life, I was always looking for things to do in the art world. One of our accomplishments, while in Tuscany, was to help the University of Georgia establish a summer art program in Cortona. The program's head had procured a hotel in town for the students' boarding the first year. Imagine my amusement when I got an S.O.S. call the first evening from one of the girls reporting that there were men at their doors! The professor had unknowingly rented the only brothel in town! From then on, I helped to arrange to put the students up in the local convent, and they have remained there ever since. The program was such a success that the university has since added full spring, summer and fall semesters in Cortona.

Every summer we hosted an annual dinner for about a hundred guests—eighty from the University of Georgia, and twenty from Georgia Tech. The students called it the "Tara" party, and the girls brought special dresses for the occasion. We even grew watermelons for their American Fourth of July football matches in Cortona.

One year we brought our daughters to the American International School of Florence. We took an apartment in the Palazzo Benci on the Arno, which was run by the Grand Hotel. Our apartment was charming. Billy insisted on returning home to Shenandoah every Friday, in spite of the fact that weekend driving was not permitted due to the oil embargo. This meant we had to get up at an ungodly hour on Monday mornings to arrive in time for school in Florence. But it also meant that Giulio could fill the car every Monday morning with fresh fruit and flowers from *Shenandoah's* garden. Even my roses bloomed till after Christmas.

A couple of those weekends Alexandra and I chose to stay in town. I loved Florence when it had no vehicles. I imagined that it resembled Florentine life at the time of the Medicis. One could *flaner* (stroll) everywhere, and even walk to have dinner with friends in their old palaces. Two such friends were Aloisia and Niccolo Ruccelai. Niccolo was an architect and Aloisia was a jewelry designer of the first order. She was so creative and had a phenomenal imagination. They lived on the top floor of the *Palazzo Ruccelai* in Via delle Vigna. Niccolo had rebuilt the apartment around the famous Paolo Uccelli's frescos which they found under layers of stucco on top of the palazzo. After a cocktail party, Aloisa would keep a few friends over for her special spaghetti al pesto. We ate off solid silver plates. She had taken all her not-so-favorite wedding presents and exchanged them for silver plates because they never broke! Around the corner from their *Palazzo Ruccelai* was Via Tornabuoni with the *Palazzo Antinori* and its cantina. We went there often on our shopping trips, as well as to the famous *Ditta Leopoldo Procacci* for our white truffle snacks.

The first weekend Aloisia and Niccolo visited us at *Shenandoah*, Niccolo asked Billy whether he had ever heard of an American painter named

Whistler. After Niccolo rifled through his mother's things in the attic, he found not only drawings, but also paintings by Whistler.

"Do you think they have any value?" Niccolo asked. Billy very quietly went to the bookcase and came back with one of our books on Whistler, and said, "Take a look at this upstairs while you are dressing for dinner!"

When Whistler lived in Venice, Countess Ruccelai—nee Miss E. Bronson, Nicolo's mother—was Whistler's friendly backer. She wrote: "He used to say Venice was an impossible place to sit down and sketch, there was always something better around the corner!"[2] We know Whistler found Venice cold, but beautiful. He would take a room in *Palazzo Rezzonico* where he would paint the sunset and then swear at the sun for setting. He found Veronese and Titian great swells, and Canaletto and Guardi, great masters. Niccolo found out something quite amazing that weekend.

I wish I could find some Whistlers suddenly in my attic! But, what we do have, which is even more important to me, is a wonderful guestbook. It contains not only guests' thank-you notes, but also their photographs on the day of their departure. Now, that's a real treasure!

In the summer of '75, we had a full house of guests, both invited and uninvited. On top of running a bed and breakfast, so to speak, I had to have a benign tumor the size of a grapefruit removed from my hip. The procedure and recovery only lasted a couple of weeks at the Blue Nuns' Hospital in Florence, but afterwards it was difficult to pack. The wound had to be kept open to heal from the inside-out, which took over two months.

Part of the furniture was to be shipped to the States, but because the house was listed as furnished, the rest was sadly left behind. The banks were intermittently on strike. We obtained an American Express card in order to leave. When we tried to use it in Florence to pay for our tickets, however, they could only authorize $500. They had to ask Rome. The connection was down. When finally we got through, they could only go to $1000. They had to get through to the office in England, but the computers were down. I asked whether the telephone couldn't be used. Oh, no! Frustrated, I insisted on paying for the damn telephone call, called myself and was transferred to one of their idiotic nincompoops. Finally, it was arranged.

It happened to be the last Atlantic crossing of the *Queen Elizabeth II* that year! At the end we had won because "I never took *no* for an answer." We had come to the conclusion that we would cross on the *Q.E. II*. The transition would be less dramatic for the children and Billy, who hated air planes. That meant we had to take the overnight train from Florence to Paris. There I reserved a station wagon with a roof rack so we could drive from Paris to Cherbourg with all the luggage and Polly, our beloved Yellow Labrador. The leg to Florence went fine—the train trip was no problem. But when we arrived in Paris, there was no station wagon. I called the car-rental company. For the first time I received the brunt of French rudeness. They did not honor our confirmed reservation. Because of our large amount of luggage, we had to take two taxis to go to the car rental office. Billy was livid. The girls were tired, only Polly seemed unperturbed. I wondered what to do. After all, it was the last Atlantic crossing of the *Q.E. II* that year. For all eventualities I had added an extra day. The young French men, however, were not helpful at all. Suddenly, I saw the manager arrive. I noticed his name was Portuguese. I immediately started to speak to him in Portuguese, won his sympathy about our plight, and things started to move. Their station wagons had no racks, but the manager was willing to buy and install one. He suggested that we go out for lunch and he would take care of our luggage. He would meet us for tea at some hotel at five with the luggage and the car. Billy was nervous, but very proud of my vamping in Portuguese. At 5:30, we were finally on our way. We stopped at *Pont L'Eveque* for a one star Guide Michelin dinner, and Billy's mood brightened several degrees.

We crossed on the *Queen Elizabeth II* from France for a five-day voyage. My dearest friend, Durru Shevar, The Princess of Berar, accompanied us. I had recently undergone surgery for a cyst on my hip and the wound had to be kept open for two months. This virtually incapacitated me, so the princess dropped everything to lend me moral support during the trip. I was extremely grateful for her company.

During the voyage we all dressed elegantly, sat at the Captain's table and enjoyed caviar and champagne. For the girls there were, of course, other goodies. These little luxuries helped alleviate the sadness our family felt having had to leave Europe and our dear Tuscan home. Overall, it was a really delightful crossing. Only our beloved Yellow Lab, Polly was not so happy. We walked her on the deck as much as possible.

Five days later we landed in New York, and it was with a heavy heart that I had to say goodbye to Durru Shehvar. From the time I was an 18 year-old in London, she had been such a part of my European life. I could only hope she would come to see us in the States as she often did when we lived in Italy.

Many of my most important memories are associated with Italy. The 14 years I owned *Shenandoah*—from 1964 to 1978—were the happiest. I had my loves and my children there, and there they were raised. I dream of the beauty of Tuscany, but most of all I shall never forget the wonderful people who made my everyday life so meaningful. These many years later I feel that part of my soul still lives among the wonders of that very special part of the world. Whenever I return, I "recharge my batteries" as my Italian friends would say.

Cincinnati – First American Home

GOLD PINE CONE

A car awaited our arrival in New York. Fortunately, it had a luggage rack on the roof. Without it we could not have fit four people, a large dog, plus our baggage into a Mercury Station Wagon. Nobody bothered to advise us that air conditioning was a necessity for cross-country traveling. It was mid-August and we were taking the southern route to Cincinnati. Although extremely hot, I thought my whole family behaved like saints, including Polly. She was squeezed in between the luggage behind the seats.

The Cincinnati Post published the following in-depth article written by Polk Laffoon, Jr. Not only was he a well-know journalist and author, he was also the son of a great friend and had spent several weeks, along with his brother, Nathan, that last summer at Shenandoah. He knew the details of our story better than most; we trusted him completely and he did not disappoint with his article titled: *New Life for Harrisons:*

After 25 years of expatriate living, Billy Harrison is back in Cincinnati. Inflation and the leftward slide of Italian politics drove him home.

His story is not an average one. Indeed, as the wealthy American living abroad, it would probably win little sympathy from less privileged countrymen in either nation. Yet it's worth telling, not only for the insight it provides about what is happening in Italy, but for the depiction of a lifestyle that may be vanishing forever.

Born in Cincinnati 58 years ago, Billy is linked to one of this city's oldest families. Learner Blackman Harrison founded the First National Bank in the mid-nineteenth Century, and Billy is a cousin. He grew up in Hyde Park, spent winters in Aiken, South Carolina, and then during WWII met and married Eloise Fiamingo, of Rome. Her father was an Italian, her mother was born Stettinius from Cincinnati.

The marriage lasted until 1962 when Billy and Eloise were divorced. Two years later Billy married Evelyn Prebensen, daughter of the Norwegian Ambassador to Great Britain and Italy, and a painter of some note. A striking woman of enormous sensitivity and perception, she stands by Billy today as he vows not to dwell on the past. "I cannot, we cannot allow ourselves to look back," he says resolutely. But then he tells you about Shenandoah.

Shenandoah—the house, the place, the way of life that he and Evie had created for themselves and their two children. I was in Cortona, one of those fawn colored hill towns that travel books dote on. When the Harrisons bought Shenandoah, it was nothing—just an abandoned convent with weeds for a view. Yet, by the time they left it this past August, it was a showplace that stunned their Tuscan neighbors.

The façade was wide and white, punctuated by dark blue chalet shutters, and soared three stories to a red tiled roof. Inside the polished brick floors shone up as burnished wood and custom-ordered fabrics that are as rare in Italy as Giottos are here. All around were leather objects and old world antiques, the residue of a generation's collecting. The grounds, with their loggia and gardens and several thousand newly planted trees, finally looked lived in.

They lived, Evie says, the life of gentleman farmers. Most of their waking hours were spent caring for the place, in company with four servants inside and three field hands. Only 80 miles from Florence, they traded visits with their friends from town and from Rome and Siena.

At home, their social life, such as it was, revolved around people like Umberto, a kind of cultural prime minister for the Italian government, and the Passerinis, a manor family that had tilled the same soil for 900 years. "Old Italy, *not new," Evie says simply. Once every winter the family went skiing, and once every summer to the seashore.*

"Five years ago if you had asked me when I was going to leave Italy, I would have said, 'Never,'" Billy said. "That house was our life and we planned to keep it forever. Except we would come back here, while the girls were at school."

The girls, Alexandra, 9, and Elizabeth, 6, are the Harrison's daughters. It was their schooling abroad which gave the family a first hint that it might have to come home permanently.

During the winter of 1973, when the oil crisis first loomed large, the girls were in school in Florence. Five days a week, Billy and Evie lived in the city and on weekends drove back to Cortona with their children.

Suddenly the price of gas doubled; driving was prohibited on Sundays and commuting became impossible. Evie, who kept the family ledger, found it more and more difficult to maintain their standard of living. In time they could not afford meat. The cost of heating Shenandoah rose to more than 5000 American dollars a year.

"Our first thought was to sweat it out. We went home and built a chicken coop." Billy called it, "A chicken palace," with idea of raising chickens, ducks and guinea hens for consumption." Evie's vegetable gardens, which already grew every-thing from grapes to olives, were expanded, and Billy was optimistic.

Evie was not. With the European's instinct for trouble, she read the vibra-tions. "I've gone through occupations. You feel it when there is something coming up. Practically, it couldn't go on. You can't cut every resource and pretend it will go away." That winter Evie did something she had never done before. She applied for an American Express card on the chance that they might be forced to evacu-ate quickly.

With increasing apprehension, both Harrisons watched Italy's Communist Party win over the minds of the people. "Intelligent men were saying democracy has failed," Billy recalls. "So much so that in June, in the provincial elections, the Communists gained 10 per cent in all the big towns and cities, and the Christian Democrats lost 7 per cent.

Part of it, of course, was the oil crisis. Ignorant people don't like rises in the cost of basic commodities. In six months, we saw gas go from $1.30 a gallon to $2. Inflation was galloping—up to 300 per cent on some things, although the official rate was 24 per cent annually. The people took it for a time, but then all hell broke loose. Wildcat strikes. Bombings. Kidnappings. And the Commies said, 'If we were in power, we wouldn't have raised prices.'"

Billy and Evie asked the people around them—servants, butchers, florists—how they felt, and invariably the answer came back: "Well...you know, democracy has failed us...and the Communists never have been in. So let's see what they can do. If we don't like it, we'll vote them out." Italians, Billy says, insist that theirs will not be a Russian or international Communism, but rather an Italian brand different from the others. The thought makes him cringe.

He remembers talking one night with a young acquaintance that had come to say goodbye. Billy believed the man to be more than a little naïve in the best of times, but what he heard on this particular night shocked him:

"Maybe it's good thing if the Communists take over," the visitor said. "Maybe, finally, Italy will belong to the Italians and not to the tourists. America doesn't have a lot of tourists. Why should we?" "Do you realize that Italy has no natural resources?" Billy responded. "No iron. No oil. No steel?" "We have geniuses," his guest countered. "We have Fermi (famous atomic scientist) and Agnelli (head of Italy's powerful Fiat Motors) and we are big in tires." "You may have geniuses, but no raw materials. If you withdraw as a nation, how do you expect to get those materials?" "Oh, I didn't mean we should withdraw from Europe..." "Well," Billy persisted, "it certainly sounds like you're suggesting getting out of the Atlantic pact." "Oh no," the other said. "Just out from under U.S. domination."

Billy pointed out that the one natural resource Italy does have is its heritage—its beautiful art, architecture and countryside. Could they afford to lose the tourist revenues these bring in, he asked. But it was hopeless. The youth was not to be persuaded.

And so it went. All over Italy Billy glimpsed the future and was frightened.

A friend in Rome, an executive in a big manufacturing company, demoted himself to shop manager, thus joining the ranks of the blue collar workers. He thought it would do better there under the coming regime.

In a speech delivered by the head of the Italian Communist party, Billy counted the word 'democratic' used 13 times and 'liberty' eight. The gist of the diatribe: "Italians, under the domination of Americans and the so-called democracy of Italy, vote for us who will guarantee your liberty. Vote us in; vote out the victims of imperialistic U.S. influence."

For years Billy had watched Italians refuse to invest in their own country, buying stocks in the U.S. of Britain instead. Suddenly the trend worsened. He saw young men with weapons, waiting for the revolution, and learned that the Vatican told its parish priests to prepare for Communism. "Know the enemy; infiltrate by joining him; instigate a counterrevolution," is the Church's position.

Billy says now, "It's inevitable that Italy will go Communist. The takeover will not be achieved through revolution, but through economic chaos. They will get the country down and step in."

The evidence was all around him; his wife had confronted it and make up her mind; but still Billy was not convinced. It took a trip to Venice to persuade him.

The trip was last May, for the benefit of the girls, who were worn out from a long winter of too little heating oil and too much New Zealand flu. Despite the warnings of friends Billy and Evie wanted Elizabeth to see Venice, and so they headed north.

They stayed for four days and three nights in a none-too-fancy motor inn on the autostrada between Padua and Venice. The bill, for lodgings and three breakfasts and dinners, was $450. Lunch on San Marco Square was $50. Adding it all up, with gas, the trip cost $700. And Bill knew he had to leave.

But how to tell the children? "You must understand that living in Shenandoah they've been raised like Scarlett O'Haras," he said. "They loved their home and the people on the place...the animals...this was their entire world, if only because we hardly ever went out of it."

And Evie: "A house here isn't the same thing. It's just something you trade in when you need a bigger one. Here a house isn't you. But the girls had been colored by the kidnappings, the bombings and the insecurity. And they were all for going to school in America. They knew the one in Cortona wasn't adequate. So that's how we approached them. But we didn't lie. We told them that if we returned to Italy, it would only be for visits."

Getting out was not easy. The Harrisons agreed that they had to be gone by the middle of August—the Italian counterpart of our Labor Day—when people return en masse from their seashore vacations. They had to put Shenandoah up for sale and arrange to ship half their furniture to the United States. The other half would be left in Italy forever because they knew it would be impossible to sell an unfurnished house.

Psychologically, they determined, a boat trip home was essential. An airplane would have been too fast, the change of environs too sudden for Alexandra and Elizabeth. So, with only the luggage they could carry, they took a train to Paris, a car (rented with the American Express card that Evie had providentially acquired) to Cherbourg, and boarded the Queen Elizabeth II for their long voyage.

Today, they live in a small house in Hyde Park loaned to them by a friend; soon, they will break ground for an unspectacular frame home in the country. Readjustment pains have been eased by an array of friends from Billy's youth, and Evie speaks laughingly of trying to open a department store charge account. Born in Moscow, Russia, with her nationality Norwegian, she underwent more than the routine credit check.

Still, reminders of the past are everywhere. Billy drives a small American car in place of a Lancia he adored. When he tried to export it, he found that its double glass windshield (instead of triple) and lack of a torque bar made it unacceptable according to American safety standards. Recently, the furniture arrived, but only after the greatest difficulty for the exporter, and the greatest expense for the Harrisons. They know that selling Shenandoah for any price will be difficult and maybe impossible.

Now and again at odd moments, the girls have trouble sleeping, or begin to look sad, and one of them will say, "Poppy, I miss Shenandoah." In response, Billy is comforting, and almost philosophical. After 25 years abroad, he has acquired something of the European life view; he smiles frequently, takes time with every person and exudes in all things a gentle acceptance of what is to be.

As much for his own peace or mind, perhaps as for the girls', he alludes often to some advice given them on the eve of their departure. The speaker was Germaine Greer, the feminist leader who had come to Cortona to write, and to be isolated, and in doing so had become close friends of the Harrisons. "Elizabeth and Alexandra," she said, "I know it is going to be hard for you to leave Shenandoah, but you will always remember a lovely childhood in this beautiful house in this beautiful country. It will be hard, but I want you to realize that you will find a great deal of bad and a great deal of good in America. It is competitive and harsh in a way Italy is not. But that is what makes a great country. And America is the greatest country in the world."[1]

I had kept up correspondence with Billy's stepmother, Aunt Ted, and she formally asked us to come to America. She was 93 years old, unwell, and requested Billy's help with the Harrison family Brill Road property. For tax purposes, Aunt Ted gave us a three-acre parcel in a corner of the property. On it we built a one story white frame house with a two-car garage. It was bought as a pre-cut house through the Pease Company. I changed out the windows for a more European feel. We called it the *Mouse House*. We had gone to the Pease Company (a building supply store) one day to get ideas. We not only found solutions, but a contractor as well. He was a former school teacher of German extraction. It was the best business relationship we ever had. The house had a spacious living room/dining room open to the kitchen, a master suite, dressing room, and a kids' room and bath. A two-car garage completed the project. As the children grew, and our time in Cincinnati extended into years, they each got their own room and we added a study and a walk-in closet. One view faced down the lawn to a brook and the other toward the stepmother's twenty-two-acre garden.

When we first started construction, Billy's cousin, Lucien Wulsin very generously lent us his townhouse. I don't know how we would have managed without it. One evening in 1975, Lucien gave a dinner. Our host was tending the barbecue. I talked to a man sitting on my other side at the table. I thought I was keeping up the dialog well because he kept smiling. Suddenly, I noticed he had an earplug wired to a transistor radio hidden by my skirt. He was listening to the Reds' baseball game! It's no wonder he was smiling as they won the pennant that year. Quite frankly, I thought he should have stayed at home. This encounter lowered my view of my ability to converse at an American dinner party! I can still remember my sharp discouragement.

I had never lived in the United States and everything was strange and new. Lucien's mother, Aunt Peggy kindly gave me a couple of her husband's cookbooks, which were not useful at the time because Uncle Lucien was a great gourmet chef. Paul Ilyinsky and Dudley Taft tried me out on my spaghetti our second night, which was a success. I quickly realized I needed more culinary help and bought two yards of both simple and advanced cookbooks. I still have them. Having lived in diplomatic life, I knew how food should taste and I knew how to read. I only needed time to experiment, which I did in between carpooling and house building. My Tuscan cook would have been proud of me. I had taught her a great deal in theory, and now I could put it into practice. Throughout the following ten years we entertained often.

In the mean time, we still had not sold *Shenandoah*. It was too difficult for Billy to go back to Italy, so I returned for three consecutive summers to oversee the selling. It was a jewel that nobody wanted because nobody could afford it at the time.

I had requested citizenship through a lawyer's office, received the promised papers by February, but not yet the little green card! Therefore, I conferred with the lawyer who conferred with the authorities, and was told I could go to Italy on business using my Norwegian passport. Nobody, however, mentioned that I would not be able to re-enter the US!!!

My first trip to Shenandoah was in 1976. I returned to my heavenly home in Cortona, visited with friends, and hoped someone would walk up and buy the property. After a month I went to visit my mother in Oslo, Norway. Upon leaving, my brother, Chris and I took an early breakfast, and then he drove me to the airport. I had a pleasant flight out the Oslo fjord over my childhood's bays and islands south to the bustling Kastrup Airport in Copenhagen. Then we boarded SAS for Chicago. The good service and company lulled me into the feeling that life was friendly and pleasant.

After a beautiful flight over the eastern U.S coast, I had a brutal awakening at O'Hare Airport in Chicago—a dreadful experience never to be repeated. Upon landing, I was refused entry into the United States due to not having a green card. I was set in a corridor, and not allowed even into the immigration office. A Nazi-type woman kept me sitting on the floor. After half an hour I finally obtained the permission to talk to her superior and was let into an office. I was allowed to sit on a chair and was told I had committed a crime by leaving the US with a running visa in my passport, but not the proper re-entry papers. I would be deported from whence I came, namely Copenhagen, 8 hours away, which made no sense at all!

I was exhausted and knew that my impatient husband and two daughters were waiting for me at Boone County Airport in Cincinnati, Ohio. There had to be a way out of this problem. I asked to call my American lawyer, it was denied. I asked to call my senator Robert Taft, also denied. Well, since I was a Norwegian citizen I asked to call my Norwegian ambassador in Washington D. C. No, they had no obligation to allow me to call anyone in the U.S. I was desperate, but I had to find a loop hole. Finally, the man I was dealing with softened a little bit and said he could call his superior in Cleveland as to whether I could be given parole!! I felt like a prisoner from SING-SING. Fortunately, it was early afternoon and the man in Cleveland was still in his office and he did give me 6-day parole! It took me over ten years before I felt like asking for US citizenship, in fact the year was 1987, just before my husband Billy died of a heart attack!!

After several hours at Chicago's O'Hare airport, once finally in the air, our plane ran into bad weather, including dodging tornado accumulations. Big cottony clouds bullied each other around us. The airport in Cincinnati was closed, so we landed in Louisville, Kentucky. The captain then asked if anybody was game to fly up the Ohio River underneath the heavy cloud cover. Ten of us volunteered. Billions of small lights helped us, and the plane finally reached Boone County Airport around midnight. Thankfully, Billy and the girls were still there waiting.

Back when Alexandra was born in Rome, I was horrified that my own child had trouble with her citizenship. The hospital threatened that she was not any kind of citizen at the time. I called William Reinhardt, the American Ambassador, and cried that they were saying Alexandra was not legitimate, although I'd been married for two years. It was a technicality. He said to give them hell and that he'd be right over to confirm her American citizenship and even give her a passport.

The second trip in 1977—which Billy would still not accompany me on—I made sure that I had my travel papers in proper order! This trip was a pleasant peaceful reunion. My beloved friend, Aloisia Ruccelai invited me to stay in Positano along with our mutual friend, Durru Shehvar Berar. Aloisia's father, Admiral Aloisi had a house right next to the Hotel Sirenuse. Dinner was always served on the terrace overlooking the ocean. Lunch was usually Vesuvius tomatoes and mozzarella bought at the Trattoria on the beach. Positano has a splendid position on the rocky Amalfi coast along the blue Mediterranean. Admiral Aloisi was one of the great characters in Positano for years. We were so sad when he died later that summer.

I returned to the states with my mission to sell unaccomplished because there were absolutely no buyers for my beautiful estate. It wasn't that I didn't try; it was a time when big houses were not desirable or practical. Billy and I were still paying the Falinis and the Ferris to maintain the huge compound. We did this while establishing our own house and life in Cincinnati.

Upon the third trip in 1978, we finally had to scale down. The market was terrible for selling big houses. That year I brought Alexandra and Elizabeth and a bunch of friends. I told them their duty was to keep me laughing; I so hated having to sell my beloved home. Durru Shehvar Berar visited, as she had through all our Tuscan years, so did Adele Emery, and Michael and Lucy Ainslie. I kept life running in good old *Shenandoah* style.

One day, my neighbor, Silvio Passerini, came over on horseback and said he had a lawyer interested in the property. That evening he brought the potential Roman buyer. He wanted to buy the villa that very evening for a country club group. I had invited guests including Princess Berar to visit. We all changed into evening clothes for a candlelight dinner on the terrace. The lawyer sat upstairs in my library and peered down at us while drawing up a contract. I was nervous and wanted to contact legal advice of my own, but one of my guests, who worked in real estate, exclaimed, "Grab him, and grab him fast!" That was how bad the market was that summer. The country club never materialized, but the lawyer, Romano Antonioli, bought and still owns *Shenandoah!*

When we finally got paid for *Shenandoah*, at a time when one could not bring the money out of Italy, I invested in a pair of Aloisia's famous tiara diamond ear clips and carried them across the ocean. I had to get the rest of the money in cash. When I received the money at the bank, the director asked me how I dared to carry it out. I had Lucy and Michael Ainslie with me, both over six-feet tall. I pointed to them and said, "My body guards!"

In Florence, "my bodyguards" went shopping at Gucci, Ginori and so on. Every time they bought something, I disappeared into the restroom and took a wad of money out of my girdle! The rest of the money I gave to a friend of mine with connections (without getting a receipt). It mysteriously appeared in my brother's bank account in Switzerland through channels a few weeks later. You can imagine our conversation when my brother called me and said, "What the hell is all this money in my bank account?" "It's *Shenandoah!*" I said. I shall never know how, but I can say I did not sleep very well while the money was en route.

After the sale of the house, I returned to Cincinnati. We celebrated my 50th birthday at the *Mouse House* with a lovely dinner and our closest friends. Among them were Angie and Paul Ilyinsky, who were there for us from the very beginning. During our first Christmas, Angie let me wrap and store presents in the guestroom of her house (the *Kremlin)*—which was extremely valuable having young children. One was nine and the other six. Paulie would come over for morning coffee after we had taken the kids to school. This was also a great help in our transition.

On Billy's 65th birthday, I invited 36 people for a seated dinner in what was referred to as *The Madwoman of Chaillot's Banqueting Hall*. It was named after a popular play in London, and yes, I was the madwoman because no one in their right mind would entertain 36 people. It had been built as a two-car garage. The English dining room table was in the center with a 17th-century Russian chandelier hanging from the high ceiling. Twenty of the guests had come to the Camargo Indoor Tennis Club for our private tournament. The atmosphere in *Mouse House* was spirited as we brought over all the dishes from Aunt Ted's large refrigerators next door. The rain poured down, but thanks to brother, Chris who was visiting from Europe, we managed everything beautifully.

One year we had arranged to meet my brother, Nicken for dinner in New York. He was living in London at the time. The day before we were planning to meet, I had run around New York City shopping all day. About five in the afternoon I rushed up Madison Avenue when a tall man ran out of a building and collided with me. It happened to be Nicken! Talk about coincidence!

The next day Billy and I invited Else and Nicken to have lunch at the famous French restaurant, Lutece. Nicken had certainly eaten at many good restaurants over his ten years in New York's shipping industry. Wanting to impress him, we asked my friends who owned La Maisonette (the best restaurant in Cincinnati) to introduce us to Andre Soltner, the owner-chef of Lutece. Andre visited our table twice during lunch, and Nicken—as we had hoped—was indeed impressed. He thought that we belonged to the restaurant's inner circle. Mission accomplished!

Our true purpose for moving to Cincinnati was for the children's education. I had taught Alexandra first grade at *Shenandoah* using curriculum from the Cincinnati Country Day School. At the American School of Florence, where she completed second grade, I received full marks for my teaching, and the child passed beautifully. Since the headmaster of Country Day was a former schoolmate of Billy's, it did not occur to us that he would deny our girls' admittance—especially since we had used their books. I had no idea why the headmaster refused the girls. I think he was one of those dull

Americans who grew backwards. With only one week before school started, in desperation, I called my old friend Lela Emery Steele, Jack Emery's daughter. "Well," she said, "I am sure we can help. My husband, John, is on the board of an excellent private school called Lotspeich." Within two days John Steele had resolved the matter. Again, I was so grateful for good friends!

We had another problem, however, in that our youngest didn't speak English. She had only spoken Italian while in Italy. To help her learn the new language, we sat her down in front of American television all day long. It helped somewhat, but the school still felt they had to keep her in first grade, which she had already passed in Italy. Without a word, she endured the humiliation of being three grades below her sister, instead of two.

One day, at the end of the school year, Elizabeth asked me come with her to see her headmaster. I was perplexed and wondered what trouble she had gotten into. She started by asking the headmaster whether it was true that she could skip a grade if she enrolled in summer school. He answered that it depended on her finding a willing teacher. "I already have found one," she said, and turned to the teacher who had come in with her. The headmaster quickly agreed to the proposition. I nodded, feeling very proud of Elizabeth's initiative at the young age of seven. We changed our summer vacation plans, and in one month, she passed second grade with flying colors.

Alexandra, on the other hand, enjoyed being bi-lingual, and seemed adept at mastering other languages and subjects. With that advantage, she graduated High School Valedictorian at the School for Creative and Performing Arts, and then went on to Georgetown University.

After five years of giving Cincinnati the chance to get "used to me," as Billy would say, I seriously took up civic duties. The girls had attended private elementary school. But in high school, they auditioned for the public School for Creative and Performing Arts and were accepted. I was asked to be on the board, and eventually became the President of the main fundraising organization, which is called The Friends of SCPA. We even raised funds to finance the salaries of 13 extra teachers.

William Dickinson was the school's dedicated headmaster. They had a brilliant choreographer named Jack Louiso. Year after year, each school musical was a huge success, and groups of guests were asked to attend performances. It bothered me that there was no media coverage for these outstanding productions and was determined to improve promotion. At one point the school was invited to take *The Wiz* to the Washington D.C. National Theater. To accept the offer, however, we needed to raise $82,000 in two weeks! My motto was and always will be, "Never take no for an answer!"

I happened to be visiting Palm Beach when I received a call from the school. They informed me that they were unable to raise the necessary money. Undaunted, I replied, "Wait, I am taking the first plane back in the morning. We will find a solution!" And, sure enough, somehow we reached our fundraising goal. Among others, Taft Broadcasting donated $20,000 and the Baldwin Piano Company provided two 18-wheelers with which to transport our revolving stage. Thanks to Michael Ainslie, head of the National Trust for Historic Preservation, a convent in Washington was willing to offer room and board for the 300 students at ten dollars a person. And lastly, round-trip via Greyhound Bus to Washington D.C. was funded.

Headmaster, Bill Dickinson and I flew to Washington for opening night. We both were extremely emotional to have reached our goal. The day of the first show, students marched from the National Theater, across the square, to the mayor's office on the "Yellow Brick Road," (a yellow carpet we had laid). The media was present as the cast paid their respects to the city. It was with pride that we watched how well the students performed. For five great performances, "The Wiz" got standing ovations from sophisticated theater audiences! Glowing reports went back to the Cincinnati Newspapers. As the saying goes, "No one ever becomes a prophet in their own land!" After the Washington tour, the local media made sure to report the school's future performances! Alexandra took part in most of the musicals, went to Washington with "The Wiz;" and also sang in the Gospel Choir—which was a great honor. Her role in "Little Foxes" was as the meanest Regina that I can remember!

As long as we lived in Cincinnati, I worked for the school. And now I often recognize names of former students on television and Broadway. I must admit that it gives me a great sense of joy and satisfaction to have had a hand in their development.

During the children's school vacations, Billy loved to take us sightseeing by car. It was a welcome break from Cincinnati's extreme climate. In the summers, we visited Canada and New England, and in winter, the Southern States. One year we drove to the plantation country of New Orleans to see magnificent estates. We also visited Aiken, South Carolina where Billy grew up. Many of the people we went to visit had been our guests at *Shenandoah*.

One of the people we visited on our trips east was Alexander Spotswood Daley, my dear old friend from Rome days. Randy was in the American Navy then, ADC to the admiral, but spent a great deal of time with us at the Norwegian Embassy. He had returned to Harvard and in 1977, became the minister at the old brown frame church in North Andover, Massachusetts. During our visit, an atmosphere of warm and gracious living enveloped us from the moment we arrived till the moment we left after a leisurely breakfast and a lot of catching up. Randy was such a special friend, I even asked him to be Elizabeth's god-father.

It was a sweltering day and we were most grateful to be taken to the beach for a swim before lunch with Francise Rawls, our Labrador, Polly's god-mother. Singing Beach Club was very exclusive, but the water was an invigorating 59 degrees! Cabot Lodge's sister was there with her daughters and granddaughters from Belgium. Alexandra and Elizabeth were whisked away to play at *Traffic House*, their home overlooking the harbor. In the meantime, we took Francise Rawls home to Beaver Pond Road. In her very tastefully decorated sitting room, we talked about the old days in Italy. Two wonderful yellow Labradors reminded me of how Polly came to be with us in Tuscany.

We drove up to Biddeford Pool, Maine in the evening, settled in with our friends, the Ittmans and dined late. I relaxed on the beach early the following morning. The sea has always been my escape when I needed help in any way, mentally or physically. I was alone with the seagulls. The waves were breaking against the shore at low tide. The path back to the house went through fields of wild flowers and raspberry bushes. A mixture of pink wild roses added to the ambience. That evening, people were arriving for drinks. We went to see Aunt Anna Black in her charming house on the golf course. While we were there, Marion King came by. Here were two of the three graces we had found after our honeymoon sitting on the Spanish Steps in Rome, resting their weary bones! We all assembled for a beach picnic. The children searched for sand dollars. Seagulls sailed overhead. Evening breezes cooled the air and the view out to sea was spectacular as the sun went down. The only problem was that we were eaten alive by bugs!

Then we went on to Camden, Maine. Freddy Chatfield, Bill Chatfield's son had taken over the family property. It was good to see the long, white Chatfield house again. Freddy's children, Biz and Alexander arrived in time for dinner. Early the next morning, Alexandra and I went down to the beach. Like me, the sea always gives her something special. She is like a mermaid, happier in than out of water! As we looked out over the ocean, we felt a delightful peace.

Seven Hundred Acre Island was so close we called on our beloved friend, Adele Emery, Jack Emery's second wife, who was summering there. The Chatfields and the Harrisons took off in the whaler. It was flat calm. We had drinks and lunch under the large trees. We deeply missed our old friend, Jack, but pictured him sitting in his yellow sweater on the bench outside having tea with us as he had just done the year before!

Janneke and Hank Nelson had visited us in Tuscany on their honeymoon with their four children, so we decided to visit them in North East Harbor, Maine. Their lovely house, *Over-the-Way* awaited us. They were the best of hosts. One gorgeous summer evening we celebrated Hank's birthday on that special, private Cranberry Island.

Another summer, as a graduation present to Alexandra in 1984, our family of four traveled to Europe. We stayed with Aloisia Ruccelai at her mother's villa in Impruneta outside Florence. We spent three weeks with Aloisia as she and I shared a venture in a jewelry business. One day while shopping in town, I went to the bank to take out cash for a trip to Venice and was masterfully robbed on Via Tornabuoni in broad daylight. They got one of my wallets out of my *zipped* handbag, which I carried carefully on my shoulder. I carried the four passports and the train passes. Fortunately, I had photocopies of all our important papers in my suitcase in the country. At the American Consulate, because of the photocopies, we had new passports in half an hour! When Billy tried to say that his stupid wife lost them, the Lady Consul took him to task. She had been robbed the same way the evening before. Very vindicating!

When, one day in Impruneta, I had not been able to wake Aloisia from a nap, I had a suspicion that she was in some physical trouble, but was totally taken aback when a couple of weeks later my lovely Renaissance friend died suddenly of an aneurysm. She was one of the most alive people I have ever known, my most delightful friend, and I shall never forget her.

It was always lovely to escape Cincinnati's intense heat. Being situated on the Ohio River, it was too hot in summer and too cold in winter. The extreme weather was bad for my health. The university hospital found my unique medical case so interesting that they asked to study it at no cost to me. Over the ten years living there, I had done my best to overcome the effects of the weather—tolerating it for the sake of the children's education. The climate, however, finally took its toll on me and once again, the doctors advised us to move south.

We had originally planned to move when Alexandra entered Georgetown University, and Elizabeth was a senior at the School of Performing Arts. Our decision was solidified when Billy's step-mother died in the spring of 1985. Unfortunately, the step-mother's nephew—with the help of the nurse—had made her change her will, so it became impossible to stay in the house on Indian Hill. Forced out by unexpected succession taxes, we sold the house and property lock, stock and barrel and left for Florida.

Palm Beach – Tropical Haven
BLUE ENAMEL EGG

During those hard winters in Cincinnati, Paulie and Angie Ilyinsky had invited us to visit in Palm Beach. Those escapes from Ohio's harsh temperatures simply saved my life. During the coldest months, I would find myself thawing out in their sunny Palm Beach house or on Paulie Ilyinsky's yacht, *Angelique*. It soon became clear that Palm Beach was the place to settle. We figured our grown children would happily travel there to spend the holidays.

We found a lovely Mediterranean house near the center of town. To Billy's delight it needed renovating. Even if that meant having to camp in the upstairs bedroom for a while, he'd be in seventh heaven. It took us a year and a half to rebuild. Unfortunately, Billy only enjoyed the fruit of his labor for a few months after that. Still, I knew he was greatly satisfied with the outcome of both the home and garden architecture.

My mother, brother, Nicken, Else and their entire family spent Christmas, 1986 with us. These family reunions had always been wonderful. Sadly, this one proved to be our last.

For ten years, I was a member of Cincinnati's Garden Club of America, and was grateful to continue as a member in the Palm Beach Chapter. In March of 1987, our house was featured in the Garden Club of America's "House and Garden Day" tour. Billy was excited and loved the attention. As one of five houses, we were honored to have had our home chosen for the annual paid tour. In fact, Mary Bolton, a grand dame of Palm Beach and a great friend of mine (whose mother-in-law was a pioneer of women legislators), wrote an article about the house that was published in the Palm Beach Garden Club's catalogue for the annual tour.

Around this time, Helen Cluett, my old garden club friend, encouraged me to become an American citizen. She needed another Republican vote for her favored candidate, George Bush, senior! I gathered the necessary study books. Next, I was called to Miami for an oral interview, which turned out to be very disappointing. I was a bit put off. The head of the office seemed to be against me for some unknown reason. At the time I felt it was because I was a middle-aged female. The fact that I had been married for over 20 years to an American citizen whose family had settled in colonial Virginia did not seem to make any difference. Nor did it matter that I had accomplished a long list of civic work in Cincinnati. It only seemed to irritate him. The fact that I spoke English apparently worked against me. And finally, when he questioned me on facts from the study books, and I answered correctly, he became so unpleasant that I almost cried. Alexandra was waiting outside of the office and was horrified when she saw the state to which I'd been reduced.

A few weeks later I received a notice to return to Miami to see a judge. Neither Billy nor I could guess what it was about. I drove by myself to Miami in our Lancia. At one point, the car exhibited a fuse problem. I had to abandon the Lancia at a gas station near the courthouse. I thought I was in for another inquisition. But, instead I was sworn in as an American citizen! It was not what I'd expected it to be, and Billy was sorry not to have been there with me. The somewhat anticlimactic event took five long hours. Since the courthouse was not located in the best part of Miami, I had worried what might happen to my Italian Lancia. Not only did I find the car safe, but washed as well. The mechanics—who incidentally refused my tip—were unable to fix the car, but they referred me to their Cuban cousin who owned an electro-auto shop nearby. When I arrived, the gentleman had the fuse ready, said he loved working on the Lancia, and once again refused any remuneration. Not bad for my first day as an American citizen!

Much changed three weeks later. One very early September morning in 1987, I suddenly heard a kind of snoring. I touched Billy's arm very lightly, and said, "Please turn over," as I had done a million times before. But this time, he didn't move and I got worried. I tried to lightly shake him and he expelled some air. I was certain I could still do something for him, but I sensed it was already too late. I looked up our doctor's number, and he quietly said, "Dial 911 at once!" I did and before the old grandfather clock struck five, the paramedics were there with flashing lights. But, as I'd suspected, it was too late. Billy had died of a heart attack.

As soon as the paramedics pulled the sheet over Billy's head, which was such a final gesture, a very unpleasant police officer who had come with the paramedics, turned to me and sneered in a most threatening manner, "How did you do it? You better call your lawyer." So I called my lawyer, Tom Mettler, at 5:30 a.m. because I knew his wife was abroad. He asked to speak to the policeman, and as soon as he heard the policeman's tone of voice, he got me back on the phone and said, "I'll be there in five minutes. Just let me put on a shirt and a pair of pants." Under such circumstances, a lawyer who also is a friend is invaluable.

Tom stayed with me until his office hours called. I believe the policeman was not heard from again on the island of Palm Beach. Then, another lawyer friend, Rod Titcomb, took over and before I knew it, my Garden Club friends came, as well. They jumped to handle telephone duties and sent me out to walk Bellina, my yellow Lab.

My immediate family was away, so, in their absence, I shall never forget what a difference these friendships made. I had to call Elizabeth who was in Tampa and Alexandra who happened to be in Italy for her junior year abroad. Elizabeth's fiancé, Marc, drove her down to Palm Beach late that afternoon. Alexandra was with our good friends in Tuscany, which is where Billy had been the happiest. I begged her to stay in Italy and promised I would join her as soon as I could.

My dear nephew, Preben and his wife, Annie, living in New York at the time, flew down as soon as they heard the news. They were of invaluable help and support. I shall always be very grateful to them.

Angie Ilyinsky came to answer telephone calls. She was so efficient that my brother Chris called back from Brussels and quipped, "Who was the sergeant major?" I told him it was Angie. Chris replied, "I could have used her to answer my phone during last week. We had two hundred members of NATO and their press here on delicate matters. A voice like that might have kept them in check."

When my good old friend, Paul Ilyinsky offered to accompany me to Cincinnati for the funeral, I gratefully accepted. Elizabeth came too, and as I mentioned already, we stayed with John and Roz Wulsin. Adele arrived with letters to "Nonna Bella" from the grandchildren. Stett and Adrienne arrived from New York just in time for dinner.

The large gathering of friends and family that turned up at Spring Grove Cemetery in Cincinnati was heart-warming. Billy was buried right under his grandfather George Torrence Harrison. The rain held off through the service, which included passages from 1st Corinthians and Tennyson's "Crossing the Bar." We then had a short goodbye at the grave site, and I knelt for a moment of silent prayer.

On our return to Palm Beach, we held a memorial service at Bethesda-by-the-Sea Episcopal Church. Billy had loved that church because the same architect that designed it had designed his school chapel at St. Georges School in Rhode Island. During the service, I gazed up at the beautiful wood ceiling with a sense that Billy approved of the memorial arrangements. Many friends came to the house for lunch afterwards. Helen Cluett assisted in both events in Palm Beach. She had been a tremendous help on so many occasions.

My two brothers had been in constant touch from Europe. Friends called from around the globe, which helped fend off loneliness. Dinners arrived from various corners. I was pampered, and really appreciated every sign of support.

With immense help from my friend, Prince Michel of Yugoslavia, I sold the house within a few months. Charlot Foster's son, Ridgely, had helped us buy it, and Michel helped me sell it. The house and garden were both in excellent shape. It was extremely hard to let it go; we had poured so much of ourselves into it. When for weeks, however, I had woken up at a quarter to five every morning—the same time Billy had died—I realized it was time to change my surroundings.

Billy died on September 22ⁿᵈ, and soon thereafter we experienced the 1987 stock market crash. If he had survived, he certainly would have had a heart attack then. We lost more than 50 percent of all we owned. It was in the hands of trustees and lawyers! Need I say more? While they were all still fighting over what remained, I took off for Italy because there was nothing more I could do. I have written about the heartwarming time that followed in another chapter.

When I returned to Palm Beach, friends remained close. I was asked to be on the Board of Hospice, where I have stayed for over 30 years to the present day. Tennis matches at the Bath and Tennis Club kept me in shape both mentally and physically. It has always been my favorite sport. The club became my home away from home for various reasons, and also because I have always been happiest by the sea.

One day, Princess Maria Pia di Savoia and Marie-Charlotte Vidal-Quadras and I went orchid shopping. They brought along their friend, Louise. She was the daughter of the famous polo player, Tommy Hitchcock. From the beginning of my marriage, I had heard a great deal about Tommy's mother, the matriarch, Louise Hitchcock. Billy had worshipped the ground she walked on. She had visited him in the infirmary at school in Aiken when he was ill; she had put him on his first horse, I believe. He never stopped talking about her. Mrs. Thomas Hitchcock *was* Aiken and had started Aiken Preparatory School. Well, I could go on and on, but I had gotten quite tired of her name. Every time I did something Billy disapproved of he would say, "Louise Hitchcock would never have done that!" Yet, here I was with her namesake and granddaughter, Louise Hitchcock Stephaich, meeting just a few weeks after Billy died. It was quite uncanny—especially because, from that car ride on we became very close friends.

A year later, Louise spent three months on and off with me because she was remodeling her house. It was the start of a very special friendship, which has meant so much to me—and for which I am extremely grateful!

Several times I visited Louise both in New York and Canada. We worked on projects such as the garden at Beaumaris, Canada. In 1991, I was headed back up to finish a job, when a medical issue stopped me in my tracks. Because of some especially bad headaches, the doctor ordered an MRI. I was called back that evening for a second MRI. I was getting nervous—and rightfully so, because the doctor said I had a brain tumor. It was just before Memorial Day weekend. An operation was immediately ordered, and I was told that travel was out of the question. I asked whether any of the physicians would be there over the holiday. When their response was negative, I decided that if I had survived up till then that I could live another ten days. So, off I went to finish my landscape work in Millbrook and Beaumaris, Canada.

After I returned to Palm Beach, everyone was eager to help me find the best surgeon. I felt that a good head nurse was equally important. The Professor of Surgery in Miami was recommended. He was also head of the university department, so my decision was made. Surgery was to be performed at Mount Sinai Hospital in Miami Beach. The doctors scared me to such a degree, that I had to call Alexandra to come back from London where she had been working for several months. They informed me that I might not be able to walk, see, or recognize anyone. In fact, they said I probably would not survive the operation! I was told to make my last will and forget about it! Charming!

The operation was a success. While the doctor and head nurse were excellent, the hospital and its post-operative care were severely lacking. In the ICU, they had failed to notice that the anesthesiologist inserted two needles into the same vein, which caused my whole arm to turn black. It was Alexandra who called attention to it and informed the head nurse who was horrified. Next, something between a doctor and a nurse marched around in high heels making a hell of a noise on the marble floors. They wore white doctors' coats, but were not helpful. The second day one of them came to perform a spinal tap. When she unsuccessfully attempted it three times, I called the real doctor and had two words for him: "Never again!"

For recovery, I received my requested single room with a bath, but the rather important telephone—which could put me in contact with Alexandra and others—was broken. Instead of replacing the phone, the staff insisted that I call a Florida Bell repairman to come to my hospital room. And I had just spent two days in intensive care! Sheer insanity!

The hospital also assigned me a nutrition specialist. My cholesterol was sky-high due to prescribed steroids for the brain surgery. I thought it was great that the hospitals had started thinking about nutrition at all and listened politely when she suggested I stop eating bon-bons! (By the way, I do not eat sweets!) So she set up a meal plan for me. The next morning the kitchen sent eggs and bacon and butterscotch pudding for breakfast. I sent it straight back. Despite selecting my order on the daily menus, this happened every day until, finally, poor Alexandra had to bring me healthy food from the local market. I was told that the communication between the departments did not exist!

After enduring a week of similar issues, I asked my surgeon when the stitches could be removed. He said he would do it after his impending trip to Boston. Unflinching, I insisted the stitches be removed before he left so I could be discharged as soon as possible. His sad comment was, "I don't blame you."

Alexandra drove me back to Palm Beach to care for me over the next few months. The hospital had shaved the back of my head, leaving a little hair in front, so I did not look too bad in a scarf. However, they neglected to remove a piece of plastic, which is still there to this day!

I had bought a charming turn-key, single story house on Fairview Road in 1988. With no renovations needed, I only had to move in the furniture. There was a wonderful garden with orchids hanging in the trees bordering the north fence; bougainvillea and a huge fichus tree along the road. A free form pool reflected a large Hong Kong orchid tree. The covered patio gave us opportunity to entertain outside, and the exterior lighting was a work of art. This was where I recuperated splendidly with Alexandra's help.

Despite the doctor's dismal prognosis, I was able to walk, talk and recognize my friends! The gloomy warnings I'd received before the operation could have discouraged the strongest of people—even to the point of losing their will to live. But, being a Viking, I just got angry and was determined to be a hearty weed, not a fragile plant, and difficult to kill. I understand that medical professionals fear being sued. What a sad state of affairs! My experience motivated me to work even harder at my highly-regarded Board of Hospice.

As was my first house in Palm Beach, my Fairview home was hospitable and always brimming with friends. Early mornings the tall, stately palms stood guard all around. Only a few birds twittered until daylight lit the sky and turned it to a turquoise blue beyond the emerald palms. Tiny, wooly clouds sailed by. Pink hibiscus still slept unfurled before the long hot day ahead. Then, sunbeams peeked through the dense green to start a new, peaceful and hope-filled day. I adored sharing my attractive tropical home with the constant flow of visiting friends and family.

It was all perfectly lovely until Hurricane Andrew—our first strong hurricane—occurred in 1992. As we faced our first mandatory evacuation, we were invited to ride out the storm with Paulie and Angie Ilyinsky. As Paulie was the proud town mayor and owner of a menagerie of animals, he and his wife had decided to stay on the island and not evacuate. With their usual style, the invitation included champagne and caviar, especially since the storm was to hit on my birthday. We were each given a guest room on their second floor, along with the opportunity to bring over whatever belongings we wanted to try and save. As the storm neared, though perhaps not developing into a direct hit, we were promised major flooding. Alexandra ended up dealing with the stress by bringing over seven Jeep loads of items—photos, paintings, even clothes—deemed too precious to replace. Most of the island lost power, but luckily, the Ilyinskys never did, and we survived the 90 plus mile per hour winds, comforted by the constant TV coverage. We were elated

to find out that our low-lying one-story house and garden had escaped flooding, but upon return, we were shocked beyond belief. The Florida Power and
Light workers had cut down all my trees on the entire north border, including
all my magnificent orchids! The orchids, which I was known for, were left in
a heap, like garbage. To me, the property had lost a great deal of its appeal.

One evening, while entertaining guests for dinner, I was burglarized—
even though there were staff in the kitchen, and several cars parked on the
road. I felt the all-too-familiar sense of being violated yet again. To make matters worse, a few days later, I was mugged and robbed at a fruit and vegetable
market. The thieves took the keys to both my house and car. The locksmith
was able to change my house lock, but the car had to be hidden in my friend,
Phil Whitacre's gated community for the next couple of days.

Police Chief Terlizzese told me I needed a man—if not a husband—at
least a doorman! The latter seemed the easier to find at that moment. Friends
advised me to move to an apartment. So, another change of residence ensued;
this time there was no garden to cheer me, except for some potted hibiscus
and bougainvillea on a terrace. Often times since, I've lamented the loss of my
garden at Fairview, and the spirit of my flowers and trees. In exchange, after
moving to the Trianon I enjoyed instead, the wonderful air and view of the
ocean from the 16th floor.

Virginia – Harrison Territory

GOLD HORN

From the very beginning, my husband, Billy proudly told me all about his father's family heritage. Apparently, the Harrisons arrived in Virginia in the 1600s. Over the years, they would establish three plantations on the James River near Richmond: *Berkeley, Brandon* and *Upper Brandon*. The 430 mile-long James River begins west of the Blue Ridge Mountains and joins the Chesapeake Bay at Hampton Roads. There are 33 plantations listed in the National Registry of Historic Places located along the James River and its tributaries. They are often referred to as American architectural treasures.

The Harrisons also left quite a mark on American history. William Henry Harrison, born at Berkeley, became the ninth President of the United States. His father, Benjamin Harrison V, was one of the signers of the Declaration of Independence. William's grandson, another Benjamin, became the 23rd president. One of Benjamin's sons moved west to Cincinnati, Ohio where Billy's branch would settle.

William Henry Harrison's presidency was the shortest in history. After so many accomplishments, including having become Secretary of the Northwest Territory, governor of the Indiana Territory, and a famous major-general in the US Army, his presidency lasted a mere 31 days. Determined to show that he was still a military hero at the age of 68, he rode to his inauguration ceremony on horseback without overcoat or hat rather than in a closed carriage. He proceeded to deliver the longest inaugural address in US history—all in the freezing rain. Shortly after, he became ill and lost his last brave battle against pneumonia on April 4th, 1841. That was also the day that Vice-President John Tyler would assume the presidency.

"Tippecanoe and Tyler, too!" was the popular song and slogan shared by the two men during their campaign. Tippecanoe referenced one of Harrison's most famous army battles. Tyler, another proud Virginian, had many accomplishments of his own. Among other achievements, he served in Congress and then as Virginia's governor. He was married twice and had fifteen children!

Incredibly, the year after Billy (William Henry Harrison III) died, whom should I meet but Francis Payne Bouknight Tyler! We met by chance at a Garden Club of America zone meeting in Richmond. We hit it off immediately and soon discovered that our families were very much related! She was married to Harrison Ruffin Tyler who, amazingly, was only the grandson of President John Tyler. Harrison's father and grandfather both had children around the age of 70!

After our delightful meeting, I returned to Palm Beach and Payne and I kept in close contact. When the following spring came, the Tylers came to spend a few weeks at the Palm Beach Polo Club. I invited them to first come for several days as my houseguests. I loved having them. We had lots of fun. Harrison played tennis in the mornings, and Payne and I would meet him for lunch at the Bath and Tennis Club. A few days later, Alexandra joined us on her spring break from Georgetown University, arriving at the B&T in time for Sunday Brunch. Those weeks in Florida built a strong bond with the Tylers. Alexandra and I were invited to go and stay in their Virginia home, the famous Sherwood Forest Plantation, anytime. Payne even suggested I work on my book in their charming little hunting lodge called *Lion's Den* on the James River near their plantation. She was so enthusiastic about my memoir and was most eager to read it. In fact, she would go on to write a beautiful book of her own. We happily took them up on their offer many times since I regularly drove Alexandra to and from Georgetown.

Of those trips to the Tylers' part of Virginia, several stand out in my mind. The first was a Christmas holiday at Sherwood Forest with Harrison,

Payne and family, including their two sons, William and Ruffin. It was so tastefully and historically decorated for the holidays. The property had been in the Tyler family since it was purchased in 1842. When her time came, Payne lovingly, yet painstakingly restored the house—the décor, furnishings and landscape—based on detailed information gathered from 47,000 letters.

We discovered so much about Sherwood Forest, Payne being such a wealth of information. She shared so much, including the fact that William Henry Harrison had owned the property when it was called Walnut Grove. Years later, when Tyler bought it, he renamed it Sherwood Forest because he related so much to Robin Hood, often feeling like a political outlaw. Once the Virginia reel ballroom was added to the main house, it became (and remains to this day) the longest frame house in America—over 300 feet long!

The night of the big Christmas party arrived, along with one of the biggest blizzards on record. It was absolutely freezing everywhere, inside and out. But we kept warm dancing the Virginia reel in the famous ballroom! The beautiful decorations inside and out, the glowing fireplaces—not to mention all the charming guests and neighbors—truly made it a warm and memorable Christmas.

On one summer visit at Sherwood Forest, representatives from the Library of Congress came to Virginia to plant a Tyler family tree. When they found out that Alexandra would be there, being a Harrison, they graciously planted two trees: one in honor of the ninth president, William Henry Harrison; and one in honor of John Tyler, his successor. It was a special and important moment.

At that time, Harrison Tyler was restoring *Pocahontas Fort*. He bought an old house in Southampton County. He moved it lock, stock and barrel across the James River and enlarged it to become a small museum of artifacts, weapons and the like. I was very happy to donate our 16th-century Roman front door that we had brought all the way from Italy. What a journey that door has enjoyed. Billy would have been thrilled!

Besides the many lovely families and beautiful properties we were introduced to near the James, Virginia has always brought me many other great adventures. From Charlottesville's horse country to historical Williamsburg, I was always impressed and very kindly received.

Once I visited another lovely southern lady named Connie Ingles. She invited us to her plantation, *White Marsh,* and became a dear friend. In her house, a very handsome old library looked out to magnificent, huge trees. One of the oldest was an enormous gingko tree by the front door. My room was right at the top of the stairs with a sweeping view of the water. I spent the night in my lovely four-poster bed, while Steven, the lonely peacock, sat screeching in the gingko tree.

As an accomplished pianist, Connie treated us to a wonderful recital one evening. She also gave a luncheon for us at her yacht club on a glorious sunny Saturday—another memory of perfect southern hospitality.

But, throughout all our visits to Virginia, we learned that true southern hospitality—as shown to us by the Tylers many times—was really about making us feel like family, always.

The Year 1989 – The Good, the Bad and the Ugly

MALACHITE PENDANT

1989 was a particularly dramatic year. It began in January when I drove with Alexandra and all of her luggage the usual 1,000 miles back to Washington, D.C. for her last semester at Georgetown University. On our way to spend the night with our great friends, the Moores at the *Combahee Plantation* in South Carolina, we encountered a fierce ice storm. Our car sailed on the slick roads, including their long driveway. But we somehow managed to arrive in one piece. The storm persisted and the next morning we found out that the roads in North Carolina were impassable. Alexandra still had to reach Georgetown on time, so we flagged down the train bound for D.C. at Yemasee Station and threw her on! I brought her belongings back to Palm Beach and sent them via FedEx.

In early spring, the Garden Club of America held its national annual meeting in Palm Beach. As I had been the head of the food and beverage committee when Cincinnati had hosted this meeting, I was asked to do the same for the Palm Beach event. Thank goodness it was again a great success. I would remain on the executive board of the GCA in Palm Beach for the next ten years.

Later that spring, I met my friend, Bill Mirkil, for lunch at the Bath and Tennis Club then drove him out to Wellington to watch some excellent polo. We drove back to Palm Beach and had supper with Louise and her mother, Mrs. Thomas Hitchcock. Afterwards, I was asked to drive Bill back to the B&T to pick up his car. We drove slowly because he didn't like driving at night. As we crossed the wide street at the north bridge, a car barreled across the bridge, ran the red light and broadsided us mid-ship! The driver's name was Tim Killen. What an appropriate name because he killed my Lancia and nearly killed us! Fortunately, Bill was basically alright even though he wasn't wearing a seatbelt. This was a great relief because Bill was using a blood thinner and could have bled to death. He fell over me instead. Sadly, I then realized that my lower right leg had gotten caught by the gearshift and split open—an injury that would haunt me for the rest of my life. The plastic surgeon that would perform the initial skin graft actually made it worse. Killen was anything but apologetic that night and never, ever admitted any wrong-doing. Yet it was his insurance company who paid me so we know who was actually responsible.

I was on crutches for some time, but was back on my feet when in May the time had come to drive back to D. C. for Alexandra's college graduation. Sadly, she couldn't wait to leave. Among other things, she had been mugged, attacked by a taxi driver, even robbed at gunpoint on campus housing! The university never helped her, never took my phone calls, and has swept it under the rug ever since. Although she had previously taken a year off, studying on her own, she was determined to get her degree. Receiving her diploma meant a lot to both of us. There was an award ceremony given by the GU School of Languages and Linguistics that followed after the formal graduation ceremony. She wanted to skip the awards event, but since I'd come such a long way, I insisted we attend. She received eight awards and I was so proud of her.

We briefly celebrated with friends in D. C. and then were off to Virginia to stay with the Harrison Tyler's for a few days. From there we drove home via the Moores at the *Combahee Plantation* as usual. Good friends always make everything better, but it was not enough.

Elizabeth, on the other hand, was at the onion-domed university in Tampa. Before Billy died, she had become engaged to a boy she met at the university. His mother was American and his father was Guatemalan. The latter proved much the better of the two. Unfortunately, the engagement resulted in a short and tragic marriage.

Our European summer escape started in Brussels where my brother Chris was serving as Executive Secretary of the North Atlantic Council. Among the highlights was a fun lunch with his wife, Anne and his two children, Christian and Anne-Sophie at NATO's staff center. On the last evening, we dined just off the Grande Place in old Brussels.

Three days sped by. We boarded the super train to Paris, "L 'Etoile du Nord," had a delicious lunch, and made it to Paris before we knew it. *The City of Lights* was preparing for the great festivities in honor of the 200th anniversary of the French Revolution (1789), the 100th anniversary of the Eiffel Tower show, as well as the 20th anniversary of the Vidal Quadras marriage.

Paris was spruced up for us. I repeated memories and Alexandra made new ones. In 1989, because the first year of Elizabeth's unfortunate marriage to Marc was so hard on the family, all we wanted to do was to escape to Europe. The elegant Monsieur Lucien met us at the station and took us to Alejo and Marie Charlotte Vidal-Quadras' charming apartment. It had previously housed another great artist and had a guest-studio apartment next door, which was ideal for us.

Gael d'Oncieu, my chic and youngest 76-year-old friend in Paris came for a Vidal-Quadras 20th anniversary dinner. That night the fireworks lit up the sky. It felt so good to be back in Paris.

A trip to Paris wouldn't be complete without a visit to Ile Saint-Louis. We lunched at a "Brasserie sur le Coin," which was very French and delicious. We even had a praline ice cream at the Gelaterie. There was quite a queue to see the Sainte Chapelle. I had promised the children five years before—when it had been closed for repairs—that we would go back. I enjoyed enormously the blue starry ceiling and the stained glass windows.

Guy and Marina de Brantes gave a buffet supper in their lovely apartment next to the Rond-Point of the Champs-Elysees. I was seated next to Jean-Louis Faucigny-Lucinge, the most popular older gentleman in Paris and

I had the Paul Claudel's son sitting on my other side. I was quite amused as the beautiful ladies of Paris were most attentive.

Since I was expected at a dinner party another night, I went to Laurent, the famous hairdresser on Rue de la Paix. He worked miracles. I looked fabulous and felt like a million dollars. The dinner was at Sheila de Rochambeau's on Rue Torneau. Sheila was a wonderful cook and hostess and had a beautifully decorated home. Among the guests were the very charming designers, Pierre Venet and Hubert de Givenchy. Michel Paulmier drove me home. I say, if you have a hairdresser as famous as Laurent, you can charm almost anyone. As a dress designer, it was marvelous to be among fashion's greats!

Another evening we went to a barbecue in Versailles with Princess Maria Pia and Prince Michel de Bourbon Parme. The guests included Ghislaine de Polignac, the Francois Mitterands, Jimmy Douglas, Jean-Pierre Dotti, Betsy Bloomingdale, Marie Christine de Bourbon Parme, Olympia Rothschild Torlonia, John Bowes-Lyon and others. Alexandra was seated next to Francois Mitterand, the president's brother, and she had such success that he sent her his book, *Frere de Quelqu'un* with a dedication the next day. Pia showed a movie of her father, King Umberto, whom I had known in Lisbon.

On my last day in Paris, I picked up my repaired emerald 3-stone ring at Bulgari. When I had asked a Bulgari jeweler in the United States for a repair estimate, I had been quoted several thousand dollars. Imagine my happy surprise when the man in Paris told me the damage was only 450 French francs—about $84 in those days! With my unexpected savings, I went and bought earrings for Alexandra at Dior's Boutique! Monsieur Lucien arrived at 10:30 p.m. and brought us to the railway station. We left France and journeyed on to Italy by wagon-lits.

I had always loved driving "Sur les belles routes de France," where one could see a village through the trees lining the roads six to seven kilometers away. But one summer afternoon a few weeks later, when Alexandra and I drove back towards Paris on the Auto-route, we experienced heavy traffic in all the lanes, and suddenly our rental car blew a tire. At great speed, we swung around twice and hit the cement center divider. By some miracle, there must have been a lull in the traffic. A man jumped out of his small Fiat and stopped the cars, so we could get over to the right side. He then asked a lady to tell the police in the next town of Auxerre what had happened to us. A police car came after a short wait. We felt a bit nervous. Instead, the three policemen insisted on changing our tire, and we became such friends with them that we exchanged cards, and later wrote them a thank-you note from Florida. Back in Paris, we returned the car at once, got a partial refund and took a taxi to our destination. We were again staying with Cha-Cha who recommended a coupe de champagne to cheer us up! Seldom has anything tasted so good. We were well familiar with her charming apartment. But now she lived there alone, as her husband, the great painter, Alejo Vidal-Quadras, had died. One could still feel the presence of a skilled artist in that apartment—something that lingered long after his death, and gave me creative inspiration.

We continued our journey by wagon-lits to Italy on to our great stay of over three weeks with my very old friend, Pia Baricalla on the Lake of Garda. From there we took trips both to Venice and Milano where I visited my doctor—another renown specialist. Every day we enjoyed Palladio's country. Time went but too fast and we continued on to Switzerland to stay with Monique and Alfy Kinsky in Verbier surrounded by a very interesting international group of friends among the beautiful mountains.

Once more we boarded the train. This time we went south to Rome, changing trains to go to Maremma and also to Porto Ercole. While in Maremma, we spent a few days with Toineau and Pier Luigi Gaspari. Alexandra had spent a wonderful birthday weekend two years before and was very happy to be back. Imagine our surprise when Toineau was suddenly less than friendly. Due to her exhaustion and frustrations with other guests she treated us quite rudely. She screamed at us for touching the dogs. She accused me of putting Pier Luigi in danger of heart trouble because he had offered to row me to another island. When we rented a car instead of accepting her invitation to use hers we apparently started WWIII. So we packed. The last night we were so scared we barred the bedroom door with a chair. We thought that Toineau was so unstable she might even come after us with a knife. We arranged to have our friend, Giulia Borghese, call us and ask if she could borrow us for a few days. Giulia to the rescue! Toineau was obviously experiencing some kind of mental and emotional breakdown and we never saw her again.

We enjoyed our stay with Guilia Borghese Cornaggia at Porto Ercole. Guilia was a dear old friend of mine from our years in London. She had the charming old Forte Santa Caterina between the two ports with bougainvillea cascading over the ancient walls and a view of the Mediterranean. It was a most wonderful time with her and her children.

From sea to hillside our next stop was Cortona—The Etruscan City— the grandmother of Rome. We met Alain in the town's main square at "La Logetta." He owned an apartment three floors above that trattoria. The steps were truly steep. But after getting help with all of our suitcases we happily settled into our rooftop flat with a direct view of the town hall's famous clock tower. It was so different from our former life at *Shenandoah*. It felt better that way; somehow, easier to bear. Since there was no telephone in the apartment, we had to make all of our calls from the nearest bar. My, how the world of communication has changed! We spent the rest of the afternoon roaming around Cortona, ending up in the town square sipping cappuccinos.

On Sunday, we went to mass at Pergo's church, San Bartolomeo. It was so inspirational to see the congregation and hear our beloved priest, Don Giuseppe presiding beautifully as ever. Even the sweet nun, Benedetta, who played the organ was very moved to see us. After church, we had lunch with the Falinis, followed by a theatrical production starring their son and my godson, Enrico.

The following day we enjoyed a most pleasant visit with the Ferri family. We then had tea with my old friend Mario and his family at Umberto Morra's villa. After which we were treated to soufflé and champagne with Alain, Ben and their new family member, German shepherd puppy, Bobby. Since we had rented a car we took in as many sights as possible. We visited Montepulciano's San Biagio (Alexandra's favorite church), the town of Assisi, Lago Trasimeno, as well as Florence for a devoted day of shopping!

Incredibly, the brilliant lawyer who bought *Shenandoah* found out from the Falinis that we were coming to town. He invited us to lunch at *Shenandoah* and discovered that it was almost my birthday. The champagne flowed. The Falinis had continued to work at the estate part-time and Marcella prepared all my favorite dishes in my honor. It took a lot of courage not to cry because of everyone's kindness and the comforting surroundings of my favorite home. Alexandra and I waited until later that night to have a good cry in private.

The day before we left we simply had to stop by *Villa Passerini*. Silvio Passerini had married a beautiful Belgian translator for the United Nations. We also met their son, Gianluca, who was every bit as attractive as his parents. On the way back to our hotel, we talked with Don Giuseppe who was as inspirational as ever! We parted sadly and headed to Rome.

Toward the end of August, we flew from the Eternal City to London, another home away from home. On arrival, we were given the keys to my old friend, Monique Kinsky's vacant apartment in Chelsea, where we would spend our first week. We met my brother at his office the following morning at Three King's Yard in Mayfair. He then treated us to lunch in honor of my birthday at *Le Gavroche* and even gave me a lovely Hermes scarf. The lunch was divine and Nicken was so pleased to be immediately recognized at the famous restaurant.

The coming weekend would be spent full of family at Nicken and Else's country home, *Barberry Cottage* in Rushden. My brother Chris traveled from Brussels to join us. Saturday featured lunch at the riverfront boat club in nearby Cambridge, followed by a hearty celebration of my 60th birthday back at the cottage. On Sunday, my niece and god-daughter, Karen, her husband, Roger and baby Oliver, came up from London to see us. In the evening, Chris returned to Brussels and we to London the following morning.

We enjoyed another fun-filled ten days in London with friends, even taking in a couple of theatre productions including *Cats*. Most important were my two appointments with the highly-recommended, Dr. Bick. He administered a combination of western and eastern medicine including acupuncture,

therapies that addressed my recent accident-related leg injury, as well as my
overall circulatory issues.

On September seventh it was time to take a train to Shropshire. My
old friend, Pempe, the now dowager Countess Lindsay, had invited us to stay
for a weekend at her thirteen-century estate, *Combemere Abbey*. Jamie and
Heather, the current Earl and Countess Lindsay, met us at the train station
and we arrived in time for dinner. We spent the next day in cozy fashion gardening and walking around the property in old Wellington boots led by our
Labrador guides. Pempe's daughter, Gigi arrived that evening with a shooting
party. We hadn't seen either Gigi or Jamie (one of Alexandra's first crushes),
since their visit to *Shenandoah* back in the early 70s. They were as charming
as ever.

I have always loved Scotland, perhaps because I am a Viking—or
an Eskimo—as Ian Moncreiffe used to call me. For him "the Blacks start-
ing at Calais" and anyone north of that was an Eskimo. I often visited the
Moncreiffes in Perthshire during my London years. In fact, one day I heard
Ian ask the neighbor whether he could bring an Eskimo for drinks! Ian
Moncreiffe's wife, Diana Erroll, was Lord High Chief Constable of Scotland.
I was highly impressed with this long title. In fact, her title made her responsible for the queen or king's safety whenever they visit Scotland. We called
her Puffin.

On one of my visits in the 50s, Puffin's uncle was there too. I was afraid
to ask his name for fear of being thought of as a stupid foreigner. Some of
my friends who knew Puffin's uncle had referred to him as Jimmy or James.
Consequently, I returned home from Scotland never knowing his august title.
While having breakfast with my father the next morning, he asked me who
had been at the Moncreiffe's. I answered, "Puffin's uncle. I think his name was
James." Horrified, my father said, "Did he not have a second name?" "Well,
how should I know?" I said as an excuse. "Nobody ever introduces anyone
at house parties." Later, I noticed his picture in the *Society News* and said to
Father, "I believe his name is the Duke of Atholl, the only man who had the
privilege of a private army." Father was scandalized at my lack of manners.

"He was such a terribly nice man," I said. That was what mattered most to me—then, now and always. In England one cannot just ask who anyone is. You are supposed to know!

"You'll take the high road and I'll take the low road." These were the Scottish lyrics that I thought of during my beloved trips to Scotland. One of the first times I went up from London, was the day after Christmas, Boxing Day, in 1949. I had been invited to stay at *Glentanar* in Aberdeenshire. Lord Glentanar had been married to my father's cousin—the lovely Grethe Thoresen. Their daughter, Jean, was my age and since her mother had died very young, Jean was the hostess of the house. The family name was Coats, of the sewing thread fame. Tom Glentanar was an avid music lover. He played both the piano and the organ. He often had other pianists staying at the house and would play duets with them on his two impressive grand pianos. There were always large house parties at Christmas and New Year. Among the young men staying at *Glentanar* the first year, was Robin Warrender, with whom I became lifelong friends. From *Glentanar,* we continued north together. Robin went to Cawdor Castle and I stayed with Jo Gordon-Cummings nearby. Her family used to own the land of the famous Gordonstoun School where the royal princes attended. One evening, while at *Glentanar* we were invited to a dance at a well-known castle. It was 50 miles away and the winter night was cold. But the Scots think nothing of driving miles and miles for a good party. The castle legend was that, for generations, no eldest son had ever received his inheritance because he had died violent death before the age of twenty-one. A few weeks after the ball, the then present heir came through London to ship out to Malaya with his regiment. Just before his 21st birthday, we celebrated over dinner how he would prove the curse wrong. He left for Malaya. A couple of days before his birthday, he was caught in an ambush. He was the only one who died. I had trouble accepting his death, yet aware that there is much between heaven and earth we will never understand.

In those days, staying with people gave the wonderful advantage of really getting to know them. The disadvantage was that sometimes the old English and Scottish country houses were absolutely freezing. We used to stand in front of the open fires, and lift the back of our long skirts in order to thaw. At one particular house party, I learned what to wear to beat the cold. The Marchioness of Lothian, Tony and her younger sister, Arabella had an Italian mother who advised me to wear a uniform comprised of a long dress with long sleeves covering half of the hand—à la Mary Stuart. The dress was of the finest silk velvet, with a layer of mohair lining and another layer of pure silk lining. The dress had a generous décolleté and—not to be dowdy—also a separate stand-up collar, like a small cape. The collar was backed with beautiful lace. This marvelous uniform saved me from many an unhappy moment on bitterly cold nights.

On this trip we stayed with Sheila de Rochambeau which proved to be quite an experience. From Crewe, we arrived at the Aviemore Train Station where Sheila fetched us. She was accompanied by her cousins and my great friends, Angie and Paulie Ilyinsky, who were traveling on a luxury train through Scotland. They came with us to *Ballachronan*, Sheila's Shangri-la, and stayed for lunch. When we deposited Paulie and Angie back on their beautifully restored train, the steward awaited us on the platform with a tray of pink champagne and roses for the ladies. Paulie, of course, was served his favorite vodka!

Sheila, Alexandra and I took the high road back over the heather-clad hills. We passed Cawdor Castle, made famous in Shakespeare's Macbeth. My old friend Hugh Cawdor had, by then, become the owner of the entire vast area. On the edge of a river, we switched vehicles to an old land rover, forged the river and climbed the hills on the other side. If the water level was too high, pedestrians would be lifted across the river by bucket.

Ballachronan was the most beautiful place detailed with marvelous *trompe l'oeil* paintings, as well as an extraordinary collection of whimsical decorations. Sheila was famous for her cooking and entertaining, and designed her large, open live-in kitchen to accommodate her skill. She hosted the Drummonds and other neighbors to a dinner party. Unfortunately, a petty argument with our friend, Hugh Cawdor, kept him off the invitation list.

One day, Alexandra and I mustered enough courage to forge the river by ourselves in order to visit Hugh. Happy to see us, he opened a wonderful bottle of Veuve Cliquot in our honor. We gossiped about old times including the New Year I'd spent at the castle. We recalled one time when it was so dreadfully cold that we played cards on the eiderdown duvet on my bed to keep warm. The only tiny single electric heating bar in the whole house was in my room. We did have to put shillings in the machine, but it was certainly well worth it. I spent a lot of my time that New Year beside the enormous fireplace in the spacious downstairs living room. Dancing the Scottish reels at the Northern Meeting in Inverness was the only thing that kept us warm. In spite of the cold, I always loved my trips to Scotland.

From *Ballachronan*, we first visited my dear friends, Charles and Jane Mowbray in Morayshire, and then visited Gina and Patrick Tellfer-Smolett on the banks of Loch Lomond. We had picked up a rental Ford in the Highlands, left Nairn, and passed through Grantown-on-Spey, Tomlinson, Balmoral, Braemar and Kirriemuir. From there we took a dual carriageway, stopped for tea at Finavon Hotel and arrived at Marcus in Morayshire in the late afternoon. Charles and his wife, Jane, were so happy to see us. As we perused old photographs, we sipped a glass of German white wine. Jane, unfortunately, had been very ill for quite some years, but was up and cheerful. The old-fashioned dinner was satisfying to both body and soul. Charles served the finest clarets and an equally good port. Their house was simply divine with its huge family portraits and paintings. My room looked out over a delightful walled garden. It had rained the day we arrived, but the sun shone brightly in the morning. After breakfast we said goodbye to the dearest of friends from my early youth and continued our trip through Scotland, past Glamis and Gleneagles to Cameron.

Both Gina and Patrick had also been part of my life in London, where Gina and I were debutantes together. Gina was, in fact, one of the prettiest debs of our year, and greatly admired by my cousin, Harald. Patrick was my loyal defender during the first difficult year in London when many of the girls, being jealous of a foreigner, were really quite beastly to me. Patrick and Gina received us with champagne on the "Bonny, Bonny Banks of Loch Lomond." After the Tellfer-Smoletts left their old castle—which was later converted into a hotel—they lived in what had been the first castle-turned-family home. Gina gave us a tour of the attractive garden she had created down towards Loch Lomond. The garden boasted the bluest of hydrangeas and the most beautiful rhododendrons and azaleas. Gina had a fantastic cutting garden and a greenhouse. A big bouquet of my favorite sweet peas greeted me in my room.

One day Gina took us to *Inverary Castle*, seat of the Duke of Argyll. It was a beautiful trip, and the clouds parted just as we crossed the wonderfully named pass, "Rest and be Thankful." The pretty white village of Inverary gleamed in the sunlight. By the time the rain and wind returned we were seated cozily inside for a delicious dinner with Gina and Patrick. When we left Loch Lomond, it was sad to say goodbye to the dearest of friends, to the white pigeons, the Australian cockatoo and the dogs. The sun appeared again as we crossed the huge bridge to arrive at Glasgow Airport. British Midlands Airlines served an excellent lunch on our way south.

We spent another week in London. Amid several events with family including dinner with Adele, Antonello, Giacomo and Giulia in Chelsea, we also had lunch with Durru Shehvar in her majestic flat in Queens's Gate Gardens. She had just returned from Hyderabad, India, where she celebrated the opening of The Durru Shehvar Children's and General Hospital. To this day it is run by the Princess Durru Shehvar Children's Medical Aid Society. The last evening we enjoyed a most amusing dinner with friends at Harry's Bar sitting next to Roger Moore, Michael Caine and their wives. Soon after, the time came to return to the States.

Beginning of October, we were back in Palm Beach. I had not received any news from Elizabeth since her wedding. I did not even know her address. I had heard she and Marc had planned to go to Macon, Georgia to study at Mercer University, but I knew nothing for sure.

Then, one day in November I got an early Christmas card from Elizabeth signed only by her. I immediately felt something was wrong and sent a card right back via FedEx! She called as soon as the mail arrived. Marc had left her after less than five months. He had taken all of her significant belongings, everything, including her car! Without an explanation, not even a good-bye, he just disappeared. She also learned that he had never gone to any classes at the college. There she was without any identification papers, no passport or birth certificate. I presumed it was his way of preventing her from pursuing him in any way. She eventually told me that Marc's best friend, Harold, became her salvation those first few days. Harold literally talked her out of shooting herself with a gun—one of the few items Marc had left behind.

I decided to locate Marc as soon as possible. His American family in Tampa was, of course, no help. They were obviously complicit with at least one of his many crimes, afraid to be found out. Marc had forged Elizabeth's signature and run off with all of her money, not to mention her heart. To her credit, she found the strength to finish the entire school year at Mercer. Her studies served as her Linus' blanket.

One day during the search my old Parisian friend, Jean-Louis Faucigny-Lucinge, told me he was going to Guatamala in order to accept a great honor on behalf of The Order of Malta. It just so happened that Marc's father was of an old Spanish noble family in Guatemala City. Jean-Louis was most amused to act as a "spy" for our benefit. Posing as her grandson's friend, he phoned the Asturias grandmother and asked where Marc was now living. No clear answer was given except that he was living in the States.

The fact that Marc had always been a mama's boy meant that he would stay in contact with his conniving mother. I hired a private investigator who, after a few months, found out that Marc had made frequent calls from Biloxi, Mississippi. He actually thought he could remain unaccounted for by joining the Air Force. One day, I received a call from Biloxi. It was the dreaded Marc asking for Elizabeth. I told him that of course she wasn't staying with me. He insisted that she had to be there as she was incapable of masterminding a search for him. It was with great satisfaction that I was able to inform him that since he had diabolically brainwashed her and estranged her from her family, I knew nothing of her whereabouts. He then told me he had been arrested by the military police. "Oh," I said, "Really? She does call once in a while. I shall pass on the message," then hung up!

A little while later, Papa Asturias, Marc's divorced father now living in Guatemala, called me. He pleaded with me to release his son. He had realized that the sum of money that Marc had transferred to him was not a gift, but a "loan" from Elizabeth. If Marc could get released from his current situation, the father promised he would return the money. I promptly told him I would speak to my lawyer. In fact, I told him not to contact me ever again. All future discussions would have to go through my lawyer. From then on the lawyers took over the case.

Elizabeth eventually recuperated some of her stolen inheritance, but between lawyer's fees, capital gains taxes, transaction fees, etc., the financial detriment was huge. To add insult to injury, years later we would find out by sheer chance that—while Marc and Elizabeth had been staying with his grandmother on their Guatemalan honeymoon—he had rekindled a relationship with an old girlfriend and fathered a baby! That is what I call…class!!

Santa Fe – Writing in the Desert
GOLD FISHING CREWEL

One day in 2003 while living in Palm Beach, I received a phone call from my close friend Natalie Campbell Walden, who asked me to share their house in Santa Fe, New Mexico. So, I went to stay with them with the intent to write this memoir in the southwest desert mountains. Medical doctors had advised me many times to try the dry climate. I found the sky as wide and imposing as it is near the ocean. The same starry sky spoke to me at night and the same fabulous moon shone as well.

Azure skies, adobe architecture, and red sandy rocks revealed a mosaic of not just scenic beauty, but also stories of New Mexico's ancient civilizations. The pueblos, built thousands of years ago, demonstrated a continuity of culture and spirit. Revealed in the landscape were stories of desperados who gave rise to the term "Wild West" and of cattle-barons who tamed the southeast plains and traded along the Santa Fe Trail.

Three friars, who later had been slain by the Indians in 1583, named the region New Mexico. Then in 1598, Don Juan de Onote founded the first Spanish colony and a Franciscan Mission. Seven years later, as governor of the recently founded kingdom of New Mexico, he camped with an expedition at Agua de la Pena. It has been described as a huge sandstone rock towering above the valley floor like the fin of a monster shark. Just outside Santa Fe, the Don Juan de Onate statue had the inscription, "Paso por acqui el adelantado Don Juan de Onate del descubrimiento de la mar del sur a 16 de abril

1605" carved 15 years before the Pilgrims landed on Plymouth Rock. And it is still there!

Don Diego de Vargas left another inscription stating that here was the general Don Diego de Vargas, who conquered for our Holy Faith and for the Royal Crown, all of New Mexico at his own expense, year of 1692. This was especially interesting to me because that was the year my home in Tuscany had been renovated!

In late July, Alexandra and I drove from Florida on Interstate 10 via New Orleans and Texas to New Mexico. After days of driving and hours of gazing, the mountains finally appeared on the horizon. We took the 285 north, and arrived in Santa Fe. Natalie, her husband, Russell and daughter, Susanna were waiting for us.

Before Alexandra returned to Florida, we enjoyed a marvelous Walden concert. First, we listened to a Wagnerian CD that their son John, (who was away at school) had sung and recorded. Then Susanna sang, accompanied by her father on the piano. Natalie warmed up her amazing voice by singing "Alfie," which we remembered so well from her stays with us in Shenandoah. The concert ended with Natalie singing the *piece de resistance*—Russell's new arrangement of "Ave Maria" by Rachmaninoff. Besides being a talented arranger, Russell accompanied Judy Collins and still does to this day. While I was there writing, he would tour with the famous folk-singer.

Natalie and I often reminisced about our days in Cincinnati, where we first met. One day during my writing, I received the message that Roz Wulsin, our close cousin and friend from Cincinnati, had died. It was unexpected and so final. I was glad I was able to speak to her on the phone before I'd left Florida. I had met Roz 40 years prior when she came to Rome to look over the girl (me) that her old friend, Billy, had decided to marry. She and I got along splendidly from the start, and she had remained a dear friend and cousin ever since. When Billy and I came to Cincinnati on our honeymoon, she was among the first people to make us feel welcome.

From the 60s to the mid-70s, some of Roz's children attended Le Rosay School in Switzerland. Because Switzerland was so close to Italy, Roz's family often took many vacations with Billy and me in Tuscany. We loved it. Billy was a very good museum guide. In fact, he prided himself at having gotten the Uffizi Museum in Florence down to 23 minutes!

I always counted on Roz for strength and good advice, especially when we moved to Cincinnati after the trouble in Italy. Roz, along with Lela Emery Steele made certain I was admitted into the Garden Club of America, Cincinnati chapter—before I even arrived in the country! This was such an extraordinary honor, very few believe the story. Born as a foreigner, the Garden Club of America has meant the world to me. I admire it as an exceptional organization. I recalled how Roz and John had lent us their summer house at Campement d'Ours, opposite Desbarats, in Canada. The vacations were a huge help for us, not to mention a tremendous joy for Alexandra and Elizabeth, as well as our Labrador, Polly.

The summer house in Canada was an old captain's house on a bluff overlooking the North Channel, between Sault Ste. Marie and the Georgian Bay. We had wide views up and down the channel. On early mornings we'd tramp the trails of Campement d'Ours, our island. After breakfast, we played doubles tennis until the "love bugs" drove us off the court. In the afternoons, we would take the boats to fetch the mail at Richard's Landing in Desbarats, or visit friends on other islands. The terrain, rocky, dotted with islands and waterways, and covered in white birches (my favorite tree) reminded me of Norway.

One notable trip to Canada, I had not yet been given my green card, I was traveling with my good, old Norwegian passport. The Canadian border control kept us for 45 minutes. They suspected that I was a Russian spy because I was born in a Moscow Embassy. If I had known how easy it was to swim from America to Canada, I would not have bothered with the unpleasant border formalities!

I have such fond memories of those early Canadian morning walks, when the sunbeams played with the birch leaves. We walked out on a dock, listened to the gulls and gazed far across the water. Breakfast on the porch overlooking the channel tasted especially good after a hearty hike home. As a favorite pastime, I often sat and sketched at the boathouse with all the flags flying in the wind. All this was made possible because of Roz. She insisted that we came and visited every year. She and Billy held a precious, enduring friendship.

In 1987, when Billy had died so suddenly of a heart attack in Palm Beach, Roz was the first to invite us to stay with them. She also volunteered to provide the post-funeral luncheon in Cincinnati. The trip from Palm Beach to Cincinnati with the ashes went smoothly. I was so grateful our old friend Paul Ilyinsky traveled with us. He helped us avoid extra security questions about the urn at the Palm Beach Airport. At Boone County Airport in Kentucky, we rented a car which happened to be maroon-colored. Billy would have hated the color! We deposited Paulie at the home of Frank and Kakie Hamilton. The Hamilton's were a great support during my ten years in Cincinnati. My step-daughter, Adele arrived with letters addressed to Nonna Bella (me) from both of her children, Giacomo and Giulia.

I was still carrying the bag with the Etruscan-shaped, charcoal gray marble urn over my shoulder as we left for Spring Grove Cemetery. The gravesite was prepared under the statue of Frank Perin. Frank was Billy's great-uncle. The burial site was right under his grandfather, George Torrence Harrison. Good friends gathered. The rain held off while Jim Metzger, the minister, gave a short, but beautiful graveside service, which included passages from 1st Corinthians and Tennyson's "Crossing the Bar." After a few psalms, we said the Lord's Prayer together, and I knelt in a silent prayer before I left Billy in the town where he was born.

Unfortunately, I was not able to attend Roz's funeral, but I knew she would be the first to understand. Instead, my special messenger, Natalie—who sang at the service—delivered my personal letters to each member of the family!

I spent the next few months working in John's room on my laptop in the company of Natalie and Russell and their menagerie. They had two Bichons Frisee (Ella and Misty), two cats (Thomas and Six Toes), a dove and a snake. Thomas, the huge yellow cat, talked constantly to Duke, the dove in his cage as well as to the snake in his glass cage. The Walden family had me under their spell in their adobe home on a hill. Music filled the house as Russell composed downstairs, which hugely inspired me upstairs. Misty and Ella, the two Bichons usually sat watching me from the bed while the snake only seemed to move when they fed him live mice. Ella was pregnant. With preparations for puppies downstairs, Grandmother Misty and I felt a little out of it and sat together on the stairs. Then Ella was taken to the vet because she needed a c-section. She had three puppies. Natalie took care of them until she left with Russell for a concert in Telluride, which meant that I was kennel maid for three days. The breeder was supposed to babysit them, but thought the litter was better off with me.

After one fitful night pet-sitting, I went to read as usual. It was early and Thomas sat outside my window on the roof and loudly complained that he was not allowed in. So, I put on some pants and a sweater and let him in. Misty was already outside my door and jumped two feet in the air for pure joy in anticipation of food. Ella joined us in the kitchen for the big breakfast preparation. I had my hot tea and picked up the paper in the morning sunshine. The dogs and I had a quiet day before I went to a dinner party at Leslie and Ruckey Barkley's house.

I drove Guadalupe, Alameda, the Old Santa Fe Trail, Old Peco's Trail and Old Las Vegas Highway. From there I was off on a smaller road until I arrived at the Barkleys' house. Large antique gates led to an inner courtyard. From there another beautiful wooden door opened into the most charming house. Leslie and Ruckey greeted me, joined by the twins, who both reminded me so much of their father, my old friend Guido di Carpegna, in Rome. It was a most lovely evening. The next day Ruckey Barkley invited me to have lunch with Donald Lamm, a literary agent and a friend of his. He read my manuscript and offered some useful criticism, which sent me back to the drawing board.

It had been an arid summer when I arrived in Santa Fe. By the time the snowy-white winter arrived, Natalie and I drove east via New Orleans and I returned to Palm Beach and my beloved sea.

I have kept in close contact with Natalie ever since. The last time we got together was in November, 2018. Natalie and Russell came to Palm Beach for another Judy Collins concert (featuring Stephen Stills of Crosby, Stills and Nash) at the Kravis Center for Performing Arts. Russell, still Judy's accompanist and musical director, invited us to attend and go backstage. Alexandra and I thoroughly enjoyed the concert and were able to spend a few days catching up with our best friends.

While Russell continues his life in music, Natalie pursues her love of all art forms. Once focused on the performing arts, she currently finds herself not only studying the masters of drawing, painting and sculpture in Florence, but is creating her own masterpieces. Her many talents forever inspire me.

Haiti – The Hospital Albert Schweitzer

HAS TIFFANY HEARTS

One of the most meaningful endeavors I shared with Louise Hitchcock Stephaich was working at her Aunt Gwen and Uncle Larry Mellon's hospital they had founded in Haiti. The Mellons had visited Dr. Albert Schweitzer's hospital in Africa. They wanted to do something significant for humanity. So, on Dr. Schweitzer's advice, Larry Mellon became a medical doctor and his wife, Gwen became a trained nurse. In 1956, they established a hospital in the poorest country of the world—Haiti.

It was my privilege to help his niece and my dear friend, Louise, with her fundraisers for the hospital here in Florida. For three years, Louise gave these events in her Palm Beach garden, and featured the work of local Haitian artists. They were hugely successful. As attendance grew, the wonderful friends of HAS (Hospital Albert Schweitzer) also hosted fundraisers in area clubs.

One year, Louise invited me to join her and Gwen Mellon's daughter, Jenny Grant, to go to the Haitian hospital in Deschapelles, north of Port-au-Prince. It was a pleasant flight, but once we arrived in Port-au-Prince, it took forever to get our luggage. The huge crates and plastic boxes full of medicine that we had brought had to be unloaded first. Following our leader, Jenny, we made our way through the sea of young men offering valet services. This was an indication of the job shortage in Haiti.

Our driver came from Deschapelles in Jenny's jeep bearing a sign that said, "Hospital Albert Schweitzer" in bold letters on its side. Driving Haiti's roads to the hospital offices in Port-au-Prince was a brain-jarring experience. When we reached the office compound, there was a rifle-armed guard behind the heavy iron gate. Jenny had brought frozen meat from the US and left it in the office freezer.

We were to spend the night at Villa Creole, a hotel situated in a garden of huge trees, hanging bougainvillea and orchids. We were served a "welcome" lemonade by the pool before the dark night descended.

Having changed into flowing evening dresses, we were met by our host's car and driver. He gave us an exhilarating ride as he darted his way among the cars, carts and Tap-Taps—a type of Haitian bus. We traveled terrible roads, narrow passageways, colorful markets and throngs of people, pushing, steaming. I lost my sense of direction as we passed a garden and went up and down hills and arrived at another iron gate. Two armed guards whisked it open to a well-lit gingerbread house. Wide verandas encircled both floors. Because it had suffered a fire, the house recently had been renovated by our hosts, Ingrid and Hans Peter Hackenbruck. Hans Peter was the Austrian Consul to Haiti.

The house was a Shangri-La in a strange world of poor, but precious people who were dominated by serious drug-trafficking and corrupt politics. Outside the estate walls was a city void of infrastructure, consisting of abandoned, half-built houses and unfinished buildings. None of them even had windows.

We had drinks on the patio in front of the charming guest wing. The French ambassador, the United States representative and their respective wives were our dinner guests. Conversation in French and English flowed during the delicious Moroccan dinner and well into coffee on the terrace.

Back at *Villa Creole,* I watched some U.S. news on TV—which seemed a million miles away—and saw scenes from the "Trumptials" (Donald and Melania Trump's Wedding in Palm Beach). Who knew what the future would bring?!

The next morning, our driver from Deschapelles fetched us and took the Route Nationale, which goes north from Port-au-Prince to Cap Hatien on the north coast. It took three hours to go 40 miles due to the disgraceful road. The potholes were as big as craters, and we were often forced to drive slalom to navigate the pits and falls. A thick layer of white dust covered everything; animals, houses, trees, bushes and people. I thought this had to be terrible for their lungs and was determined that something be done about that road. I was told there was money allocated for it, but that work was halted for political reasons—as if the people in the hills knew what that meant. There were several road blocks, but the Hospital Albert Schweitzer car was waved through. Quite happy to leave the main road, we took off for Deschapelles at San Marc. There were still ten miles of kidney-shaking travel.

Clothing dangled from walls, trees and carts along the way. The abundance of roadside markets was evidence of the country's main commerce. Haiti operates entirely on its local economy. The markets are its lifeline. Haitians outside of their country send in about a billion dollars a year straight to families and villages. Yet, at every turn there were signs of extreme poverty. At St. Marc we turned inland to a green valley. Dr Mellon had built not only the hospital, but also a dam at the top of the valley.

Kay Mellon met us under pleasant, sunny skies. There was an extraordinary feeling of peace surrounding this charming house that had been home for Larry and Gwen Mellon over the years. Bougainvillea, huge flanbwayan and fichus trees encircled the estate. *Kay Mellon* sat on a rise overlooking the valley and the Chaos Mountains. The porch, which was shaded by the most famous of the fichus trees, was the main eating area. The living room was large, open and welcoming. The hallway between the living room and the front door held some of the best Haitian paintings. The dining room was separated from the living room by three steps, a Chinese screen and hanging plants. A Californian architect had designed the house, which also boasted a flower-filled courtyard between the hall and the kitchen wing. Fortunately, we had bathrooms at *Kay Mellon* and could wash up in the mornings, but the water came and went. In all the other dwellings, there was not a drop of hot water, ever!

Frederique, who was assisting Dr. Mellon and later Gwen Mellon, brought our luggage in from the car. Kay Mellon also had two *securities* night and day. Louise and I were installed in the two large bedrooms in the guest wing. Two of the walls in my room had louvered doors made from Cuban wood, as were most of the walls in the house.

The first evening we had been invited to a birthday party for Raji, the wife of the new head of the hospital. Other guests included the head physician, Bob Carroway and his wife. We were served a wonderful Indian meal with more inspiring conversation.

It was quite cool when we returned home to *Kay Mellon*, so we were most grateful for the new blankets Jenny had brought from the States. The villagers nearby played their instruments and sang late into the night.

On one of our first outings, we toured an orchard. The lemon, papaya and banana trees had been planted in memory of Gwen Mellon on her specific wish. Levy, the tall, enthusiastic Haitian in charge of the orchard, had done a remarkable job over the prior two years. A locked gate kept out the wild goats. The grounds also grew coffee.

Roosters constantly vied for attention in early mornings. Birds joined in, as well as stray dogs. Guards talked loudly in Creole and the sound of garden watering added to the music. After breakfast, we met Dr. Suresh at the hospital and he showed us every nook and cranny. I was impressed with the cleanliness. Suresh said under his breath, "Sunday is a good day!"

We were routinely included in the doctors' morning briefings, and afterwards we would visit the various parts of the hospital. I shall never forget the small two-year old boy curled up on the corner of his bed, covered with tubes because of severe malnutrition. He cried in fear and loneliness. It was heartbreaking. We also visited dispensaries where the patients were given two day's worth of food and medicines. We counted pills and performed other useful services.

Dr. Larimer Mellon's HAS complex covered 625 square miles, and he employed over 900 people. Courtyards and gardens separated the various wards and offices with hibiscus hedges bordering the paths. The outpatient area for children—designed by the Swiss—was open to the breeze. It was a great space for families to gather. Next to it were more fruit trees.

One Sunday afternoon at *Kay Mellon* we held a reception with beer and soft drinks, nuts and crackers. Jenny gave a talk on Dr Schweitzer, Larry Mellon and her mother. There were several young physicians there—many of whom were European.

We woke up early to go to the physician's 7 a.m. briefing and lecture in the library. The large group met to hear a talk on lung x-rays, which greatly interested me. As the physicians left for their rounds, I met with Raji, who was in charge of the gardens, to see what gardening advice I could offer her. We had three gardeners following in our footsteps. We inspected every bed, tree and flower. Raji had done a fabulous job and cleared away all the garbage and debris. Stones delineated flowerbeds and paths. Bougainvillea draped several walls; ixoras and lantanas dotted the grounds.

Come afternoon, we returned to the hospital and I left the t-shirts I had brought with Debbie, the office manager. Most of the shirts were going to the orphanage, but some white ones were reserved for the women in the hospital to wear while their other clothes were being laundered. We then walked to the pottery, furniture and the weaving shops. Work had stalled for the weavers because they were out of cotton. The trip continued up through the very colorful, noisy market and up the very dusty road to L'Escale, a small village which acts like a half-way house. It means two more months of food and medication. Their only source of water was a spigot at the bottom gate. A smiling young man wheeled a huge tub of water up the hill to the communal kitchen. L'Escale was supposed to have had a deep well drilled and installed. The man contracted to do the job had disappeared to the States for a while. He was supposed to return and finish the job, or else forfeit the money.

Back at *Kay Mellon* I was offered a hot bath. Aware this was a luxury, I gratefully accepted after all the dust I'd encountered. I never really got friendly with the shower. I think we only met when the water was cold, lacking power to warm it. That night, our dinner guests included Dr. Jim Fett and Dr. Len Christie who had traveled all the way from the northwest US.

I woke up even earlier than usual to Voodoo drums and roosters. At 6 a.m. the gardener joined in with his watering. After a breakfast of grapefruit and local eggs, we were off to the 7 a.m. briefing. Dr. Joe Keeley's lecture on the placebo effect of certain medications was most interesting.

At the house Raji joined us and we piled into the jeep. Jenny drove with a young Haitian next to her. Louise, Raji and I sat in the second seat and another young Haitian man sat in the far back. He was afflicted with a large, terrible looking growth on the back of his head. It could only be operated on in the States.

We arrived at the Liancourt Health Center and toured one small fruit and vegetable garden after another. Most of the plots were extremely dusty with pigs and goats tied to the hedges nearby. Thankfully, we found a healthier field of green beans, which would replenish the soil with nitrogen. The woman in charge of this large garden was suffering from a bad fall. Her leg, shoulder and wrist were in bandages. First, we took her to the health center, an extension of HAS, and from there we went to the hospital. I was very impressed with how clean and well-run the health center appeared.

One morning trip took us up to Dr. Mellon's Tapion Dam and Aqueduct located in a green fertile valley. On the road we passed a "Save the Children" distribution center for pregnant women, breastfeeding mothers and small children suffering from malnutrition. It was set up a year prior, but was to be discontinued by the end of the year—a disappointing end. Raji stayed with us for lunch. At 1 p.m. Levy's brother, Watson, came to see me and we had an hour-and-a-half talk on sketching and art in general. I had brought sketch pads, pencils and pencil sharpeners to be shared with his artist friends. Watson was a good artist and brought one of his painting to show me. He was employed at the hospital's garage.

In the 60s, the Mellons had planted a stick without roots or leaves. The stick grew into a fichus tree of gigantic proportions with one branch measuring over 60 feet long. There were several flanbwayan trees around the house and a large shade tree in the middle of the front courtyard. In her later years, Gwen Mellon liked to sit under the shade tree so she could follow all that was going on, see the people and encourage them.

One night at *Kay Mellon*, the full moon rose majestically behind the Cayo Mountains and peeked in through the tree branches. Two doctors from the Mayo Clinic had come to dinner: Dr Kelly with his two grandsons, Colt and Peter, and Dr. Karsell. Dr. Karsell had led the briefing that morning on lung and heart x-ray methodology.

The next day, I began to work on the bougainvillea behind the guest wing by cutting out the dead parts. I found that several large branches of the huge flanbwayan tree had infiltrated the bougainvillea and were putting the *Kay Mellon* roof in danger. So I scheduled someone to fix it that afternoon. At 10 a.m., Frankie came to fetch us to visit the elementary school. One hundred and thirty of the most charming uniformed boys and girls were studying. They had to squeeze four classes into two rooms with one teacher per room. Each room had a wooden door which had to be kept ajar to provide light, as there was no other source of light. There were no sanitary facilities of any kind. All the teachers were volunteers, but they have to follow state books and programs. There were no books, only blackboards. Nonetheless, the children remained cheerful and looked adorable in their cotton uniforms. The girls even had bows in their hair. As we entered each classroom, the girls and boys got up and sang a welcome song. One of the young teachers was a former student. We ended up in the office to the headmaster, Mr. Fortini—a man with a mission and a huge heart. He gave Louise a great thank you speech for all that she had already done.

Back at the house, Larry Mellon's secretary, a very elegant Haitian lady, came to lunch. This lovely, immaculately dressed woman had worked for Mr. Mellon since 1964, and she is still there. After lunch, the three big men with machetes arrived to disentangle the bougainvilleas and remove the branches from the roof. Tall, good looking and charming Levy came to direct traffic. He was married and had four children who were left in the north near Cap Haitian. He was appreciative that he had a job with HAS. The next day, Levy was also the one who caught us running late after breakfast to the daily briefing like tardy school girls. He was terribly amused.

The Mayo Clinic doctor talked on leukemia and the latest medicines, which could prolong life, but not cure the disease. After the lecture, I went to sketch the ruins of the old aqueduct. Four school children came to talk to me in Creole. They wanted me to photograph them. So I went back to the house to fetch my camera while they eagerly waiting at the gate.

That evening we had our last soiree at *Kay Mellon* for all the doctors and head nurses. We needed a couple of flower arrangements. There were no vases, but I found some modern wine carafes. So we went to the orchard to get some elephant leaves. There, Levy gave me his first beautiful orange lily of the season. Suddenly the water was shut off until 6 p.m., so dinner was postponed for 30 minutes. We found some water elsewhere to wash off the dust before the party. Water was gold here. We had music, but no one danced. The atmosphere, however, was joyous. The moon was up and the night orchestra of cicadas, barking dogs, and the guards' Creole conversation serenaded us.

At our last morning briefing, Bob Carraway honored us as if we had been in the same category as the departing physicians. The room applauded all of our efforts.

The final evening, Raji and Suresh, Debbie and her husband joined us for dinner. Raji brought us lovely Indian bags as parting gifts. There was a light breeze and the sun was bathing the mountains across the valley. Dinner was served early as we had to get up at four in the morning.

We said good bye to Frederique and the girls before taking off at 5 a.m. for Port-au-Prince. The Route Nationale was as bad leaving as it had been driving in. We uncomfortably traversed the area of "White Death" where dust cakes even your eyes.

Once one has felt the atmosphere of HAS, one never forgets it. The beauty of the people, despite the poverty, was so special. Their smiles are unforgettable. My lovely gold heart charms will forever remind me!

Home in Palm Beach – Back to My Beloved Sea

GOLD TURTLE

In 1994, upon my return to Palm Beach, I moved across the bridge to West Palm Beach to the sixteenth floor of the *Trianon*. The apartment not only came with a pool and doorman, but a large balcony with an incredible view that included the Intracoastal Waterway (from smaller boats to yachts), the island of Palm Beach and my beloved Atlantic. In fact, the location was so attractive that it prompted Alexandra to give up her water views of the Venetian Causeway in Miami for her own apartment in the *Trianon*.

Besides writing, I occupy myself with charity work whenever possible. I also enjoy participating on the board of Palm Beach's much-admired Hospice Guild. Alexandra and I co-chaired its annual 1994 gala fundraiser. I thought it would be great to invite the Duke and Duchess of Norfolk to the gala as guests of honor. Anne, the Duchess of Norfolk, had been the head of England's Hospice for years. She had been a friend of mine since 1948 when London had hosted the Olympic Games. Norway's Crown Prince Olav, family and entourage were staying with us at the embassy, and my parents gave a wonderful dinner dance for many of the other visiting dignitaries and royalty in town for the first games after WW II. Sixty-two people were seated for dinner including Princess Margaret, Anne, as well as some of our other closest English friends. It was an amazing evening and I was so proud to be Norwegian.

Miles, the Duke of Norfolk, was a Fitzalan-Howard and his large family was also among the first friends who stood by me in England from the very beginning. As a recent arrival from Norway who spoke little English, assimilation was not easy. The Fitzalan-Howards were more than helpful during that difficult period.

The gala invitation was accepted with enthusiasm, and an especially lovely time was had by all. Along with the elegant fashion show brought down personally by Carolina Herrera, the gala was a huge success! So were the Norfolks, as I knew they would be. They were wined and dined by many of my good friends.

It was sad to see them leave. The loyal, lifelong friendship with Miles and Anne was one example of how very exceptional my twelve years in England had been. In fact, my family's diplomatic stay in London had afforded me friendships from all over the whole world. I feel I have been very lucky.

During these later years in Palm Beach, I traveled whenever possible. Two of the most memorable trips were taken with my great friend, Louise. In 1999, she and I met in Paris. We took the TGV with Marie-Charlotte Vidal-Quadras to Avignon, where we rented a car. Vicky de Cervera lived not too far away at d'Eygalieres then, so we spent a few pleasant days with her. *Mas de la Rosere* was a charming, beautifully remodeled place with an ingenious pool. We drove under Vicky's guidance to les Baux, and admired some strange rock formations. Vicky now lives in Africa. Marie-Charlotte went back on the train to Paris and Louise and I drove over to Nicken and Else's at Chateauneuf for a couple of days. Aagot, Else's sister, was there as well and everybody got on famously, as I knew they would.

After our visit in France, we drove east and had lunch on the sea just before we crossed over to Italy. The south of France was as charming as ever. As we crossed the border into Italy, I felt the usual butterflies in my stomach. Thanks to the good *autostrada*, we made it to Portofino by the afternoon. We settled for a hotel on the harbor because my beloved *Splendido* was now out of reach. First, we had a drink in the port and then dined at my favorite restaurant in the square. As we leisurely ate a delicious meal, we watched the sailboats bobbing, the children playing and old fishermen still fiddling with their nets. Then I asked for the check, not once, but four or five times. The owner was so busy talking to other people that I finally raised my voice and said in Italian, "If you don't bring me the check now, we will leave without paying!" The owner came right over to us, took my hand and said, "Signora, may I offer you this dinner? It is so nice to see you again." He was so genial we could do nothing but accept his gracious offer. We thanked him profusely and later on again from New York.

From Portofino we drove to my old Etruscan hilltop town of Cortona. Our hotel for four days was situated on a very steep street off the main square. Cortona had recently enjoyed a new level of fame thanks to the film *Under the Tuscan Sun*. Most mornings, fog covered the Val di Chiana, but sunshine always reigned in Cortona.

While there, I took Louise to the famous Fra Angelico Museum and the Etruscan Museum. The square in front of the theater was full of market booths. Wherever we went, it was heart-warming that people recognized me in such a joyful way. One such person was the shoe shop owner who said I'd been away for far too long!

I also got to see many of my old friends. Alain Vidal-Naquet, the finder of *Shenandoah*, invited us to dinner twice, both in town at the trattoria by the old city gate and at his hillside house behind Umberto Morra's villa. There we saw my great old friends, Juan Carlos and Daphne Katzenstein. Juan Carlos and I had been in Rome in the early days when he was in the embassy. His last ambassadorship from Argentina had been to Bangladesh. After the turmoil of Bangladesh, he and Daphne had come to retire in "our" peaceful valley! Sadly, we were forced to move away shortly thereafter.

My dear Anna Ferri served us afternoon tea one day with her family. Then beloved Giulio and Marcella had us for drinks. These two families had been dear to us during our *Shenandoah* years and have remained so ever since. It was so wonderful to be back in Cortona and introduce Louise to my long-time friends.

Four days passed quickly and we were off to Florence for the wedding of the daughter of Payne and Enrique Middleton. Once in Florence we also had lunch with Simonetta Chiaramonti. It had been my old shopping town when I lived at *Shenandoah,* so we could not resist Via Tornabuoni's many boutiques, as well as the delicious tartufati at the Ditta Procacci.

On to Rome, we stayed at the Grand Hotel Plaza on the Via del Corso. I had asked for a room toward the back on the 5th or 6th floor in order to get the superb view of Trinita dei Monti and the rooftops around the Piazza di Spagna. Again, it was my joy to show Louise all my favorite places in the Eternal City.

At the Vatican, we had difficulties gaining entrance because of an Italian presidential visit to the pope. Again, never taking no for an answer, at the Swiss Guard's office, we were able to send a telephonic message to Father Allen Dunston, and he joined us for lunch at a nearby trattoria. He later showed us his impressive office and arranged a visit to the Sistine Chapel at eight in the morning escorted by his charming Texan assistant. Alone, without the usual crowds, we were able to lay flat on our backs to admire Michelangelo's masterpiece. It was literally divine.

After a couple of days, we drove with one of Louise's old friends, Gucky Lichtenstein, to visit her home in La Puglia, often referred to as the heel of Italy. Her Castello di Depressa was located in the middle of the town of Tricase, its courtyard covered in bougainvillea. Lots of sightseeing, coming and going, and after a week it brought us back to Rome.

On Louise's last day, we took a sentimental tour of Rome, including the Trevi Fountain, the Forum and, of course, the Colosseum. That evening we dined with Vanessa and Frech Vreeland (the son of Vogue's Diana Vreeland), who had been an American ambassador to Morocco. Following refreshing drinks at the Vreeland's chic apartment, my old friend Guido di Carpegna (having not seen him since 1961 when he accompanied me to visit my father in the hospital) joined us at a local trattoria. It was so divinely Roman.

Louise flew back to Paris and I remained for another week staying with my Canadian-born friend, Judy Caracciolo. I walked every morning from her apartment on Via Giulia, past Palazzo Farnese (the French Embassy), to Campo dei Fiori, where my mother used to live. I had to have my cappuccino on that corner. The rest of the time friends continued to wine and dine me, reminiscing about the good old times until the day came to leave Italy yet again.

As always, many of my dearest memories are associated with Italy, especially in Rome and Tuscany. After all, the twelve years I lived at *Shenandoah* were the happiest. I often dream of its beauty, but most of all I shall never forget the wonderful people who made my everyday life there so meaningful. These many years later, I still feel that a piece of my soul remains in that part of the world.

The second trip came in 2009 when—in honor of my 80th birthday—Louise invited me to join her for an incredible cruise along Norway's extensive west coast. I had been staying for a week with my brother in Oslo, when on June 21st, Louise and her childhood friend, Laura Ault, joined me. As they were staying at the Grand Hotel for five days, I was able to show them some of the most interesting places in Oslo. We went to several museums beginning with the Edvard Munch art museum. We also visited the

Viking Ship Museum, the Norwegian Museum of Cultural History and the Kon Tiki Museum. The latter was famous for housing the raft that brought Thor Heyerdahl from Peru across the Pacific Ocean, all the way to Polynesia in 1947. Of course, I showed them the beautiful Vigeland Park, which is known as the world's largest sculpture park made by a single artist, Gustav Vigeland. The last day, we went to see the new Oslo Opera House, home to the Norwegian Opera and Ballet. A most exciting architectural structure, it is a true masterpiece. It is like an iceberg emerging out of the sea, a mixture of steel, glass, marble and truly amazing variations of woods, in one word… fabulous!

On our last night in Oslo, My beloved brother gave a wonderful reception for my 80th birthday. Surrounded by family and friends, it meant the world to me.

The following day we boarded a train for Bergen. The train west afforded a view of the spectacular mountains and stunning scenery. Once there, to my delight, according to my well-traveled friends, we had the best dinner ever at Potetkjelleren. The next morning we boarded the cruise ship, *The Midnattsolen* (the midnight sun), which also doubled as a mail boat. For eight days we sailed north stopping at coastal towns and small villages delivering mail. The famous fjords and waterfalls like "The Seven Sisters," "The Suitor," and "The Bridal Veil," offered the most magnificent of sights. We were lucky to enjoy daily sunshine and clear skies every night for the entire trip—something that doesn't often happen.

We had several opportunities to go ashore as we sailed from port to port. One of the main stops was Trondheim, the third largest city in Norway where we visited the majestic Nidaros Cathedral, the church where the Norwegian kings have been crowned.

Later on, sailing northward, we crossed the Arctic Circle. We received our official "baptism" and certificates in our suite while resting and watching TV. The thought of watching Roger Federer play tennis at Wimbledon while in the Arctic Circle was quite amusing.

Another of the many highlights was the navigational feat our ship completed by sailing in and out of Trollfjorden just after the town of Svolvaer. The ship literally had a couple of feet on either side entering and exiting the channel, not to mention the 180 degree turn it had to make in between.

It was time to continue northward toward the North Cape. We sailed to the island of Mageroya where we were taken the remaining 34 kilometers by bus. What a view! On the way back to the ship, we stopped at a large Saami camp. The Saami, also known as the Lapps, are a northern semi-nomadic people famous for their reindeer. The reindeer calves were only a few weeks old and simply adorable.

The last leg of the journey brought us past the port of Vardoe a few short miles shy of the Russian border. It was quite moving to hear the captain tell us that my great-uncle and godfather Nicolai Prebensen's house was still standing on a road that was named after him. At the end of WWII, while retreating, the Germans had burned most of Finmark. Uncle Nicolai had been the governor of the strategically located Finmark, also the largest county in Norway, for several years. In 1906 he became the Norwegian Envoy to Czar Nicholas' Russia until the revolution in 1917.

Soon after, like all good things, our cruise had to come to an end and the time had come to fly back to Oslo. On the way to the airport, we were reminded how very close we were to the Russian border. A highway sign written in both Norwegian and Russian read: *Exit west to airport. Exit east to Murmansk.* It made quite an impression on all three of us. Louise and Laura returned to the US while I remained for another week in Oslo.

I was so very happy to show off my beautiful Norway. At every stop, whether it was night or day, I took photographs or sketched. Photography and sketching have been two of my greatest joys wherever I have lived or traveled.

Another country I was lucky enough to visit most summers was Canada. Besides visiting Louise several times on her family's *Squirrel Island* in Lake Muskoka, I also had the pleasure of staying with two other great friends, the talented and handsome Brett Sherlock and James Booty in

Niagara-on-the-Lake. Their present home, *Hill House,* couldn't be more charming. I always felt very welcomed there, and am now very honored to know that a large Hugo Caballero drawing of me hangs on their staircase wall.

Upon returning from each and every trip, the conditions at the *Trianon* seemed to deteriorate progressively. It was more and more apparent that the property was not being adequately maintained. We suffered three major floods, due to issues with neighboring apartments that ruined most of our furniture. In 2004 and 2005, Hurricanes Francis, Jeanne and Wilma battered Trianon. When Ivan came through we had to move in with Louise because there was no electricity, which meant cold water and complete darkness. Due to the apartment building's heavy shutters, it was not possible to open any doors.

I especially missed the garden during the latter years when the *Trianon* management forced me to remove all my heavenly flower pots due to renovations. Every year they worked six-months on construction projects, which made it impossible to use even the balconies—not to mention how we suffered from the menacing noise of machinery! The good thing was that the *Trianon* sat on the Intracoastal with a superb view of Palm Beach Island. Our 16th floor unit also provided a sprawling vista of the Atlantic.

I have always adored the ocean. Any time I have felt blue or been in pain, a gaze at the watery turquoise expanse has always restored me. Although my apartment was not on the beach, Mary Bolton—who was the very first Palm Beach person who so heartily welcomed us—gave us an open invitation to use her beach at her estate on Blossom Way. Our car was the only car parked there at times. I am ever grateful to her and considered it a great privilege to have her beach available at any time. She also invited me often to the theater and ballet, which I have always loved. In fact, we attended the ballet only a couple of weeks before she died. She was in her 90s.

As mentioned before, I am an artist at heart. In addition to my passion for the arts, I have always adored having my lovely gardens and belonging to the Garden Club of America. I was accepted into the Garden Club even before we arrived in the States, and it has been an immense joy to me. It is such a great organization, in which I am proud to be involved. The ladies in both the Cincinnati and Palm Beach chapters have shown me great talents and accomplishments. And I have always felt that I could depend on these friends in good and difficult times.

Then, for many years, I have belonged to a unique group of friends—a reading circle we called the Palm Beach Reading Group. Apart from reading and discussing interesting books, we have shared open and inspiring ideas "en petite committee." Many of these lovely ladies are now gone, but have left me wonderful memories.

For nearly three decades, I was a member of the Bath and Tennis Club. It truly became my home away from home in so many ways. Having always adored the sea, its ocean side location provided many life-restoring walks on the peaceful semi-private beach, not to mention the large and oh-so-therapeutic salt water pool. Tennis games in the morning, three times a week so often kept me going. That is until my hands, legs, neck and back ultimately gave up on me! Being part of the tennis committee brought me great joy on and off the court. To this day they still invite me to various tennis championships where the incredibly friendly atmosphere continues to inspire and encourage. The genuine friendships I made there, not only with so many members, but also with the charming people who work there, have been priceless.

In addition to my love of sports and the arts, my deep faith has helped me to survive. From the early years in London with the spiritual help from Father Guerrin, I became a Catholic. Another great help was my being sent to the south of Europe during the winters to alleviate my allergies to the cold. The times I spent with these wonderful families restored a great deal of my mental and physical health. Also, thanks to a few fabulous visionary physicians, I was given treatments that were truly out of the box. All of this led to the joy of having two beautiful daughters who, as mentioned before, were born in Rome, the Eternal City. They were christened by our wonderful parish priest, Don Giuseppe, in Tuscany, who also officiated in our private chapel at my beloved Shenandoah.

In my later years, I would continue to rely on my faith to get me through further medical trials. Besides having legs with paper-thin skin, making my constantly on-the-go lifestyle very challenging, my love of the sun and outdoor sports resulted in several skin cancer procedures. The worst two involved my nose and my back. My nose required extensive radiation which meant saying goodbye to my eyebrows. The removal of a large melanoma on my back required a more serious surgery. Despite warning the doctors of my past reactions, I nearly died due to the anesthesia. Alexandra actually witnessed my turning completely grey! The recovery was longer and more unpleasant than expected. Since then, I have become an advocate for various forms of sun protection, especially pointing out the most effective ingredients in sunscreen for all skin types.

Despite these challenges including operations on both eyes, with every sunny morning, the possibility of new adventures gives me the courage to keep going. Nearing my ninetieth birthday, I still dream of Norway where I spent my childhood and England where I grew up, as well as my cherished home in Italy and hold those thoughts close to my heart.

Life Comes Full Circle

I never dreamt I would be able to see my beloved family and friends in Norway and Italy ever again. Surprise, surprise! In honor of my 90th birthday, my great friend Louise gave me the first class airfare to Europe! Following this wonderful gift, came invitations from Norway and Italy to celebrate. Of course, I couldn't travel alone so Alexandra happily volunteered to join me. Off we went!

On Friday, the 23rd of August, our long flight from the US via Copenhagen made its way up the Oslo Fjord. The visibility was amazing and all the well-known sights were crystal clear. It was a trip I had flown so many times throughout the years. Coming back to Norway to celebrate my 90th really struck home. We were welcomed at Gardemoen Airport by my dear brother, Chris and my beautiful niece and goddaughter, Cecilie. The airport express brought us to the small town of Sandvika, a suburb of Oslo where Chris lives. His wife, Anne was still out of town, so Cecilie made a cozy dinner for the four of us. Our week there was spent with close family and friends, old and young. Since the youngest generation, age two to six, couldn't join us for the evening events, we planned to meet them and their parents at a park in Sandvika the following day, where a Viking festival was in full swing. There were Viking games, historic booths and various circus performers for all to enjoy in glorious sunshine. Needless to say, the Prebensen grandchildren, Mathias, Augusta and Benjamin, were more than adorable!

That evening, being my actual birthday, Chris and Anne took us to a charming little restaurant on the river, where a surprise outdoor concert of opera songs and violin music serenaded us.

The next birthday celebration came in the form of a lovely sit down family luncheon for 25, chez Chris and Anne. It was so very moving to see everyone. An unexpected delight was seeing my sister-in-law, Else, who happened to be visiting from England. They even surprised me with a birthday cake, presents and Happy Birthday sung in Norwegian by all.

Monday was supposed to be a more restful day, but an invitation came that was too tempting to resist. My cousin, Thorvald, asked both of us to join him and his old friend, Peder Meidell at the famous gentlemen's club, Det Norske Selskap. The food was delicious; the company delightful, and the superb well-known art collection was an added treat. Tuesday brought us another pleasure. We were invited to lunch at the Bristol Hotel by my former sister-in-law, Inger. Cecilie, her daughter, joined us and both were in great form. Inger's unique birthday gift followed lunch. She brought us to the office of Nordmanns Forbundet/Norwegians Worldwide, where she arranged a year's membership for both of us. It was most appreciated. The next day we enjoyed a cocktail reception at Chris and Anne's for cousins, cousins and more cousins! There were friends attending also, including my long-time friend, Rikke, whom I had known since first grade in 1935! Like all good parties, it was over too soon.

Chris had arranged for a place for us to stay in Rome. His old friend, Sissel, offered her apartment in old Rome near the Coliseum. We went to see her on Thursday to pick up the keys and all pertinent details. As well as being a lovely person, she is a great artist. Her eclectic apartment in old Oslo, with all of her paintings, couldn't have been more charming. As you can imagine, leaving Oslo was emotional, but we could not have had a better time. It simply was over too soon. Of course, Chris, the saint, accompanied us to the airport. I have called him a saint since he was three years old because he has always taken great care of me. He can hardly see and walks with a cane, but gives of himself just the same. As we said goodbye, we concentrated on how Italy would present another journey of soul renewal.

We found ourselves in Rome in a mere couple of hours. Sissell's sixth floor apartment had large windows and a balcony with views over the rooftops that afforded many beautiful sights of the city including the Coliseum. So many memories flooded my mind, especially the painting of the large cross in the middle of the Coliseum that I was inspired to create in 1960. In fact, it's the painting found on the back cover of this book. Alas, there was no air conditioning, and more importantly no wifi. We'd heard that Hurricane Dorian was heading directly toward Palm Beach, and frustratingly, we could get little information as to whether our U.S. home was going to get blown off the map. Through lots of phone calls and prayers, we did our best not to allow it to burden us too much and appreciated how lucky we were to be in Rome.

Despite the heat, it was so good to be back in the Eternal City. Our first night was spent with my Roman grandchildren, Giulia and Giacomo. Imagine the lovely surprise when they happened to invite us to dine at the very same trattoria where my mother brought me for my first dinner in Rome in 1947! I Tre Scalini on Piazza Navona had barely changed, apart from the fact that it was three times the size! To my delight, Giulia's son Giulio joined us.

The next night we were invited to a dinner party at the club of the Ministero degli Affari Esteri by Courtney Walsh, a friend of Alexandra's from Palm Beach, married to a charming Italian architect. It turned out to be a birthday celebration in honor of Jane Smith, another friend of ours from Palm Beach. She was only turning 103 years young, energetic and fun as ever! Our hosts' son and daughter provided the music as DJs, and Alexandra was the first to be asked to dance by our host, Michele. Soon, everyone was dancing including several ambassadors. It so reminded me of the parties I used to host at the Norwegian Embassy when my father was ambassador in Rome in the days of "La Dolce Vita."

The most important thing we wanted to do was pay our respects to my (step) daughter, Adele, at the Protestant Cemetery (Il Cimitero Acattolico di Roma). We met Giacomo who had brought roses to place on his mother's grave. This peaceful and incredibly beautiful garden was also the resting place of my father's memorial plaque. After a lovely time of sunshine and reflection, Giacomo brought us to a wonderful trattoria at Campo di Fiori, my mother's last Roman home. In the evening Giacomo and Giulia took us to their favorite Indian restaurant.

The last day, I couldn't resist going to more of my old stomping grounds including Piazza di Spagna and Via Condotti. Of course, that included a visit to Gucci and Bulgari. We even covered Via del Corso ending up in Piazza del Popolo. As usual, all on foot! Our bodies a bit worse for wear, we took Giulia's advice and got a Thai massage. Considering we were massage veterans, it was surprisingly quite torturous! Despite the pain, we'd hoped it would help in the long run. I couldn't wait to get home, but Alexandra insisted on taking some videos of some amazing hip-hop dancers in Piazza Navona. An unexpected sight. For a quick five-day Roman holiday, both Alexandra and I were so grateful and happy to have been back in the Eternal City.

The morning we left, Giacomo brought us by taxi to the station where he kindly insisted on serving us cappuccino while we waited for our train. Leave it to our beloved Italians to change tracks at the last minute. With Giacomo's help we ran with all our luggage and made the train with seconds to spare. The train took us north to our well-known station, Terentola-Cortona in our dearly loved Val di Chiana. My godson, Enrico Falini, was there to meet us and drove us straight to his parents, Giulio and Marcella's home. They were among the closest people to me during our years in our beloved home, Shenandoah. After a divine Falini luncheon, we were brought over to our old neighbors the Cancellieris. The current generation had made the Antica Villa degli Ulivi into a very welcoming Tuscan hotel, where they so generously gave us the ground floor apartment. It was all so beautifully restored. On one of the terraces above the villa, they had built a beautiful swimming pool with gorgeous views. It was so inviting that Alexandra had to jump in minutes before dinner!

That following day, we had lunch at Casa Ferri where Anna had made Alexandra's favorite childhood pasta. Anna's son, Ivo Ferri—whom I've known since he was 13 years old—drove us back to the Villa degli Ulivi. Ivo married a great gal named Vilma Pareti, and they have two charming children, Veronica and Giacomo. On top of which, thanks to all his Facebook postings, I've come to admire him as a great Italian writer.

That evening was the great birthday party. The guest list included Guilio Falini, Marcella Bertini, Enrico Falini, Tommaso Falini, and Sonia Polvani. Then, Massimiliano Cancellieri, Antonella Giardini, Jacopo Cancellieri, Beatrice Cancellieri, Danilo Pelosi, and Mattia Pelosi. Also, Ivo Ferri, Vilma Pareti, Anna Ferri, Elsa Pareti, Veronica Ferri, Giacomo Ferri and Sara Ciani. All contributed to the event, and the long table overflowed with homemade food, laughter and love Sitting at the head of the table with Giulio to my right, I looked down the table at my wonderful Tuscan friends who had meant so much to me during my fantastic years at *Shenandoah*. Tommy, son of Enrico and proud grandson of Giulio, presented me with a most lovely gift. It was a beautiful photo frame that I shall appreciate for the rest of my life. The five course dinner was the best that Tuscany could offer—all homemade. When it came time for dessert, the lights went out and the room erupted with *Happy Birthday* sung in Italian. Out came a work of art—a large fruit tart over two feet in diameter decorated with pineapple, kiwis, peaches, bananas, grapes, blackberries, even red currents. It was literally breathtaking.

The following day, after a dip in the wonderful pool, we lunched with Enrico while visiting Cortona. The famous old Etruscan town has always been so close to my heart. As we left Cortona, the sky clouded up and it began to rain, putting a possible damper on our upcoming visit to *Shenandoah*. When we arrived back at the Villa degli Ulivi, Mattia (Massimigliano's nephew and Beatrice's son) surprised us with a personal concert showing off his exquisite double bass playing in the country kitchen. He was hoping to further his music studies in Norway, where coincidentally, I could happily make introductions for him.

After changing for upcoming drinks and dinner, Massimiliano kindly offered to take us to *Shenandoah*. Boarding the car, we looked up and saw there wasn't a cloud in the sky. God had answered our prayers. Once again, we were warmly greeted by the present owner, Romano Antonioli. We were so pleased when he immediately invited Massimiliano to join us. As we were having drinks on the terrace with Romano and his wife and daughter, Marcella and Marta and some friends from Rome, Alexandra asked if she could take some photographs of the gardens and grounds. As I complimented Romano on how wonderful everything looked, so beautifully preserved, he got up and took me on his own tour of the property. My old friend, the gazebo, was still there, not to mention all the many trees and plants that Billy and I had planted half a century ago! The sunset was spectacular and Alexandra continued to take pictures. As difficult as it was, she accepted the invitation to tour *Shenandoah's* interior. Romano encouraged her to take video on my behalf. The evening had gone so well, that he finally persuaded me to venture inside and view the first floor. The colors of the sunset were stronger than ever as we left for dinner. I was so glad that "she" was still in good hands. I well know, my old friend Giulio had a lot to do with it.

Our last day was joyful but extremely long. We first attended the annual festival at Il Santuario della Madonna del Bagno in the early morning. We saw lots of old friends and even met the current mayor of Cortona, Luciano Meoni, who, by the end of our friendly conversation, promised me a book signing party. We then not only arranged to see one of Alexandra's elementary school friends, Emanuela Scarpaccini and her very charming fiancé, but finally got a hold of my old friend, Silvio Passerini! We all gathered in Cortona at Tonino's Restaurant, reminiscing about the good old days. Once again, we had lunch with the Falinis in order to see Enrico's sister, Elisabetta, her husband, Roberto and beautiful daughter, Lucrezia, who had returned from their ocean vacation just to see us before we left.

We were driven back by Enrico for our last moments at the Cancellieris. As we finished our packing, guess who showed up again? Good old Silvio Passerini, as always! With very heavy hearts, we said our good-byes, and Enrico drove us to the train station. Thank goodness, our new friend, Danilo, also came to see us off. He came to help with luggage, but he did so much more. I think Alexandra and I would have collapsed emotionally had he not been there.

Around 9 pm, after having been highly amused by the very Roman banter between taxi driver and son, we arrived at my granddaughter Guilia's lovely apartment. Our time with her was short, but precious. Sadly, we had to leave for the airport by six in the morning; we were already looking forward to seeing her and the boys in the near future. Our flight home went via Oslo where we spent three hours at Gardemoen Airport. My brother, Chris, of course, came to the airport to see us again. It was a sad and difficult goodbye.

On our return to our US apartment, we had high hopes to publish this book by Christmas. Instead, we were met with several incidents that delayed those plans. Arriving at 2 am, we were met with a terrible stench as we walked into our apartment. Hurricane Dorian had spared us, though sadly it had hit the Bahamas over and over again. The hasty preparations by the maintenance staff had turned our apartment into a small disaster. Not only had they taken all the damp patio furniture and plants and thrown them haphazardly into the living room, they had also turned off the air conditioning and left it off! After being gone for three weeks, we found the apartment smelling like mold and mildew. It took forever to clean up, and the air quality remained toxic for weeks, then months! We don't believe the friendly maintenance crew intended to make such a mess. Being under the threat of a hurricane always breeds chaos. Nevertheless, it was a terrible welcome home present.

During the following weeks, I simply didn't feel like myself, so I went to see my dear friend and doctor, John Whelton. He reassured me that— apart from all my usual life-long ailments—incredibly, I had the heart of a sixteen-year-old! Sadly, that heart was soon to be broken when Dr. John suddenly passed away. At the funeral, I not only mourned the loss of a great friend, but the loss of my entire sense of medical security.

Our Florida fall weather had been mostly grey and humid. So on December 6th, when a beautiful bright sun broke through the clouds, Alexandra and I ran to the ocean. It was truly one of the nicest afternoons at the beach in ages. As Alexandra swam, I took more photos than usual of my beloved ocean. Little did I know I would not be returning anytime soon. The next morning, coincidentally Pearl Harbor Day, I went to the kitchen to make my daily cup of coffee. That's the last thing I would remember for quite some time.

According to Alexandra, the following took place. Miraculously, she happened to be home and literally walking by when I silently dropped to the floor. I had hit my head on the tile floor, but she soon realized it was the least of her worries. I was unresponsive and not breathing! Thank God her instincts took over and she started CPR immediately. As luck would have it, she had recently viewed the latest CPR techniques on the Doctor Oz show! Since there was still no visible response, she grabbed her phone, dialed 911, put it on speaker, and continued pumping my chest. The 911 voice kept her going until the ambulance arrived. Once she saw those five strong EMTs, she was able to let me go. Alexandra was first told to go to our familiar St. Mary's Hospital. But in the interest of time, I had been rerouted to the even closer JFK Hospital North. When Alexandra arrived at the ER, no one could tell her what had happened.

The next morning, still unconscious, they moved me to JFK Hospital South where they specialize in cardiac care. As the day progressed, Alexandra grew more and more horrified by the inefficiency of most of the staff, and was determined not to leave my side. When she wouldn't leave, they finally rolled in an old lumpy bed, so she could sleep next to me. After nearly a week, they were ready to transfer me to rehab, but thanks to Alexandra's insistence, they begrudgingly checked my lungs. Being in Intensive Care, with constant lights and sounds, Alexandra was unable to sleep most of the time. Therefore, she could witness my unusual coughing, and difficulty in breathing. The doctors and nurses hadn't seemed to notice. Literally, one hour before my discharge, test results confirmed I had double pneumonia with an excess of fluid in both lungs! So, I stayed another week in their understaffed care (the Christmas and New Year holidays seemed to be their first priority), and was finally moved to rehab. I was just grateful to have survived not only a heart attack and pneumonia, but also the hospital!

Several days into rehab, my daughter Elizabeth came to help for a few days. Though Alexandra and I were both looking forward to see her, unfortunately she arrived with a bad cold. She did what she could, but Alexandra continued to be my primary caretaker.

Alexandra hardly told a soul about me, as I really wasn't up to seeing anyone. Of course, Louise visited several times, and on Boxing Day, she brought our good friend Laura Ault. Very few of Alexandra's friends found out. TJ and Neil Fisher were the first to come. Simone and Chuck Desiderio came by as well bearing flowers, food and cheer. By the way, I shall always be grateful—although unconscious at the time—that on the second day at JFK South, TJ Fisher asked her friend, Father John Mericante, to perform last rites. Now that is friendship.

Unfortunately, the rehab facility was under new management. Although it was more pleasant than the hospital, by the time I left, Alexandra referred to the place and most of the staff as 'orchids and idiots!'

The following months of recuperation at home were steady but slower than expected. Growing old is not for the faint of heart! I often think that, although I technically died for a spell, I was blessed to continue living for many reasons—especially to finish this book.

Shortly after my health incidents, I was able to do just that—with the help of Alexandra and our editor. However, the arrival of the deadly serious Corona virus (COVID-19) posed another significant delay. Executive orders to quarantine at home to contain the disease, forced us to work remotely by phone and computer. Technical difficulties went unrectified as help was not available, delaying the project further. I cannot imagine what would have happened if I'd suffered my heart attack just a few weeks later when COVID-19 became a worldwide pandemic. Dear God! Good or bad, timing seems to have been so very crucial during my entire life.

The 90th birthday trip to Norway and Italy brought the realization that another chapter had to be written. This last chapter was what brought my life—and the bracelet—full circle.

Now residing close to a lovely lake, on clear Florida nights when the full moon gleams on its still waters, I often reflect on the blessing of having had friends of all ages and from every corner of the world. Their positive spirit and soul have supported me my whole life. Despite vast distances, modern technology has allowed us to continue to be in close contact.

In spite of all of my challenges, as well as having arrived at 90+ years of age, I will continue to say for the rest of this charmed life, "Never take *no* for an answer!"

NOTES

Chapter 3 - London

1. *Champagne: The Wine, the Land and the People,* Patrick Forbes, (London Gollancz, 1967)
2. *London Daily Newspaper,* December, 1954
3. *The Illustrated London News,* June, 1947
4. *The Illustrated London News,* June, 1947

Chapter 4 – Ireland

1. *The Splendor Falls,* Alfred Lord Tennyson, Public Domain
2. *The Rural Life of England,* William Howitt, Public Domain
3. *The Galway Bay,* Dr. Arthur Colahan

Chapter 5 – Denmark

1. *Henry IV,* Part 2: Act 3, Scene 2, pg 10, Public Domain

Chapter 7 – Sicily

1. Johann Wolfgang Von Goethe, 1787
2. *The Islands of Italy,* Barbara Grizutti Harrison, pg 330, 1991

Chapter 8 – Sweden

1. Henrik Ibsen

Chapter 12 – Portugal

1. *This Delicious Land, Portugal,* Lady Kelly
2. Ibid

Chapter 13 - Morocco

1. *The History and Description of Africa,* Leo Africanus (1600's)
2. Chapter 17 – Shenandoah
3. *Shadows and Images,* Marchesa Origo

Chapter 18 – Cincinnati

1. *New Life for Harrisons - Cincinnati Post,* 1975